Praise for *Capitalism at the Crossroads*

"*Capitalism at the Crossroads* is built on strong theoretical underpinnings and illustrated with many practical examples. The author offers a pioneering roadmap to responsible macroeconomics and corporate growth."

—Clayton Christensen, Professor of Business Administration, Harvard Business School and author of *The Innovator's Dilemma*

"*Capitalism at the Crossroads* clearly reveals the essence of what sustainability means to today's business world. Hart's analysis that businesses must increasingly adopt a business framework based on building sustainable value speaks to the entire sustainability movement's relevance. Sustainability is more than today's competitive edge; it is tomorrow's model for success."

—Don Pether, President and CEO, Dofasco Inc.

"Stuart Hart has written a book full of big insights painted with bold strokes. He may make you mad. He will certainly make you think."

—Jonathan Lash, President, The World Resources Institute

"A must-read for every CEO—and every MBA."

—John Elkington, Chairman, SustainAbility

"This book provides us with a vast array of innovative and practical ideas to accelerate the transformation to global sustainability and the role businesses and corporations will have to play therein. Stuart Hart manages to contribute in an essential way to the growing intellectual capital that addresses this topic. But, beyond that, the book will also prove to be a pioneer in the literature on corporate strategy by adding this new dimension to the current thinking."

—Jan Oosterveld, Professor, IESE Business School, Barcelona, Spain
Member, Group Management Committee (Ret.), Royal Philips Electronics

"*Capitalism at the Crossroads* captures a disturbing and descriptive picture of the global condition. Dr. Hart constructs a compelling new corporate business model that simultaneously merges the metric of profitability along with societal value and environmental integrity. He challenges the corporate sector to take the lead and to invoke this change so that the benefits of capitalism can be shared with the entire human community worldwide."

—Mac Bridger, CEO of Tandus Group

"Stuart L. Hart makes a very important contribution to the understanding of how enterprise can help save the world's environment. Crucial reading."

—Hernando de Soto, president of The Institute for Liberty and Democracy and author of *The Mystery of Capital*

"Stuart Hart's insights into the business sense of sustainability come through compellingly in *Capitalism at the Crossroads*. Any businessperson interested in the long view will find resonance with his wise reasoning."

—Ray Anderson, Founder and Chairman, Interface, Inc.

"This stimulating book documents the central role that business will play in humanity's efforts to develop a sustainable global economy. Professor Hart presents an attractive vision of opportunity for those corporations that develop the new technologies, new business models, and new mental frames that are essential to a sustainable future."

—Jeffrey Lehman, President of Cornell University and former Dean of the University of Michigan Law School

Capitalism at the Crossroads

The Unlimited Business Opportunities in Solving the World's Most Difficult Problems

Capitalism at the Crossroads

The Unlimited Business Opportunities in Solving the World's Most Difficult Problems

Stuart L. Hart
Johnson Graduate School of Management
Cornell University

Ideas. Action. Impact.
Wharton School Publishing

Library of Congress Publication in Data: *2004114823*

Publisher: Tim Moore
Executive Editor: Jim Boyd
Editorial Assistant: Richard Winkler
Development Editor: Elisa Adams
Marketing Manager: Martin Litkowski
International Marketing Manager: Tim Galligan
Cover Designer: Chuti Prasertsith
Managing Editor: Gina Kanouse
Senior Project Editor: Kristy Hart
Copy Editor: Krista Hansing
Indexer: Lisa Stumpf
Interior Designer: Gail Cocker-Bogusz
Compositor: Jake McFarland
Manufacturing Buyer: Dan Uhrig

Ideas. Action. Impact.
**Wharton School
Publishing**

Wharton School Publishing offers excellent discounts on this book when ordered in quantity for bulk purchases or special sales. For more information, please contact U.S. Corporate and Government Sales, 1-800-382-3419, corpsales@pearsontech-group.com. For sales outside the U.S., please contact International Sales at international@pearsoned.com.

ISBN 0-13-143987-1

Pearson Education LTD.
Pearson Education Australia PTY, Limited.
Pearson Education Singapore, Pte. Ltd.
Pearson Education North Asia, Ltd.
Pearson Education Canada, Ltd.
Pearson Educatión de Mexico, S.A. de C.V.
Pearson Education—Japan
Pearson Education Malaysia, Pte. Ltd.

Ideas. Action. Impact.
Wharton School Publishing

Bernard Baumohl

THE SECRETS OF ECONOMIC INDICATORS
Hidden Clues to Future Economic Trends and Investment Opportunities

Sayan Chatterjee

FAILSAFE STRATEGIES
Profit and Grow from Risks That Others Avoid

Sunil Gupta, Donald R. Lehmann

MANAGING CUSTOMERS AS INVESTMENTS
The Strategic Value of Customers in the Long Run

Stuart L. Hart

CAPITALISM AT THE CROSSROADS
The Unlimited Business Opportunities in Solving the World's Most Difficult Problems

Lawrence G. Hrebiniak

MAKING STRATEGY WORK
Leading Effective Execution and Change

Robert Mittelstaedt

WILL YOUR NEXT MISTAKE BE FATAL?
Avoiding the Chain of Mistakes That Can Destroy Your Organization

Mukul Pandya, Robbie Shell, Susan Warner, Sandeep Junnarkar, Jeffrey Brown

NIGHTLY BUSINESS REPORT PRESENTS LASTING LEADERSHIP
What You Can Learn from the Top 25 Business People of Our Times

C. K. Prahalad

THE FORTUNE AT THE BOTTOM OF THE PYRAMID
Eradicating Poverty Through Profits

Scott A. Shane

FINDING FERTILE GROUND
Identifying Extraordinary Opportunities for New Ventures

Oded Shenkar

THE CHINESE CENTURY
The Rising Chinese Economy and Its Impact on the Global Economy, the Balance of Power, and Your Job

Yoram (Jerry)Wind, Colin Crook, with Robert Gunther

THE POWER OF IMPOSSIBLE THINKING
Transform the Business of Your Life and the Life of Your Business

113052

To all the children, yet unborn.

CONTENTS

PART TWO BEYOND GREENING

ABOUT THE AUTHOR

Stuart L. Hart is one of the world's top authorities on the implications of sustainable development and environmentalism for business strategy. He is currently SC Johnson Chair of Sustainable Global Enterprise and Professor of Management at Cornell's Johnson Graduate School of Management. Previously, he taught strategic management and founded both the Center for Sustainable Enterprise (CSE) at the University of North Carolina's Kenan-Flagler Business School, and the Corporate Environmental Management Program (CEMP) at the University of Michigan. His consulting clients range from DuPont and Hewlett-Packard to Procter & Gamble and Shell.

He wrote the seminal article "Beyond Greening: Strategies for a Sustainable World," which won the McKinsey Award for Best Article in *Harvard Business Review* in 1997, and helped launch the movement for corporate sustainability. With C.K. Prahalad, Hart also wrote the path-breaking 2002 article "The Fortune at the Bottom of the Pyramid," which provided the first articulation of how business could profitably serve the needs of the four billion poor in the developing world.

ACKNOWLEDGMENTS

This book pulls together and extends work I have been doing in the area of sustainability and business over the past 15 years, but it has actually been 35 years in the making. Indeed, there is no doubt that this work was influenced, shaped, and determined, to a large extent, by my prior experiences in college, graduate school, and the real world. I owe a great debt, therefore, to a number of people—mentors, professors, benefactors, colleagues, associates, and students—as well as friends and family.

As an undergraduate student at the University of Rochester, I would have never embarked on the path of environmental studies and management were it not for the inspiration of professors Larry Lundgren and Christian Kling. These two professors were the ones who awakened my interest and stirred my passion for this domain and set me on a course that has continued to this day. I am living proof that college professors really do have an enormously important shaping influence on their students. To them I owe a huge debt of gratitude.

At Yale, during my time at the School of Forestry and Environmental Studies, I am very thankful to have had the honor to work with the late Professor Joe Miller, as well as professors Lloyd Irland and Garth Voight. These three, in particular, helped to shape my interest and deepen my knowledge in environmental policy and management. They also enabled me to develop a much broader intellectual grasp of the history of the environmental movement and how it fit into the larger pattern of societal evolution toward greater inclusiveness.[1]

My first encounter with the "real world" (in the form of an actual job) came at the Institute on Man and Science in upstate New York in the late 1970s. As a research associate in economic and environmental studies, I worked with Dr. Gordon Enk—my first boss. This job resulted in a professional and personal relationship that continues to this day. In fact, if I had to name the one person who has had the biggest impact on me, it would have to be Gordon Enk. With his background and deep commitment both to the environment and to the economic system (Gordon holds a Ph.D. from Yale in natural resource economics), he was the first person to show me that we need not accept trade-offs when it comes to societal and economic performance. Gordon was also way ahead of his time when it came to stakeholder involvement in strategic decision making. Under his guidance, we embarked on a series of projects that sought to involve diverse voices in important social and strategic decisions. We wrote about the learnings from these experiences in a range of publications that stand the test of time to this day.[2]

Since that time in the late 1970s, Gordon and I have continued to work together: He served on my dissertation committee at Michigan;[3] I served as a consultant to him during his years as an executive at International Paper Company. More recently, he has been an active participant in the advisory boards for the Corporate Environmental Management Program at Michigan, the Center for Sustainable Enterprise at UNC, and now the Center for Sustainable Global Enterprise at Cornell. In reading the pages of this manuscript, Gordon will no doubt see the shaping effect he has had on my point of view. He should take satisfaction in knowing that he has taught me well.

During my time in the doctoral program at Michigan, I was mentored and influenced by several key faculty members. Professors Pete Andrews (now at UNC), Rachel Kaplan, Jim Crowfoot, Kan Chen, Paul

Nowak, and (the late) Bill Drake were of particular influence and importance. Rachel Kaplan deserves special mention for her encouragement and support of my dissertation work. After completing my doctoral work in 1983, I was appointed post-doctoral fellow and research scientist at the Institute for Social Research in Ann Arbor. During this time, I worked closely with Dr. Mark Berg, Dr. Don Michael, and professors Donald Pelz and Nate Kaplan. This was also the time that I met and established life-long personal and professional relationships with two other highly influential people: Professor Dan Denison (now at IMD in Switzerland) and Professor Jac Geurts (at Tilburg University in the Netherlands). They had an enormous influence on my intellectual development, especially when it came to combining interests in strategy and organizational change with a concern for social impact and environmental management. I continue to work with both of them to this day.[4]

My career as a professor of strategic management began in the mid-1980s at the University of Michigan Business School. There, I was greatly helped by relationships with professors Jane Dutton, Bob Quinn, and Noel Tichy. Professor Jim Walsh has also been a particularly helpful and special friend, confidant, and advisor over the years. Without him, it would have been much more difficult to work up the courage to take the career risks that I have taken. However, there is one faculty mentor, in particular, who deserves special mention: Professor C. K. Prahalad. By the late 1980s, I was becoming frustrated with my career: I was increasingly spending time on research and teaching that did not reflect my real interests or passions. My performance in both research and teaching was, as a result, mediocre. Where most senior faculty advised me to forget about my background and interest in environment and sustainable development, C. K. was one of the few supportive voices. I still remember how he urged me to pursue my passion and leverage my unique background in this area. Were it not for C. K., I never would have made the conscious decision (which I did in 1990) to devote the rest of my professional career to the connections between business and sustainability. C. K.'s unique perspective on strategy as innovation has also had a huge impact on how I have formulated my ideas about sustainable enterprise. For this, and much more, I owe C. K. a huge debt of gratitude.

Other early contributors who had important influence on my thinking included Paul Hawken, particularly his work *The Ecology of Commerce*; Ed Freeman, with his important book *Strategic Management: A Stakeholder View*; John Elkington, with his concept of the "triple bottom line," first published in *Cannibals With Forks*, and professors Dick Vietor and Forest Reinhardt at the Harvard Business School, who produced most of the early teaching cases on environmental management and business in the early 1990s.

Two other faculty members also deserve special mention for inspiring me to pursue this path: Professor Paul Shrivastava, of Bucknell University, and Professor Tom Gladwin (then at NYU, now at Michigan).[5] In my view, Paul and Tom were the academic pioneers in this area. They were both working this space before most others in business schools even gave it a second look. Like C. K. Prahalad, Paul and Tom provided both the example and encouragement that led me to take the bold step of dedicating my professional life to this topic. It was the best decision I ever made, and I am tremendously thankful to both of them.

Were it not for two other people, it would have never been possible to successfully develop the Corporate Environmental Management Program (CEMP) at Michigan, a dual-degree program between two previously disconnected entities. Garry Brewer, who came to Michigan from Yale as the Dean of the School of Natural Resources and Environment in 1990, and Joe White, who became the new Dean of the Business School at the same time. Garry Brewer, in particular, was instrumental in forging the relationship between the two schools and helping to secure the early support for the program. Without the commitment of Garry and Joe, the CEMP Program would have never happened. Both also helped me to better understand the challenges and opportunities in attempting to bring these two worlds together.

At the University of North Carolina, I am indebted to professors Hugh O'Neill, Rich Bettis, and Ben Rosen, and, later, Dean Robert Sullivan for giving me the opportunity to develop the Center for Sustainable Enterprise. However, it was really Professor Anne Illinitch (now York) who deserves the most credit for attracting me to UNC in the first place. It was her passion, vision, and persistence that helped to make it a reality. With regard to the center itself, however, my professional and personal relationship with Professor Jim Johnson has been especially fruitful. In his role as faculty co-director of the center with me, Jim has taught me a great deal about the social aspects of sustainability, particularly those relating to minorities and the economically disadvantaged. I also owe Jim a debt of thanks for helping to create the title for this book: For several years, the two of us discussed (but never completed) an article together entitled (tentatively) "Capitalism at the Crossroads." For Jim's unswerving support as both a friend and a close colleague, I am very grateful.

As with the creation of CEMP at Michigan, the Center for Sustainable Enterprise at UNC would have never been possible if it were not for the visionary support of two people: Professor Jack Kasarda (Director of the Kenan Institute for Private Enterprise) and Professor Bill Glaze (Director of the Carolina Environmental Program). Both showed the willingness to financially support the fledgling concept for a new Center before anyone else at either the business school or the university would pay any attention. Without them, the body of new work generated over the past seven years would have not been possible. Nor would the establishment of an MBA concentration at Kenan-Flagler Business School that, by the early 2000s, attracted nearly one-third of the admitted students each year to the school. For this accomplishment, I should also thank Jim Dean, who was Dean of the MBA program during the creation of the concentration.

For the opportunity at Cornell, I am indebted to several people: Dean Robert Sweiringa; Senior Associate Dean Joe Thomas; and professors Alan McAdams, Norm Scott, Bob Libby, Beta Mannix, and Bob Frank, to name but a few. However, the ultimate acknowledgement must be made to the late Sam Johnson, Chairman Emeritus of S.C. Johnson & Son, Inc. It was Sam and the Johnson Family who had the vision to endow both the S.C. Johnson Chair in Sustainable Global Enterprise and the new Center for Sustainable Global Enterprise. Other pioneering benefactors also deserve recognition: Dr. Hans Zulliger, Swiss scientist and businessperson, for endowing the Chair in Sustainable Enterprise at UNC; and Fred Erb and the Max McGraw Foundation for endowing the Erb Environmental Management Institute and Max McGraw Chair, respectively, at Michigan. It is important to recognize the crucial contribution that such gifts make to the legitimacy and institutionalization of this work at major universities and business schools.

There are also a number of people from the corporate and not-for-profit sector who deserve recognition for both their support and influence over the years. Paul Tebo at Dupont, in particular, deserves special recognition. Like Gordon Enk, Paul and DuPont have been involved with the initiatives at Michigan, UNC, and now Cornell. DuPont has also financially supported the initiatives at all three institutions. Dawn Rittenhouse, John Lott, John Hodgson, and Eduardo Wanick, all of DuPont, have also been key supporters of our work. Matt Arnold, originally of the Management Institute for Environment and Business (MEB) and later the World Resources Institute (WRI), has been enormously influential over the years. We began together on this adventure in the early 1990s, as he was forming MEB and I was developing the CEMP Program at Michigan. Like DuPont, WRI has been a long-term partner for more than a decade, with people like Jonathan Lash, Rick Bunch, Jennifer Layke, Rob Day, Meghan Chapple, Al Hammond, and Liz Cook providing key support. Dow Chemical Company, in general, and Dave Buzzelli and Scott Noesen, in particular, also deserve special mention. Dow was among the early supporters of the CEMP Program at Michigan and has since endowed a chair jointly between the Business School and the School of Natural Resources and Environment. Jane Pratt and Jed Schilling of the World Bank and (later) the Mountain Institute have also been key long-term collaborators and partners. Both have been indispensable champions of the content area and the programs over the years. For their business leadership and program involvement, I am also indebted to Lee Schilling and Mac Bridger of Tandus Group (Collins & Aikman Floorcoverings), as well as Sam Moore of Burlington Chemical Company, Dan Vermeer from Coca Cola, and Debbie Zemke at Ford. Jim Sheats, Barbara Waugh, and Gary Herman from Hewlett-Packard also deserve acknowledgement, as do Greg Allgood, Chuck Gagel, Keith Zook, and George Carpenter at Procter & Gamble.

While this list of acknowledgments has grown long, I would be terribly remiss if I did not directly recognize the crucial contributions of coauthors and colleagues in influencing and shaping both my thought and, in some instances, the actual words written in this book. Although the conceptual foundation for this book was clearly laid in several single-authored articles during the 1990s, later collaborations were of critical importance.[6] I would like to recognize Professor C. K. Prahalad (University of Michigan Business School) for his important influence in our joint work that developed the original idea of the bottom of the pyramid as a business opportunity.[7] This work can be found in parts of Chapters 5, 6, and 9. Professor Clayton Christensen (Harvard Business School) also deserves special note. He and I have coauthored two articles that join his theory of disruptive innovation with my work on sustainable development and the base of the pyramid.[8] This joint work can be found in Chapter 5. I have also worked closely with Professor Sanjay Sharma (Wilfred Laurier Business School) in recent years. Our joint work on engaging fringe stakeholders and radical transactiveness can be found in the pages of Chapter 7.[9]

Several doctoral students at the University of North Carolina have also been important colleagues and collaborators over the past seven years. I have known Mark Milstein for 10 years, beginning at Michigan, where he was a student in the CEMP Program. During his tenure as a doctoral student at UNC, he and I coauthored two articles.[10] Our joint work on creative destruction and sustainability can be found in the pages of Chapters 2 and 4; portions of Chapter 3 are also directly attributable to our collaboration on creating sustainable value. Collaboration with Ted London, given his extensive international experience, has also been extremely valuable. Joint work with Ted examining emerging market strategies for the base of the pyramid business entry can be found in parts of Chapters 6 and 8.[11] Finally, although Erik Simanis and I have yet to publish an article together, he has had a significant influence on my thinking over the past few years. The mark of his work, which brings economic anthropology into the business strategy field, can be found in parts of Chapters 7 and 8.

All three of these doctoral students have also made tremendous contributions to the Center for Sustainable Enterprise at UNC over the past several years: Mark Milstein has served as research director for the center and, with Monica Touesnard, has essentially run the Center for the past four years. Erik Simanis helped me to conceive the original idea for the Base of the Pyramid Learning Laboratory at UNC in 2000 as a recently minted MBA, prior to starting the doctoral program. And Ted London has served with great effectiveness as the Director of the BOP Learning Lab since 2001 and has been a close collaborator in our international work in Asia, Africa, and Latin America. Look for these three to make important independent contributions in the near future as they join the faculty ranks.

My participation as a core faculty member in the Sustainable Enterprise Academy (SEA) these past five years has also provided a wonderful venue for trying out new ideas—and learning, in the process. In this regard, I would like to recognize and thank my faculty colleagues in SEA, particularly Brian Kelly, David Wheeler, Bryan Smith, John Ehrenfeld, David Bell, and Nigel Roome, for their honest feedback and support in helping me develop and present my ideas in such a way to achieve maximum impact.

Finally, I would like to acknowledge the patience, support, and editorial skills of my publisher, Wharton School Publishing—in particular, my editor, Jim Boyd (fellow University of Rochester classmate); developmental editor, Elisa Adams; copy editor, Krista Hansing; project editor, Kristy Hart; and Wharton representative Professor Paul Kleindorfer. The book has been vastly improved as a direct result of their skilled eyes—and pens. My colleagues Gordon Enk, Ted London, Erik Simanis, Paul Tebo, Bob Frank, Alan McAdams, and Mark Milstein also provided invaluable feedback on early drafts of the manuscript.

Clearly, the writing of a book like this "takes a village," as Hillary Clinton would say. While I have done my best to recognize as many of the important contributors to my professional life as space allows, there are many more who could have been included. For my friends and colleagues in this group, please forgive me! However, no acknowledgment would be complete without recognizing my parents, Lloyd and Katherine Hart, for their support of my education, and, I'm sure what seemed to be aimless wanderings, for the better part of a decade during the 1970s and 80s. I'm just sorry that my father did not live to see this book finally come to fruition. I'd also like to recognize my brother, Paul, who set the example for me in pursuing the academic route long before I ever imagined doing doctoral work.

Finally, my wife, Patricia, has been nothing short of an inspiration over the years. She has been the ultimate enabler of my work for 30 years. Without her love and support, none of this would have been possible. She is also a very talented editor and confidante. I shudder to think how much time she has spent reading and commenting on my work.

I dedicate this book to my two daughters, Jaren and Jane, in the hopes that it is of some use to them in navigating the troubled waters ahead. For better or worse, it will be their generation that will ultimately have to ensure our transition toward a sustainable world. I wish them Godspeed and hope it is not too late.

Stuart L. Hart
Ithaca, NY
October 2004

Notes

1. See, for example, Stuart Hart, "The Environmental Movement: Fulfillment of the Renaissance Prophesy?" *Natural Resources Journal* 20 (1980): 501–522.
2. A few of these publications include the following: Gordon Enk and Stuart Hart, "An Eight-Step Approach to Strategic Problem Solving," *Human Systems Management* 5 (1985):245–258; Stuart Hart, Mark Boroush, Gordon Enk, and William Hornick, "Managing Complexity Through Consensus Mapping: Technology for the Structuring of Group Decisions," *Academy of Management Review* 10 (1985):587–600.; Stuart Hart, Gordon Enk, and William Hornick, (eds.), *Improving Impact Assessment* (Boulder, CO: Westview Press, 1984); and Stuart Hart and Gordon Enk, *Green Goals and Greenbacks* (Boulder: Westview Press, 1980).
3. Stuart Hart, *Strategic Problem Solving in Turbulent Environments* (Ann Arbor, MI: University of Michigan, 1983).
4. A couple of sample publications include Jac Geurts, Stuart Hart, and Nate Caplan, "Decision Techniques and Social Research: A Contingency Framework for Problem Solving," *Human Systems Management* 5 (1985): 333–347.; and Daniel Denison and Stuart Hart, *Revival in the Rust Belt* (Ann Arbor, MI: Institute for Social Research, 214 pp).
5. Some of my earliest published work in the area was done with Paul Shrivastava. See, for example, his (and Stuart Hart's) Greening Organizations, *Academy of Management Best Paper Proceedings*, 52 (1992):185–189.
6. Two of my most important single-authored articles were "A Natural Resource-Based View of the Firm," *Academy of Management Review* 20 (1995):986–1014; and "Beyond Greening: Strategies for a Sustainable World," *Harvard Business Review* (January–February 1997): 66–76.
7. C. K. Prahalad and Stuart Hart, "The Fortune at the Bottom of the Pyramid," *Strategy+Business* 26 (2002):54–67.

8. Christensen, Clayton, Thomas Craig, and Stuart Hart, "The Great Disruption," *Foreign Affairs* 80(2) (2001): 80–95; and Stuart Hart and Clayton Christensen, "The Great Leap: Driving Innovation from the Base of the Pyramid," *Sloan Management Review* 44(1) (2002): 51–56.

9. Stuart Hart and Sanjay Sharma, "Engaging Fringe Stakeholders for Competitive Imagination," *Academy of Management Executive* 18(1) (2004): 7–18.

10. Stuart Hart and Mark Milstein, "Global Sustainability and the Creative Destruction of Industries," *Sloan Management Review* 41(1) (1999): 23–33; and "Creating Sustainable Value," *Academy of Management Executive* 17(2) (2003): 56–69.

11. Ted London and Stuart Hart, "Reinventing Strategies for Emerging Markets: Beyond the Transnational Model," *Journal of International Business Studies*, 35 (2004): 350–370.

FOREWORD

For those of us unwilling to stick our heads in the sand like an ostrich, Stuart L. Hart's new book gives voice to an inescapable reality: that the corporate sector can be the catalyst for a truly sustainable force of global development for all on the planet.

As the chairman and CEO of a consumer products company with global operations, I see every day the value that business can bring. I see that its products can improve the health and safety of people around the world. I see that its jobs enable parents to support their children, and allow children to achieve dreams not even imagined by their parents.

I also recognize that business has provided fuel for the growing antiglobalization outcry. But despite what some see as the inevitable stain of "progress," I know there are many business leaders who share my belief that you cannot purely pursue greater profitability every quarter and have that be an acceptable mission statement. Or that improving the lives of workers in one country while degrading the environment in another is an unacceptable demonstration of civic responsibility. Short-term quarterly profits cannot trump long-term sustainability.

As the author makes clear in *Capitalism at the Crossroads*, there is no inherent conflict between making the world a better place and achieving economic prosperity for all. Maintaining a principled commitment to global sustainability is not a soft approach to business—

it is, in fact, the only pragmatic approach for long-term growth.

Capitalism at the Crossroads presents a scenario in which business can generate growth *and* satisfy social and environmental stakeholders. By focusing on the four billion people currently at the "base of the pyramid," Hart contends that companies can reap incredible growth while sowing tremendous improvement in people's lives and at the same time preserving the other species that live on this planet.

Business driving sustainability is not a new concept to me. The seed was planted and then cultivated throughout a lifetime of conversations with my father, Samuel C. Johnson. He shared stories about my grandfather, who traveled to Brazil in the 1930s in search of a sustainable source of wax for our products. He described his own 1975 decision to voluntarily and unilaterally ban CFCs from our products despite fervent opposition from colleagues and competitors alike.

My father's pioneering social and environmental efforts led to his selection as an original member of the President's Council on Sustainable Development and as a founding member of the World Business Council on Sustainable Development. He led our family company, SC Johnson, to new heights of corporate environmental and social achievement.

Perhaps most important, my father ensured that the dialogue on sustainability would continue. In 2000, he endowed the Samuel C. Johnson Chair in Sustainable Global Enterprise, and it is this Chair that Hart now so ably and deservedly occupies. He also endowed the new Center for Sustainable Global Enterprise of the Johnson School at Cornell University. By doing so, he was fulfilling a vital obligation that Hart sets forth for business in this book: being optimistic about the future and the opportunities inherent in the global challenges we face.

I share that optimism. That is why in 2001 our company unilaterally developed the Greenlist™ environmental classification system to institutionalize the selection of environmentally preferred raw materials and packaging components, far exceeding government regulation and driving our business with better products. It is why in 2003 we launched programs to attack the menace of malaria in sub-Saharan Africa and the misery of asthma among Hispanic children in Miami. It is why in 2004 we joined with Conservation International's Carbon Conservation Program to help save one of the world's most critically threatened hotspots of biodiversity. Yet we still are in the early stages of truly addressing "base of the pyramid" products.

Optimism underlies all the arguments in *Capitalism at the Crossroads*, and the author presents us with a call to optimistic action. He asks us to involve the full range of stakeholders in crafting solutions to the issues of sustainability. He demands that we embrace a new business paradigm built not on incremental change, but on creative destruction and reinvention. He challenges us to base our policies and businesses on the unassailable truth that shareholder value can be created while solving social and environmental problems.

Some might say linking "global business" and "sustainable development" is an oxymoron, but they would be sorely mistaken. All of us are tied together: the radical environmentalist and the corporate CEO, the Sudanese refugee and the British socialite, the U.S. factory worker and the Argentine farmer. We all share a stake in the future of our global environment and economy. That is the undeniable truth of *Capitalism at the Crossroads*: We are all fundamentally linked, dependent on the same finite resources and driven by the same hopes for ourselves and our children.

I steadfastly believe there is honor and value in business. In *Capitalism at the Crossroads*, Stuart Hart demands that we embrace that truth. I'm convinced this may well be the best opportunity global businesses have to ensure their long-term sustainability. And I am tremendously optimistic about the future.

Dr. H. Fisk Johnson
Chairman and CEO
S.C. Johnson & Son, Inc.

Prologue

CAPITALISM AT THE CROSSROADS

Each human generation believes that it is endowed with special importance, that it faced a particularly important challenge (for example, the "greatest" generation and World War II), that it has a special quality or character (for example, the baby boomers), or that it lived at a particularly important time (for example, the age of enlightenment). The term for this is *chronocentrism*. Although each generation earnestly believes in its own significance, there is objective evidence that those of us alive today will witness the most important time in human history. We truly stand at a crossroads.

From the dawn of our species some 2 million years ago until roughly 12,000 years ago, there were never more than some tens of millions of our brethren walking the planet at any one time. With the advent of agriculture and surplus food production, however, our species embarked on a path of population expansion that continues to this day. By the time of the American Revolution, the human family had grown to approximately one billion. Propelled further by the expansion to the New World and the industrial revolution, the population continued to grow so that by the close of World War II, there were two billion people on the planet.[1]

As a baby boomer born in 1952, I entered a world of about two bil-lion people. In less than half a century, that population had ballooned to more than six billion. If I live to a ripe old age, I could easily see eight billion or more people on the planet. Thus, in a *single lifetime*, the human population will have grown from two billion to more than eight billion. This growth is truly unprecedented. Never before in human his-tory has a single generation witnessed such explosive change. It seems self-evident, therefore, that the policies we adopt, the decisions we make, and the strategies we pursue over the next decade or two will determine the future of our species and the trajectory of the planet for the foreseeable future. That is an awesome responsibility, to say the least. It is also a huge opportunity.

The Best of Times, The Worst of Times

We are truly poised at the threshold of a historic moment. During the past decade, we have witnessed the fall of communism and the birth of a planetary economy and civilization. The United States has emerged as the world's only superpower, championing a message of liberty and democracy rather than conquest and subjugation. Multinational corpo-rations, international institutions, and global civil society have exploded onto the world stage, bringing with them state-of-the-art technology, advanced business practices, and a new accountability. Life expectancy and literacy are on the rise throughout the world.[2]

A revolution in information and communication technologies has unfolded before our eyes, changing the way we live and speeding the spread of information and ideas. The new information-based economy has greatly increased transparency, fostered local self-help, and facili-tated the spread of democracy throughout the world. Technological innovation has also led to dramatic reductions in the material and energy intensity of the economy. Consider, for example, that the U.S. economy "weighed" about the same (in terms of material intensity) at the end of the twentieth century as it did at the beginning of the century, despite being approximately 20 times larger in real terms.[3] As the Iron Age gives way to the Information Age, there is no question that we have much to be thankful for.

Yet fault lines and fissures are also readily visible. Although U.S. consumers did a yeoman's job of driving the world economy during much of the 1990s, it appears that there may be a limit even to Americans' ability to consume goods and services (witness the record levels of consumer debt). Indeed, despite some recent signs of life, the global economy has been sputtering, raising the question of where the growth will come from in the future. With few exceptions (such as oil and pharmaceuticals), most major industries have been mired in an extended slowdown, with no apparent end in sight.

In fact, a decade of economic globalization, privatization, and free trade has produced mixed results, at best. Whereas the wealthy in developed countries have grown richer, the vast majority of nations and people in the world have yet to benefit from the apparent triumph of capitalism and liberal democracy. The $40 trillion–plus world economy is simply not growing fast enough to provide jobs for the tens of millions of young people from around the world joining the labor force each year. Contrary to popular belief, the so-called "roaring '90s" was actually the slowest-growing decade in the world economy in the past 40 years.[4] In fact, the poorest countries in the world have had zero or negative economic growth since the early 1980s.[5]

And whereas developed country economies have indeed become more information- and service-intensive, globally, the use of materials and energy has exploded during the past 50 years, with dire consequences for the world environment. The underlying natural systems supporting human economies—forests, fisheries, soils, ecosystems, and climate—have all experienced significant disruption and decline.[6] The proliferation of new diseases such as AIDS, Ebola, and SARS also reminds us that the potential for a global scourge is only one plane ride away. Already our cows are mad and the birds are sick with the flu.

The Russian fiasco, the Asian financial crisis, and, most recently, the Argentinean crisis have made it clear that the so-called Washington Consensus is coming apart at the seams: The International Monetary Fund, the World Bank, and the World Trade Organization are all under increasing fire, even from insiders such as Jeffery Sachs, Joseph Stiglitz, and George Soros.[7] Lack of an international standard of value, currency instability, and wild swings in the business cycle have contributed to simultaneous recession in the three major world economies, a lack of investment in the developing world, and an ongoing conflict between the short-term financial demands of shareholders and long-term sustainability. Across the developing world, there is less enthusiasm for globalization's potential to bring prosperity to the masses.[8]

A rising tide of antiglobalization has emerged that combines concerns about environmental degradation, inequity, human rights, cultural imperialism, and loss of local autonomy. Wealthy protesters organize massive demonstrations against multinational corporations and the institutions of global capitalism, such as the WTO and the World Economic Forum. The disenfranchised become increasingly organized—and militant—in their desire to assert their autonomy. Indian-led movements in Bolivia, for example, succeeded in toppling the Western-friendly government in that country and have joined a continent-wide backlash against free-market reforms. Many, in fact, assert that the whole concept of "development" must be abandoned, in favor of a new concept that gives a greater voice to the views and aspirations of local people.[9]

Two recent events, in particular, have fueled anticorporate and antiglobalization sentiments: the Enron debacle, which has eroded the public's already low level of trust in corporate conduct; and the events of September 11, 2001, which have proven that unrest in one part of the world will not remain geographically isolated. Indeed, terrorism—the ultimate expression of antiglobalization—is on the rise, driven by poverty and hopelessness and, in the Muslim world, by a growing sense of defiance and polarization. And despite the United States' best intentions, it is not clear that a doctrine of "preventive war" can bring about democratization, empowerment, or self-determination.[10]

Implications for Corporations

The global dynamics just described have significant implications for large multinational corporations (MNCs), given their centrality to the global economy. There are now more than 60,000 MNCs (defined as any corporation with operations in more than one country) with more than a quarter-million affiliates around the world. MNCs account for more than 25 percent of world economic output. During the 1990s, foreign direct investment (FDI) by MNCs overtook official development assistance (ODA); by 2000, it exceeded ODA by more than a factor of 5. Indeed, MNCs have become the primary instruments of economic globalization, facilitating the diffusion of more efficient and competitive business practices throughout the world.[11]

However, a growing chorus of voices points out that the process of economic globalization driven by MNCs over the past decade has also had a dark side.[12] For example, the 10 largest MNCs have annual sales of more than the GNPs of the 100 smallest, poorest countries in the world, raising concerns about sovereignty and the ability of governments to determine their own fate.[13] Given the ability of MNCs to shift resources and production across borders, many have also suggested that they encourage a global "race to the bottom" by chasing subsidies, incentives, and lower costs wherever they might lead, at the expense of national and community interests.[14]

Of the top 200 MNCs in the world, the vast majority have their origins in the most affluent, developed countries of the world—in the United States, in European countries, and Japan. A growing number of critics have voiced concern that such corporate dominance is leading to a worldwide commercial monoculture based upon the values of Western consumerism and bringing with it the decline of local cultures, products, and traditions.[15] Others decry the environmental consequences associated with spreading the energy- and material-intensive industries associated with global capitalism to the rest of the developing world.[16]

And although MNCs account for a quarter of global economic activity, they employ less than 1 percent of the world's labor force, while one-third of the world's willing-to-work population is either unemployed or underemployed.[17] Furthermore, while a substantial number of Americans now hold shares in companies either directly or through pension accounts, less than 1 percent of the world's population participates in the financial markets as shareholders. As a consequence, the wealth created by MNCs accrues almost exclusively to a relatively small number of wealthy people in the world—corporate executives, employees, and Western shareholders.[18]

We can also discern a similar trend on the corporate investment side, where the vast majority of FDI occurs within the richest countries.[19] Investment in emerging markets has been limited largely to the wealthiest of the poor countries or those with the largest potential markets, such China, India, and Brazil. Even there, most MNC products are aimed at the wealthy, elite customers or those in the rising middle-class segments of the market.[20] Virtually no commercial attention has been paid to serving the needs of those at the base of the economic pyramid.[21]

The result is that, during the past 40 years, the gap between the richest and the poorest in the world has continued to widen. In 1960, for example, the richest 20 percent accounted for 70.2 percent of global GDP, while the poorest 20 percent controlled 2.3 percent (a ratio of 30:1). By 2000, however, this gap had widened considerably: The richest quintile controlled 85 percent of global GDP, while the poorest accounted for only 1.1 percent (a ratio of 80:1).[22]

Clearly, MNCs alone are not responsible for all these problems: International financial institutions such as the International Monetary

Fund and the World Bank have played a central role. Corrupt and repressive regimes in the poorest countries have also been major contributors to the problem. Still, these dynamics are increasingly being viewed as unacceptable. MNCs, for better or worse, are on the "front line" of globalization. If current trends continue, they can only become more frequent targets of antiglobalization protests, sabotage, and terrorism.

The Fork in the Road

Global capitalism now stands at a crossroads: Without a significant change of course, the future for globalization and multinational corporations appears increasingly bleak. It might be argued, in fact, that global capitalism stands at a juncture similar to the one faced in 1914. Between 1914 and 1945, world war, depression, fascism, and communism almost succeeded in eliminating capitalism from the face of the Earth. The problems global capitalism now faces (international terrorism, the backlash against globalization, global-scale environmental change) are no less daunting. Constructively engaging these challenges will be the key to ensuring that capitalism continues to thrive in the coming century—to everyone's benefit.

The Brundtland Commission defined sustainable development as that which "meets the needs of the present without compromising the ability of future generations to meet their own needs."[23] By creating a new, more inclusive brand of capitalism, one that incorporates previously excluded voices, concerns, and interests, the corporate sector could become the catalyst for a truly sustainable form of global development—and prosper in the process. To succeed, however, corporations must learn how to open up to the world: Strategies need to take into account the entire human community of 6.5 billion, as well as the host of other species with which we share the planet.

Sustainable global enterprise thus represents the potential for a new private sector–based approach to development that creates profitable businesses that simultaneously raise the quality of life for the world's poor, respect cultural diversity, and conserve the ecological integrity of the planet for future generations. Making such a societal contribution while simultaneously creating shareholder value will take real imagination and a fresh approach to business strategy. These exciting and uplifting challenges are the focus of the pages that follow.

Notes

1. For a fascinating account of the human species' emergence, see Jared Diamond, *Guns, Germs, and Steel* (New York: W.W. Norton, 1999).

2. Allen Hammond, *Which World?* (Washington, D.C.: Island Press, 1998).

3. Diane Coyle, *Paradoxes of Prosperity* (New York: Textere, 2001).

4. Thomas Palley, "A New Development Paradigm: Domestic Demand-Led Growth," *Foreign Policy in Focus* (September, 1999), www.fpif.org/papers/development_body.html.

5. William Easterly, *The Elusive Quest for Growth* (Cambridge, MA: MIT Press, 2002).

6. Allen Hammond, *Which World?*

7. See, for example, Jeff Sachs, "Helping the World's Poorest." *The Economist* (14 August 2000): 17–20; Joseph Stiglitz, *Globalization and its Discontents* (New York: W.W. Norton, 2002); and George Soros, *George Soros on Globalization* (New York: Perseus Books, 2002).

8. This point is made convincingly by Hernando DeSoto, *The Mystery of Capital* (New York: Perseus Books, 2000).

9. See, for example, Wolfgang Sachs, *Planet Dialectics* (London: Zed Books, 1999).

10. Benjamin Barber, *Fear's Empire* (New York: Ballantine Books, 2003).

11. Rajan Raghuram and Luigi Zingales, *Saving Capitalism from the Capitalists* (New York: Crown Business, 2003).

12. Perhaps the best articulation of this point of view can be found in David Korten, *When Corporations Rule the World* (San Francisco: Berrett-Koehler, 1995).

13. As Jagdish Bhagwati points out in his book *In Defense of Globalization* (New York: Oxford University Press, 2004), this comparison, while appealing, is conceptually flawed. When we compare sales volumes, which are gross values, with GDP, which includes only value-added figures for the goods and services, we are comparing apples and oranges. In other words, corporate sales figures across an entire economy will add up to numbers that vastly exceed the GDPs of the countries where these sales occur.

14. David Korten, *When Corporations Rule the World.*

15. See Colin Hines, *Localization: A Global Manifesto* (London: Earthscan, 2000).

16. Allen Hammond, *Which World?*

17. The World Bank, *World Development Report* (New York: Oxford University Press, 2000).

18. David Korten, *When Corporations Rule the World.*

19. Jeff Sachs, "Helping the World's Poorest."

20. C. K. Prahalad and Ken Lieberthal, "The End of Corporate Imperialism," *Harvard Business Review* 76(4) (1998): 68–79.

21. C. K. Prahalad and S. Hart, "The Fortune at the Bottom of the Pyramid," *Strategy+Business* 26 (2002): 2–14.

22. The World Bank, *World Development Report.*

23. Brundtland Commission, *Our Common Future* (New York: Oxford University Press, 1997).

Part One
Mapping the Terrain

1

FROM OBLIGATION TO OPPORTUNITY

This book takes the contrarian's view that business—more than either government or civil society—is uniquely equipped at this point in history to lead us toward a sustainable world in the years ahead. I argue that corporations are the only entities in the world today with the technology, resources, capacity, and global reach required. Properly focused, the profit motive can *accelerate* (not inhibit) the transformation toward global sustainability, with nonprofits, governments, and multilateral agencies all playing crucial roles as collaborators. The book is written with a practical focus and should be of direct use to executives, entrepreneurs, and technologists, as well as business school faculty and students. The contents are equally appropriate, however, for those from the nonprofit world, the public sector, and society at large, especially those interested—and inclined—to collaborate with the private sector.

The book carries an optimistic message. Despite the gathering storm of environmental degradation, antiglobalization protest, and terrorism, it envisions a central and expanding role for commerce, particularly multinational corporations, in fostering global sustainability. It foresees massive opportunities for companies both to make money and to make the world a better place, particularly among the four billion poor at the base of the economic pyramid. This book is the result of an intellectual journey that began for me more than three decades ago. My own personal evolution is reflected in its structure and flow. Allow me to explain.

Having grown up in western New York in the 1950s and '60s, I have memories of family vacations spent at destinations like Niagara Falls. Although the Falls themselves were indeed magnificent, equally memorable for a 10-year-old was the soot from nearby factories that accumulated on the porch furniture, requiring that we clean the furniture daily, lest we ruin our clothes. The accompanying stench was also something to experience. I still remember asking why, in a place of such natural beauty and splendor, did it have to be so polluted? The answer, accepted wisdom in those days, was that this was "the smell of money." If we were going to have economic prosperity, then we would have to put up with some minor inconveniences, such as soot, stench, rivers that catch fire, and mountains of waste. It was the cost of progress. I remember being singularly unsatisfied by this response.

Fast-forward to 1974. As a freshly minted college graduate headed to Yale for graduate work in the School of Forestry and Environmental Studies, I was convinced that corporations were the "enemy" and that the only way to deal effectively with environmental problems was to "make them pay" through regulation—to internalize their externalities, in the jargon of economics. This was probably a correct perception at that point in history: Large corporations, by and large, had been unresponsive to environmental issues, and it appeared that the only way to deal with the problem was to force them to clean up the mess they were making. The Environmental Protection Agency, along with scores of other regulatory agencies, was created precisely for this purpose. A mountain of command-and-control regulation was passed during the decade of the 1970s, aimed at forcing companies to mitigate their negative impacts.

Regulators and citizen activists, buoyed by their newfound power, increased the pressure on companies through fines, penalties, campaigns, and consent decrees. The courts became clogged with lawsuits aimed at halting projects that were deemed unacceptable due to their environmental or social impacts. Economists of the "environmental" variety wrote books about externalities and the public policies that would be required for them to be "internalized" most efficiently by companies.[1] In the process, companies became convinced that social and environmental issues were necessarily costly problems, usually involving lawyers and litigation. For better or worse, the message was that environmental and social issues were "responsibilities" that companies were required to deal with—and it was going to be expensive.

The Great Trade-Off Illusion

There can be no question that command-and-control regulation was of enormous importance; it *required*, perhaps for the first time, that business address directly its negative societal impacts. Since the time of the industrial revolution, enterprises had relied upon the extraction of cheap raw materials, exploitation of factory labor, and production of mass quantities of waste and pollution (think of those "dark, satanic mills"). Indeed, pollution was *assumed* to be part of the industrialization process. When economists conceived the concept of externalities, in other words, it seemed virtually impossible that firms could behave in any other manner. For the better part of 200 years, industrial firms engaged in what might be described as "take, make, waste" as an organizing paradigm.[2] Command-and-control regulation seemed a necessary and appropriate counter to the prevailing industrial mindset.

Paradoxically, this mindset also resulted in what I call the "Great Trade-Off Illusion"—the belief that firms must sacrifice financial performance to meet societal obligations.[3] A massive wall of environmental and social regulation has been spawned over the past 30 years, most of which has been written in a way that makes the Great Trade-Off Illusion a self-fulfilling prophesy. Just track the thickness (and lack of flexibility) of the Code of Federal Regulations in the United States for confirmation.[4] Too often, command-and-control regulations prescribed specific treatment technologies without regard to their efficiency or cost-effectiveness.

A generation of businesspeople was shaped by this framing of the situation. Not surprisingly, the managers and executives who rose to prominence during the postwar years were predisposed to think of environmental and social issues as negatives for business. A socially minded executive or company might "give back" to the community through philanthropy or volunteering, but such concerns would *certainly* never be part of the company's core activities! The social responsibility of business was to maximize profits, as Milton Friedman advocated, and it seemed clear that social or environmental concerns could only serve to *reduce* them.[5]

Even today, this mindset lingers. Try the following thought experiment: Imagine that you are a general manager in a business or company of your choosing. Your assistant calls saying that the environment, health, and safety (EHS) manager and the public affairs director are in your outer office, and they say the matter is *urgent*. What is your first reaction? If you are honest with yourself, you will have to admit that the first thoughts that come to mind are something like: *problem, crisis, spill, incident, accident, boycott, protest, lawsuit, fine,* or *jail time.* Your first instinct was probably to head for the back door of your office to escape.

But now try a second thought experiment: Your assistant calls saying that the heads of marketing and new product development are in your outer office and they are anxious to meet with you. Now, what is your first reaction? What thoughts or issues come to mind? In all likelihood, your mind probably flashes to images like: *breakthrough, opportunity, blockbuster, innovation,* or *growth.* Your first instinct is to run to the front door of the office to let them in.[6]

The Great Trade-Off Illusion trained a generation of corporate, business, and facility-level managers to assume that societal concerns could only be drags on their business. As a consequence, their attitude tended to be *reactive*—they would do only the bare minimum necessary to avoid legal sanction. Unfortunately, when lawmakers and activists unfamiliar with operations or market dynamics write the rules for compliance, it is a virtual certainty that the rules will not integrate well with company strategy or operations. Taking a reactive posture thus doomed companies to a decade or more of onerous regulations that treated the symptoms rather than the underlying problems. These regulations targeted specific wastes, emissions, pollutants, and exposure levels through command-and-control-style rules that forced companies to deal with problems "at the end of the pipe" rather than addressing them as part of their core strategy or operations. Unfortunately, pollution-control devices can never improve efficiency or produce revenue; they can only add cost.

The Greening Revolution

The decade of the 1980s brought with it a growing sense of unease with command-and-control regulation. Despite enormous expenditures, it was not at all clear that the end-of-the-pipe approach to pollution control and regulation was working.[7] Alternatives such as market-based incentives and tradable emission permits demonstrated that pollution levels could be reduced in a dramatically more efficient and cost-effective manner. In Europe, a more collaborative and goal-oriented approach to regulation was the norm; the focus was on actual environmental and social improvement rather than the specification of particular treatment technologies or pollution control devices.

I, too, was undergoing a transformation of sorts. In 1986, I joined the faculty at the University of Michigan Business School, having completed my doctoral work in strategy and planning in 1983. My transition from a regulatory to a business strategy orientation reflected my own growing disenchantment with the command-and-control approach to dealing with environmental and societal problems. Rather than simply trying to halt polluting projects or mitigate damage, I became increasingly interested in understanding why such seemingly bad projects were being proposed in the first place.

This change proved fortuitous: By the late 1980s, there was a growing receptivity to environmental and social issues within companies—and business schools. As luck would have it, this openness developed through innovation in another arena: quality management. As you might recall, in the late 1970s and early 1980s, Japanese companies were literally overrunning their American and European competitors with higher-quality and lower-cost goods. From steel makers to automobile firms, to consumer electronics manufacturers, companies were scrambling to match the Japanese quality advantage. Because of widespread plant closures and downsizing, there was palpable concern that the West would lose to "Japan, Inc."[8]

After three glorious postwar decades of high-volume, standardized mass production with quality *inspected* in (after the fact) rather than *built* in (as part of the design and production process), Western companies were being out-competed by a new and better way. Instead of countering with their own unique strategies, American and European companies became obsessed with learning and copying the ways of Japanese quality management.[9] Among other things, they built the capacity for "continuous improvement" (*kaizen*) into the management system by empowering workers to improve their work processes rather than blindly following prescribed procedures. Managers' mindsets changed from a fixation on centralized control and a "results" orientation (detecting defects and fixing them) to a preoccupation on decentralization and a "process" orientation (improving the management system so that employees could *prevent* quality problems from occurring in the first place).[10]

Shattering the Trade-Off Myth

The confluence of the quality and environmental movements was a marriage made in heaven: By the late 1980s, it had become clear that *preventing* pollution and other negative impacts was usually a much cheaper and more effective approach than trying to clean up the mess after it had already been made. The emergence of market-based incentives such as tradable emission permits made prevention even more appealing. Furthermore, the discipline of quality management could be easily expanded to incorporate social and environmental issues. In the early 1990s, this confluence produced a flurry of so-called environmental management system (EMS) approaches and "total quality environmental management" protocols, culminating in the advent of ISO 14001, the environmental equivalent of ISO 9000 for quality.

Community advisory panels and stakeholder dialogues, intended to involve affected parties in company affairs instead of doing battle in court, proved to be a much more effective way to maintain legitimacy and the "right to operate." Indeed, in designing its self-regulation program called Responsible Care, the chemical industry enshrined the principles of pollution prevention and community engagement as part of its product stewardship process. In short, the quality revolution taught us that *muda* (waste) was the enemy of good management. Pollution and litigation were the ultimate forms of *muda*.

As social and environmental issues became more deeply embedded in the ongoing operations of enterprises, managers began to see that corporate and societal performance need not be separated. Whereas companies previously sought to first make money through their business operations and then give back to society through philanthropy, now these two agendas could be merged. What had been a virtual firewall separating business from philanthropy was now transforming into a host of new and creative approaches to combining the two through corporate partnerships with nongovernmental organizations, strategic philanthropy, and other forms of social innovation.[11]

Furthermore, in certain situations, preventing pollution through process or product redesign could actually save money, reduce risk, and even improve products for the firm. An extensive body of research began to document the situations and contexts in which pollution prevention and product stewardship resulted in superior financial performance.[12] Not surprisingly, parlaying environmental and social performance into improved business performance required a set of supporting or complementary capabilities, such as employee empowerment, quality management, cross-functional cooperation, and stakeholder engagement. This meant that the greening revolution had not only succeeded in elevating the significance of social and environmental issues, but it also had converted them from expensive problems into strategic opportunities for certain firms with the necessary skills, capabilities, and leadership vision.[13]

Breaking Free of Command-and-Control

Accompanying the greening revolution in the corporate sector was the emergence of a new philosophy in regulation and public policy that recognized the limitations (and expense) of conventional regulation and the end-of-the-pipe mentality. In response, a slew of new *voluntary initiatives* were introduced that recognized the power of information disclosure and transparency.[14] The pioneering initiative was the Toxic Release Inventory (TRI) in the US. Passed in 1988 as a rider on the Superfund

Reauthorization (the law establishing strict liability for toxic waste sites), the TRI received relatively little attention in its early days. This seemingly innocuous provision required only that manufacturers disclose their use, storage, transport, and disposal of more than 300 toxic chemicals (all of which were perfectly legal at the time). Much to everyone's surprise, this data, maintained by the U.S. Environmental Protection agency, became an important new source of information for activist groups, the media, and third-party analysts to track corporate environmental performance. Top 10 lists of corporate polluters became *de rigeur*.

The TRI also provided, for the first time, a metric for corporate and facility managers to track their own firms' performance and benchmark it against competitors. What gets measured gets done. Ten years later, toxic emissions in the United States had been reduced by *more than 60 percent,* even though the U.S. economy boomed during the 1990s. Indeed, many companies actually saved tens of millions of dollars in the process of reducing or eliminating their toxic emissions.[15] We could argue that the TRI was one of the most important and effective pieces of social legislation ever passed. And it required nary a lawsuit, court battle, or inspector to make it happen. Since then, many developing countries have adopted a similar philosophy of transparency and information disclosure as the basis for their environmental policies, since these can be implemented at a fraction of the cost of command-and-control regulations.

Equally important was the advent of "extended producer responsibility" laws, primarily in Europe.[16] Quite simply, these laws stipulate that manufacturers are responsible for the products they create *all the way to the end of their useful lives.* Beginning with regulations on packaging waste in Germany in the late 1980s, these laws now extend to several industrial sectors, including automobiles, consumer electronics, and computers. Requiring that producers take back their products after they have reached the end of their life has obvious effects on the way companies go about designing products in the first place. This simple requirement has fomented a revolution in product stewardship and "green design" protocols, using life-cycle management as its core principle. Rather than focusing only on the phase of the product's life cycle that the company controls (manufacture or assembly), product stewardship means designing products to take account of their entire life cycle, from the sourcing of raw materials and energy from the Earth to the reuse, remanufacture, or return of the materials to the Earth. Rather than thinking linearly, in terms of "cradle to grave," increasingly, designers think cyclically, in terms of "cradle to cradle."[17]

In the process, companies have discovered that life-cycle design principles can yield competitively superior products. During the early 1990s, for example, Xerox pioneered take-back, remanufacturing, and design-for-environment strategies in the photocopier business and reaped significant competitive benefits. Given the company's extensive field presence for servicing commercial copiers, it was relatively easy to take back used machines, refurbish parts and components, and produce a line of remanufactured machines. However, it was not until the mid-1990s that Xerox actually began to *design* copiers with an eye toward taking them back. This program, dubbed Asset Recycle Management, was founded on the notion that by reusing assets as many times as possible (recall that most Xerox commercial copiers were leased, not owned by customers), the company would not only reduce its environmental footprint, but also lower its costs and increase its return on assets. It set the goal of producing "waste-free products from waste-free factories."[18] By the late 1990s, Xerox was saving close to $500 million per year through this program, a figure approaching 2.5 percent of company sales. In fact, it can be argued that, given Xerox's failure to shift its strategy toward printers (since documents were increasingly being stored electronically and printed rather than duplicated), the Asset Recycle Management Program kept the company afloat for much of the 1990s.

As the green revolution progressed, leading companies began to shift their energy and attention more toward *proactive* strategies that reduced waste, emissions, and impacts while simultaneously reducing costs and risks. Paying real money for raw materials and inputs only to dump substantial amounts of these into the environment in the form of waste made little economic sense. In fact, Dow Chemical estimated in the early 1990s that reactive efforts such as regulatory compliance, cleanup, and remediation result in returns in the range of –60 percent while proactive initiatives typically produce positive returns in excess of 20 percent.[19] The problem was that most corporate activity (perhaps as much as 90 percent) was still of the reactive variety. The challenge was to transform the portfolio so that more was of the proactive sort. Ultimately, the goal is to get out of the regulatory compliance business entirely.

It was becoming clear that, *under the right circumstances,* firms could actually improve their own competitive position by creating societal value. They could, for example, lower costs by internalizing externalities through pollution prevention. Furthermore, through product stewardship, it was sometimes possible to supply public goods and achieve superior performance. Witness Volvo's new radiator that actually cleans the air as it cools the engine, or BP's climate-change policy that reduces its greenhouse gas emissions while reducing its costs. We should emphasize, however, the caveat "under the right circumstances:" Only through creativity, imagination, and the persistent development of particular skills and capabilities can firms simultaneously optimize financial, social, and environmental performance.

By the early 1990s, the greening revolution had led to the creation of a new dual-degree program at the University of Michigan involving both the Business School and the School of Natural Resources and Environment: the Corporate Environmental Management Program (CEMP). Integrating pollution prevention and product stewardship into the management curriculum was the backbone for this program. As the founding director of CEMP, I had completed a virtual turnabout: It was now clear to me that the corporate sector itself was the key leverage point for achieving substantial and lasting change in societal performance, and that financial performance need not suffer in the process. I could finally put aside the demons from the past associated with "the smell of money." I came to realize instead that pollution was the smell of waste and poor management.

Beyond Greening

Yet, this personal reconciliation was by no means the end of the road. The corporate "greening" initiatives of the late 1980s and early 1990s—pollution prevention and product stewardship—were important first steps. They shattered the myth that business should treat societal issues as expensive obligations. Instead, seen through the prism of quality and stakeholder management, these issues could become important opportunities for the company to improve its societal and operating performance simultaneously. A growing body of research pointed to the potential for enhanced financial performance through well-executed pollution prevention and product stewardship strategies. Pioneers such as 3M, Dow, and Dupont realized significant cost reductions and enhanced reputations as a result of their activities. The World Business Council for Sustainable Development, with its mantra of "eco-efficiency," helped to erase the false dichotomy between business and environmental performance.

However, greening alone fell well short of what was possible—and needed: Incremental improvements to current product systems and production processes only slowed the rate of environmental damage. Sustainability means inventing a new form of "natural capitalism."[20] As University of Virginia architect Bill McDonough points out, greening is akin to heading in the wrong direction, but at a slower rate of speed—being less bad. Sustainability, however, means actually turning around and heading in the right direction—being more good. It is, as McDonough and his colleague Michael Braungart point out, the difference between being eco-efficient and being eco-effective.[21]

Furthermore, most corporations continued to serve the needs of the wealthy exclusively while exploiting the developing world primarily for its abundant resources and cheap labor pool. A sustainable global enterprise would instead seek to create corporate and competitive strategies that simultaneously deliver economic, social, and environmental benefits for the entire world.[22] By the mid-1990s, it was clear that the corporate agenda was much bigger than just greening—and that the business opportunity was much more substantial as well. This was the key message of my 1997 McKinsey award-winning article in the *Harvard Business Review*, "Beyond Greening: Strategies for a Sustainable World." It was also my primary motivation for moving to the University of North Carolina at Chapel Hill in 1998 to become the founding director of the Center for Sustainable Enterprise at the Kenan-Flagler Business School.

Corporations were being challenged to move beyond greening, first by pursuing new technologies that had the potential to be inherently clean (renewable energy, biomaterials, wireless IT), and second by reaching out to bring the benefits of capitalism to the entire human community of 6.5 billion people (rather than just the 800 million at the top of the economic pyramid). In recognition of this challenge, my colleagues at UNC and I launched in 2000 The Base of the Pyramid Learning Laboratory, a consortium of large corporations, new ventures, and nongovernmental organizations (NGOs) all focused on how best to serve the needs of the four billion people at the base of the economic pyramid (BOP) in a way that is culturally appropriate, environmentally sustainable, and economically profitable.

By moving beyond greening, companies hope not only to address mounting social and environmental concerns, but also to build the foundation for innovation and growth in the coming decades. In so doing, they would outperform their competitors in today's businesses and, even more important, outrun them to tomorrow's technologies and markets. In short, sustainable global enterprises would create competitively superior strategies that simultaneously move us more rapidly toward a sustainable world.

Exhibit 1.1 summarizes the evolutionary path that corporations have followed over the past 50 years. Crossing the chasm from seeing societal performance as a trade-off or *obligation* (the left side of the figure) to a possible win-win *opportunity* (the lower-right side) was the major breakthrough of the 1980s. By the mid-1990s, many large corporations had internalized the capabilities and disciplines associated with greening, although some still had a long way to go. As a result, the competitive front migrated to the "beyond greening" domain (the upper-right portion).

Exhibit 1.1
The Long and Winding Road

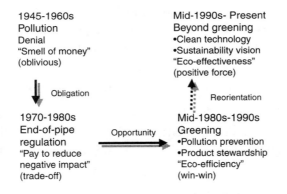

Rather than seeking incremental improvements to what already exists, moving beyond greening often means pursuing innovations that may make obsolete what currently constitutes the company's core business—it is an inherently disruptive act. Thus, given its focus on new technologies and markets, the "beyond greening" space is blessed with much greater opportunities, but also fraught with bigger risks. One case in particular—Monsanto's controversial entry into genetically modified seeds—illustrates the potential opportunities and pitfalls of pursuing such strategies.[23]

Raging Against the Machine

In the mid-1990s, new CEO Robert Shapiro sought to revolutionize Monsanto. Through the power of his vision, he hoped to convert the firm from a chemicals manufacturer to a life-sciences company focused on "Food, Health, and Hope." Consistent with this vision, Shapiro spun off several strategic business units (SBUs) associated with the organization's chemicals business heritage, retaining only those closely tied to its life sciences focus. Simultaneously, he took the company on an acquisition binge, aggressively buying up biotech and seed companies, and huge debt in the process. The more focused—and leveraged—company then set out on a rapid growth strategy to make agricultural biotechnology a practical reality.

Shapiro also articulated how Monsanto's genetically engineered seeds gave the firm an advantage in the drive toward sustainability because they could increase farmers' yields, reduce pesticide use, and help to deliver nutrients to the world's chronically undernourished poor. In the space of a few years, Monsanto convinced farmers to plant nearly 60 million acres in the U.S. in genetically modified crops. In 1997, Shapiro also launched a new Sustainable Development Sector, empowering dozens of internal champions to identify and grow the new businesses of the future that would address global social and environmental concerns in an economically profitable manner. Between 1995 and 1997, Monsanto's stock price soared amid rosy projections of blockbuster products and rapidly expanding markets for agricultural biotechnology.

As a result of these developments, Monsanto was thrust into the public eye in a way that few companies had ever been in the past. Shapiro's portrayal of biotechnology's role in the future of agriculture generated unprecedented levels of public attention and scrutiny. This scrutiny resulted in problems for Monsanto as critics cast bright lights on incidents in which company actions did not match the spirit of Shapiro's vision.

For example, when Monsanto attempted to launch its genetically modified seeds in Europe, it met intense resistance from organic farmers and environmentalists, despite the fact that all the necessary regulatory approvals had been secured. Some Monsanto managers hired private investigators to ensure that customers (farmers) were not illegally saving Monsanto's genetically modified seed for replanting the following year. These actions and others alienated many who called into question Monsanto's true dedication to sustainable development and environmental stewardship. Shapiro's vision, in other words, did not always align with the actions taken by people in the company.

Other stakeholder groups included the millions of small farmers in developing countries such as India. These farmers protested against Monsanto in the streets, fearing that the company would enforce patents on essential grains and make them pay international prices for the seed they planted. Moreover, the farmers were concerned that Monsanto's patent ownership (via acquisition) of the "terminator" gene (seed-sterilization technology) would not allow them to practice the age-old tradition of propagating seeds from their own crops.

Regrettably, Monsanto did not enable these voices to reach business decision makers. The firm consulted with its immediate customers (large-scale farmers), regulators, and consumer groups in the United States. Despite efforts by the company's Sustainable Development Sector to access other voices, the business decision makers did not consider consumer groups in Europe or small farmers in developing countries to be legitimate or persuasive, even if their claims seemed urgent.

Instead of becoming a more open, innovative culture, the firm became more defensive and had to back away publicly from several of its biotechnology initiatives under pressure from growing protest. Indeed, in October 1999, Monsanto publicly apologized for its behavior: "Our confidence in this technology (genetic engineering) and our enthusiasm for it has, I think, been widely seen, and understandably so, as condescension and indeed arrogance."[24] External support for the firm's strategy had eroded, and in late 1999, the company followed through on merger talks with pharmaceutical maker Pharamcia & Upjohn. This move effectively ended the Shapiro era of sustainability-driven corporate strategy at Monsanto.

Smart Mobs Versus Smart Globalization

How do we account for the rapid rise—and even more precipitous fall—of a major corporation such as Monsanto, which had done nothing wrong according to society's legal and regulatory institutions and had, in fact, transformed its business model to add value to its customers while reducing environmental impact?[25] Certainly, the emergent nature of biotechnology had something to do with the problems that Monsanto experienced. Indeed, an accelerating pace of technological change appears to be generating ever-faster cycles of creative destruction.[26]

Yet there is even something more fundamental at work here. The power of governments has eroded in the wake of globalization and the growth of transnational corporations with global supply chains that span several continents. NGOs and civil society groups have stepped into the breach, assuming the role of monitor and, in some cases, enforcer of social and environmental standards.[27] Today, for example, there are more than 50,000 international NGOs, compared to fewer than 20,000 only a decade ago.[28]

At the same time, the spread of the Internet and other information technologies has enabled not only these groups, but also millions of individuals, to communicate with each other in ways that were unimaginable even a decade ago.[29] Indeed, Internet-connected coalitions of NGOs and individuals—smart mobs—are now making it impossible for governments, corporations, or any large institution to operate in secrecy.[30] The varied claims of these smart mobs have created a dynamically complex business environment in which organizations find it difficult to determine what knowledge is relevant for managing strategic change; just ask senior managers at Shell, Nike, the World Trade Organization, or the World Economic Forum.

Unfortunately, as the Monsanto case illustrates, most companies still tend to focus management attention only on known, powerful, or "salient" stakeholders—those who can directly impact the firm.[31] Even recent efforts at "radical transparency," the complete and truthful disclosure of an organization's plans and activities, appear inadequate because they entail reporting only what has already been decided or, in fact, accomplished. Yet in a world of smart mobs, firms cannot manage stakeholders. Instead, swarms of stakeholders self-organize on the Net in chaotic and unpredictable ways.

Groups at the "fringe" of a firm's stakeholder network can acquire an important voice in such swarms. To avoid the wrath of the smart mob, it has now become essential to proactively seek out the voices from the fringe that had previously been ignored. To survive and compete for the future, firms must harness these voices to identify creative new business models and opportunities. The tyranny of the smart mob can yield to a new form of what might be called "smart globalization:" growth via disruptive business models that address the social and environmental concerns of fringe stakeholders.[32]

Becoming Indigenous

The Monsanto experience holds an important lesson: If corporate sustainability strategies are narrowly construed, they will fall seriously short. It is not enough to develop revolutionary technology with the potential to leapfrog currently unsustainable methods. Antiglobalization demonstrators have made it apparent that if corporate expansion is seen to endanger local autonomy, it will encounter vigorous resistance. Multinationals seeking new growth strategies to satisfy shareholders increasingly hear concerns from many quarters about consumer monoculture, labor rights, and cultural hegemony. As long as multinational corporations persist in being outsiders—alien to both the cultures and the ecosystems within which they do business—it will be difficult for them to realize their full commercial, let alone social, potential. It was with this realization that I embarked on a new professional challenge in 2003, having accepted the SC Johnson Chair in Sustainable Global Enterprise at Cornell University's Johnson School of Management.

Today corporations are being challenged to rethink global strategies in which one-size-fits-all products are produced for the global market using world-scale production facilities and supply chains. Even so-called locally responsive strategies are often little more than preexisting corporate solutions tailored to "fit" local markets: Technologies are frequently transferred from the corporate lab and applied in unfamiliar cultural and environmental settings; unmet needs in new markets are identified through demographic (secondary) data. The result is stillborn products and inappropriate business models that fail to effectively address real needs.

The next challenge will thus be for corporations to become "indigenous" to the places in which they operate (see Exhibit 1.2). Doing so will require that they first widen the corporate bandwidth by admitting voices that have, up to now, been excluded; this means becoming radically *transactive* rather than just radically *transparent*. It will also entail the development of new "native" capabilities that enable a company to develop fully contextualized solutions to real problems in ways that respect local culture and natural diversity. When combined with multinational corporation's (MNC) ability to provide technical resources, investment, and global learning, native capability can enable companies to become truly embedded in the local context.

Unilever's Indian subsidiary, Hindustan Lever Limited (HLL), provides an interesting glimpse of the development of native capabilities in its efforts to pioneer new markets among the rural poor.[33] HLL requires all employees in India to spend six weeks living in rural villages, actively seeks local consumer insights and preferences as it develops new products, and sources raw materials almost exclusively from local producers. The company also created an R&D center in rural India focused specifically on technology and product development to serve the needs of the poor. HLL uses a wide variety of local partners to distribute its products and also supports the efforts of these partners to build local capabilities. In addition, HLL provides opportunities and training to local entrepreneurs and actively experiments with new types of distribution, such as selling via local product demonstrations and village street theaters.

By developing local understanding, building local capacity, and encouraging a creative and flexible market entry process, HLL has been able to generate substantial revenues and profits from operating in low-income markets. Today more than half of HLL's revenues come from customers at the base of the economic pyramid. Using the approach to product development, marketing, and distribution pioneered in rural India, Unilever has also been able to leverage a rapidly growing and profitable business focused on low-income markets in other parts of the developing world. Even more important, through its new strategy, HLL has created tens of thousands of jobs, improved hygiene and quality of life, and become an accepted partner in development among the poor themselves.

Exhibit 1.2
Indigenous Enterprise:
The Next Sustainability Challenge

Beyond Greening ➝ Becoming Indigenous

Sustainability Vision — Radical Transactiveness
• Create a roadmap for targeting the unmet needs at the BOP ┄┄┄► • Broaden the corporate bandwidth by engaging fringe stakeholders

Clean Technology — Native Capability
• Deploy the sustainable "leapfrog" technologies of the future ┄┄┄► • Coinvent contextualized solutions that leverage local knowledge

"Alien" ⟶ "Native"

The Road Ahead

To summarize, the greening initiatives of the late 1980s and early 1990s were revolutionary, if insufficient, steps: They repositioned social and environmental issues as profit-making opportunities rather than profit-spending obligations. More recent "beyond greening" strategies are even more significant: They hold the potential to reorient corporate portfolios around inherently clean technologies and create a more inclusive form of capitalism that embraces the four billion poor at the base of the economic pyramid. If narrowly construed, however, such strategies still position MNCs as outsiders, alien to both the cultures and the ecosystems within which they do business. The challenge is for multinationals to move beyond "alien" strategies imposed from the outside to become truly indigenous to the places in which they operate. To do so will require companies to widen their corporate bandwidths and develop entirely new "native" capabilities that emphasize deep listening and local codevelopment. A more inclusive commerce thus requires innovation not just in technology, but also in business models and mental frames.

Thus, as we enter the new millennium, capitalism truly does stand at a crossroads. The old strategies of the industrial age are no longer viable. The time is now for the birth of a new, more inclusive form of commerce, one that lifts the entire human family while at the same time replenishing and restoring nature. The path to a sustainable world, however, will be anything but smooth. It will be a bumpy ride strewn with the remains of companies that variously dragged their feet, made promises they could not keep, bet on the wrong technology, collaborated with the wrong partners, and separated their social and business agendas. Only those companies with the right combination of vision, strategy, structure, capability, and audacity will succeed in what could be the most important transition period in the history of capitalism.

Overview of the Book

This chapter has provided a guided tour of the argument contained in the book. The book itself is divided into three parts. Part One, "Mapping the Terrain," provides the background and context for the chapters that follow; it describes the global situation and establishes the business case for pursuing strategies that aim to solve social and environmental problems. It also outlines the challenges and opportunities that remain to be addressed, particularly those that involve the development of new, more sustainable technologies and the needs of the four billion people who have been largely bypassed thus far by globalization. Part Two, "Beyond Greening," then develops the logic and content of these "beyond greening" strategies in more depth. Finally, in Part Three, "Becoming Indigenous," I suggest how corporations might begin to move beyond even these strategies for sustainability by learning to become more embedded in the local context. Learning to become indigenous, I argue, is the next strategic challenge on the road to building a sustainable global enterprise.

Chapter 2, "Worlds in Collision," places the global challenges associated with sustainability in the larger context. It seeks to cut through the complexity by providing a readily digestible framework for thinking about the current global situation, characterizing it as the collision of three economies or worlds—the money economy, the traditional economy, and nature's economy. Ultimately, the challenge is to develop a *sustainable global economy*: an economy that the planet is capable of supporting indefinitely, while simultaneously providing for the entire human community in a way that respects cultural, religious, and ethnic diversity. This chapter seeks to put this challenge into perspective and offers some thoughts about appropriate roles for multinational corporations.

Chapter 3, "The Sustainable Value Portfolio," closes out the first section of the book by developing a detailed framework for connecting the agendas of sustainability and value creation. Just as companies must succeed on many fronts in order to create shareholder value, so, too, must they master economic, social, and environmental challenges to achieve sustainability. These challenges affect virtually every aspect of a firm's strategy. The chapter makes clear that although the biggest opportunity for the future lies in moving beyond greening, most companies still focus virtually all their attention on greening or (worse) mere compliance.

Part Two of this book develops the strategies that move beyond greening in greater depth. Chapter 4, "Creative Destruction and Sustainability," articulates the strategic logic for pursuing leapfrog strategies to clean technology in ways that open exciting new growth markets but also often make the firms' existing technologies and products obsolete. The chapter also shows how the lens of whole-systems thinking can help to prioritize investment in the new technologies and capabilities that will be important to the future competitiveness of the enterprise.

Chapter 5, "The Great Leap Downward," demonstrates why the four billion people at the base of the world economic pyramid represent the most attractive early market for many of the most exciting new clean technologies. Because most such technologies are disruptive and will, therefore, be resisted by established markets, the vast underserved populations in shantytowns and rural villages offer the most promising places to incubate and grow the technologies of tomorrow. In the process, they also provide platforms for new growth industries that hold the potential to revolutionize markets at the top of the pyramid—and move us much more rapidly toward a sustainable world.

Chapter 6, "Reaching the Base of the Pyramid," articulates some basic principles for successfully tapping into these emerging markets and shows how effective strategies will generate not only corporate growth and profits, but also local jobs, incomes, and solutions to social and environmental problems. By removing the constraints imposed on the poor, increasing their earning power, and creating new potential in poor communities, companies can identify and pursue previously invisible opportunities. To be successful in these new markets, however, companies must pursue *business model innovation* just as avidly as technological innovation.

Finally, Part Three of this book critically evaluates early "beyond greening" experiences and offers some prescriptions for how to move toward a more indigenous and inclusive form of commerce. Chapter 7, "Broadening the Corporate Bandwidth," first describes how the existing conceptions of "development" and "modernization" reflect a Western cultural bias and a preoccupation with simply raising income and GDP per capita. Together, these shortcomings significantly hinder efforts to imagine and build healthy communities and markets at the base of the pyramid. To successfully serve the needs of the entire human community, therefore, corporations must broaden their bandwidth. Radical transactiveness is the tool proposed to enable companies to hear the true voices of those who have been marginalized or ignored by globalization.

Chapter 8, "Developing Native Capability," then shows how critical it is to expand our conception of the global economy to include not just the transactions that occur in the formal economy, but also the myriad other forms of economic activity that are typically ignored—the informal economy, household production, and the barter economy, for example. Native capability means bridging the formal and informal sectors: Development at the base of the economic pyramid does not follow traditional patterns found in the developed world. Indeed, the chapter shows that success in this space means focusing on what is *positive* in the BOP, not just what is negative (corruption), or missing (Western-style institutions). Native capability then enables global firms to move beyond the existing transnational model, with its emphasis on global supply chains, world scale, and centrally developed—and often alien—solutions.

In the final chapter, "Toward a Sustainable Global Enterprise," the problem of terrorism is shown to be, at base, a problem of unsustainable development. Only by removing the underlying conditions that lead to extremist movements will we be able to move toward global sustainability. The Middle East thus represents the biggest immediate challenge—and opportunity—on the road to a sustainable global enterprise. Most of the book focuses on *what* companies might do to pursue the sustainability path—the strategies, practices, and capabilities that are required. What is less clear is *how* to pursue this path, particularly within the context of large, incumbent, multinational corporations. This chapter therefore closes with some thoughts on what it will take to make this happen in the real world of budgets, quarterly earnings reports, discounted cash flow analysis, and the discipline of the investor community.

Notes

1. For example, Allen Kneese and Charles Schultze, *Pollution, Prices, and Public Policy* (Washington, D.C.: Brookings, 1975); and Robert Dorfman and Nancy Dorfman, *Economics of the Environment* (New York: W.W. Norton, 1972).

2. Ray Anderson, *Mid-Course Correction* (White River Junction, VT: Chelsea Green, 1998).

3. It is not my intention here to suggest that trade-offs do not exist between corporate economic and societal performance. Clearly, in some situations, command-and-control regulation is the only viable solution. In others, however, it is possible to internalize externalities or even supply public goods in a way that facilitates economic performance. The problem has been blind adherence to the belief that such "win-win" situations are generally not possible.

4. Again, my intention here is not to suggest that command-and-control regulation does not serve an important purpose. For laggards and criminals, there is no option. However, for those firms seeking to move beyond compliance, such regulation can sometimes limit degrees of freedom and slow the rate of innovation.

5. Milton Friedman, "The Social Responsibility of Business Is to Increase Its Profits," *The New York Times Magazine* 13 September (1970): 32–33, 122–126.

6. My thanks to Paul Tebo at DuPont for this wonderful illustration.

7. Indeed, the Reagan administration in the United States was bent on reforming—or, better yet eliminating—these regulations.

8. Clyde Prestowitz, *Trading Places* (New York: Basic Books, 1988); Barry Bluestone and Bennett Harrison, *The Deindustrialization of America* (New York: Basic Books, 1982); and Ira Magaziner and Robert Reich, *Minding America's Business* (New York: Vintage Books, 1982).

9. Ironically, quality management was an American invention in the first place, but it was rejected in the 1950s by U.S. companies who were making too much money through high-volume, standardized mass production. Proponents such as Deming and Crosby found willing adopters, however, in the struggling companies of post-war Japan.

10. See, for example, Masaki Imai, Kaizen: *The Key to Japan's Competitive Success* (New York: Random House, 1986).

11. Excellent examples include Bill Shore, *The Cathedral Within* (New York: Random House, 1999); and Mark Albion, *Making a Life, Making a Living* (New York: Warner Books, 2000).

12. Michael Porter and Claas van der Linde, "Green and Competitive: Ending the Stalemate." *Harvard Business Review* (September/October 1995): 120–134; Stuart Hart and Gautam Ahuja, "Does It Pay to Be Green? An Empirical Examination of the Relationship Between Emission Reduction and Firm Performance," *Business Strategy and the Environment* 5 (1996): 30–37; Michael Russo and Peter Fouts, "A Resource-Based Perspective on Corporate Environmental Performance and Profitability," *Academy of Management Journal*

40(3) (1997): 534–559; Petra Christmann, "Effects of 'Best Practices' of Environmental Management on Cost Advantage: The Role of Complementary Assets," *Academy of Management Journal* 43(4) (1998): 663–680; and Sanjay Sharma and Harrie Vredenburg, "Proactive Corporate Environmental Strategy and the Development of Competitively Valuable Organizational Capabilities." *Strategic Management Journal* 19 (1998): 729–753.

13. For an excellent and in-depth treatment of greening as business opportunity and strategy, see Forest Reinhardt, *Down to Earth* (Cambridge, MA: Harvard Business School Press, 2000).

14. A. Marcus, D. Geffen, and K. Sexton, *Reinventing Environmental Regulation: Lessons from Project XL* (Washington, D.C.: Resources for the Future/Johns Hopkins University Press, 2002).

15. Andy King and Michael Lenox, "Exploring the Locus of Profitable Pollution Reduction," *Management Science* 47(2) (2002): 289–299.

16. See Nigel Roome and Michael Hinnells, "Environmental Factors in the Management of New Product Development," *Business Strategy and the Environment* 2(1) (1993): 12–27; and Ulrich Steger, "Managerial Issues in Closing the Loop," *Business Strategy and the Environment* 5(4) (1996): 252–268.

17. William McDonough and Michael Braungart, *Cradle to Cradle* (New York: North Point Press, 2002).

18. Fiona Murray and Richard Vietor, *Xerox: Design for Environment* (Boston: Harvard Business School Publishing, 1993).

19. Personal communication with Dave Buzzelli, Dow Chemical Company, 1996.

20. Paul Hawken, Amory Lovins, and Hunter Lovins, *Natural Capitalism* (New York: Little, Brown and Company, 1999),

21. William McDonough and Michael Braungart, *Cradle to Cradle*.

22. This is referred to as the "triple bottom line." See John Elkington, *Cannibals with Forks* (Gabriola Island, B.C.: New Society Publishing, 1998).

23. Erik Simanis and Stuart Hart, Monsanto *Company (A) and (B): Quest for Sustainability* (Washington, D.C.: World Resources Institute, 2000).

24. Robert Shapiro, *Address to Greenpeace's Annual Conference*, 1999.

25. This section is excerpted from Stuart Hart and Sanjay Sharma, "Engaging Fringe Stakeholders for Competitive Imagination," *Academy of Management Executive* 18(1) (2004): 7–18.

26. Robert Foster and Sarah Kaplan, *Creative Destruction* (New York: Currency Books, 2001).

27. David Korten, *When Corporations Rule the World* (West Hartford, CT: Kumarian Press, 1995).

28. Christopher Gunn, *Third-Sector Development* (Ithaca, NY: Cornell University Press, 2004).

29. Ann Florini, ed., *The Third Force: The Rise of Transnational Civil Society* (Washington, D.C.: Carnegie Endowment for International Peace, 2000).

30. Howard Reingold, Smart Mobs: *The Next Social Revolution* (Cambridge, MA: Perseus Publishing, 2002).

31. R. K. Mitchell, B. R. Agle, and D. J. Wood, "Toward a Theory of Stakeholder Identification and Salience: Defining the Principle of Who and What Really Counts," *Academy of Management Review* 22 (1997): 853–886.

32. See, for example, Anil Gupta and Eleanor Westney, eds., *Smart Globalization* (San Francisco: Jossey-Bass, 2003).

33. Brian Ellison, Dasha Moller, and Miguel Angel Rodriguez, *Hindustan Lever: Reinventing the Wheel* (Barcelona, Spain: IESE Business School, 2003).

2

WORLDS IN COLLISION

Nearly three decades ago, environmentalists made this simple but powerful observation. The total environmental impact (I) created by human activity on the planet is a function of three factors: population (P); affluence (A), which is a proxy for consumption; and technology (T), which is how wealth is created. The total environmental impact of human activity can thus be expressed as a formula: $I = P \times A \times T$.[1]

Achieving sustainability will require stabilizing and ultimately reducing the human impact on the planet. We can do that by drastically decreasing the human population, lowering the level of affluence (consumption), or fundamentally changing the technology used to create wealth—effectively moving technology (T) into the *denominator* of the formula. The first option, decreasing population, is not feasible short of draconian political measures unless we experience a major public health crisis that causes mass mortality (such as a global pandemic created by a new disease). Indeed, while the rate of population growth is slowing, it is not expected to stabilize until midcentury, at somewhere between 8 billion and 10 billion.

The second option, decreasing the level of affluence, is also not viable; it would only make sustainability harder to achieve because poverty and population growth go hand in hand. Demographers have long known that birth rates are inversely correlated with the standard of living and level of education. Thus, stabilizing the human population will require improving the education and economic standing of the world's four billion desperately poor, particularly women of childbearing age.

Some believe that the problems of poverty can be addressed through the redistribution of existing wealth. Closer examination, however, reveals the folly of this approach: Even if all the assets of the world's seven million millionaires (totaling about $25 trillion), were divided among the world's four billion poorest, that would still give only about $6,000 to each in the form of a one-time payment—clearly not a viable solution to the problem.[2] In the end, elevating the standing of the poorest can be accomplished only by creating new wealth on a massive scale. Indeed, it might be necessary to increase world economic activity tenfold to support a population of 8 billion to 10 billion.

That leaves the third option: changing the technology used to create the goods and services that constitute the world's wealth. Although population and consumption are societal issues, technology is the business of business. If economic activity must increase tenfold over what it is today to support a population nearly double its current size, then technology will have to reduce its impact *twenty-fold* merely to keep the planet at its current levels of environmental impact. Thus, for those who believe that ecological disaster will somehow be averted, it must also be clear that, over the next decade or so, sustainable development will constitute one of the biggest opportunities in the history of commerce. And innovation will be the name of the game.

For example, bio- and nanotechnology create products and services at the molecular level, holding the potential to completely eliminate waste and pollution.[3] Biomimicry emulates nature's processes to create novel products and services without relying on brute force to hammer out goods from large stocks of virgin raw materials.[4] Wireless information technology and renewable energy are distributed in character, meaning that they can be applied in the most remote and small-scale settings imaginable, eliminating the need for centralized infrastructure and wireline distribution, both of which are environmentally destructive. Such technologies thus hold the potential to meet the needs of the billions of rural poor (who have thus far been largely ignored by global business) in a way that dramatically reduces environmental impact.[5]

The Three Economies

It should be clear from this that transformation toward global sustainability will mean the creation of trillions of dollars in products, services, and technologies that barely exist today. Whereas yesterday's businesses were often oblivious to their negative impacts and today's responsible businesses strive to reduce their impacts, tomorrow's businesses will learn to make a *positive* contribution. Increasingly, companies will be selling solutions to the world's social and environmental problems, and doing so in a way that respects diversity and cultural differences. Envisioning tomorrow's businesses, therefore, requires that we gain a fuller appreciation of a complex set of global interdependencies.[6] In fact, the global economy is really composed of three different, overlapping economies: the money economy, the traditional economy, and nature's economy.

The Money Economy

The money economy is the familiar world of industry and commerce comprising both the *developed economies* and the so-called *emerging economies*. Roughly two billion people participate in the money economy, with less than half of those living in the wealthy countries of the developed world. Those affluent 800 million, however, account for more than 75 percent of the world's energy and resource consumption, and also create the bulk of its industrial, toxic, and consumer waste.

Although industrialization has produced tremendous economic benefits, it has also generated significant pollution burdens and continues to consume virgin materials, resources, and fossil fuels at an increasing rate.[7] In fact, with its rapid growth in emerging economies, industrial activity has reached the point that it might now be having irreversible effects on the global environment, including impacts on climate, biodiversity, and ecosystem function.[8] The money economy thus leaves a large ecological footprint, defined as the amount of land and resources required to meet a typical consumer's needs. For example, with only about 4 percent of the world's population, the United States, the largest money economy, consumes in excess of one-quarter of the world's energy and materials.[9]

Despite such intense use of energy and materials, levels of conventional industrial pollutants have declined in the developed economies over the past 30 years. Three factors account for this seeming paradox: stringent environmental regulation, the greening of industry, and the relocation of the most polluting activities (such as commodity processing and heavy manufacturing) to the emerging market economies. Thus, to some extent, the greening of the developed world has come at the expense of the environments in emerging economies. Given the much larger population base in those countries, their rapid industrialization could easily offset the environmental gains made in developed countries.

With industrialization in emerging economies comes urbanization—people leaving the countryside in search of wage employment. Today, about one of every three people in the world lives in a city. By 2025, if trends continue, it will be two out of three.[10] Demographers predict that by that year, there will be more than 30 megacities with populations exceeding eight million, and more than 500 cities with populations exceeding one million. Urbanization on this scale presents enormous infrastructural challenges because the major portion of such growth is in the form of urban slums, shantytowns, and squatter communities. Consider, for example, that over the next 20 years, given current trends, more than 300 million people in China alone will migrate from rural areas to cities. This is the equivalent of the entire current population of North America moving to cities in the next two decades.[11]

Because industrialization has focused initially on commodities and heavy manufacturing, cities in many emerging economies suffer from oppressive levels of pollution. Acid rain is a growing problem, especially in places where coal combustion is unregulated. The World Bank estimates that, by 2010, there will be more than one billion motor vehicles in the world. Concentrated in cities, they will double current levels of energy use, smog precursors, and emissions of greenhouse gas. The result is that, although environmental conditions have improved on some dimensions in the developed world, rapid industrialization in emerging economies is a mounting problem, with an associated explosion of urban slums and shantytowns in the developing world. Another part of the price to be paid for a cleaner environment in the developed world has been large-scale outsourcing of manufacturing industries, with associated job loss and dislocation. Indeed, in the United States, only the wealthiest quintile has seen real income increase over the past two decades. For the vast majority of Americans, real income has actually decreased during this time.[12]

The Traditional Economy

The second economy is the *traditional economy*: the village-based way of life found in the rural parts of most developing countries. It is made up of roughly four billion people—fully two-thirds of humanity— mainly Indians, Chinese, Latin Americans, and Africans who are subsistence-oriented and meet their basic needs directly from nature, while participating only sparingly in the cash or money economy. Demographers generally agree that the world's population, currently growing by about 100 million people per year, will continue to increase until it levels off at somewhere between 8 billion and 10 billion after midcentury. Developing countries will account for 90 percent of that growth, and most of it will occur in the traditional economy.[13]

Owing in part to the rapid expansion of the money economy, existence in the traditional economy is becoming increasingly precarious. Indigenous cultures, once able to live in a self-sufficient manner based upon the principles of community, frugality, and sufficiency, have been irreversibly changed by the introduction of cash and wage employment.[14] Structural adjustment, privatization, and free trade have accelerated this trend over the past two decades. Indeed, massive poverty appeared only when the spread of the money economy eroded community ties and traditional cultures. Extractive industries and the development of infrastructure have also, in many cases, degraded the ecosystems upon which the traditional economy depends.

Rural populations are driven further into poverty as they compete for natural resources often made scarce through expansion of the money economy. Women and children in rural areas spend most of their day searching for fuel wood and drawing and carrying water. Ironically, these conditions encourage high fertility rates because, in the short run, children help the family to garner needed resources. But in the long run, population growth in the traditional economy only reinforces a vicious cycle of resource depletion and poverty. Indeed, survival pressures often force these rapidly growing rural populations into practices that cause damage to forests, soil, and water. When wood becomes scarce, people burn dung for fuel, one of the greatest—and least known—environmental hazards in the world today. Contaminated drinking water is an equally grave problem. The World Health Organization estimates that burning dung and drinking contaminated water together cause eight million deaths per year.

As it becomes more difficult to live off the land, millions of desperate people migrate to already overcrowded cities in search of wage employment, often splitting up families and fracturing village communities. Increasingly, the young are migrating to foreign countries in search of wage jobs. It is estimated, for example, that repatriation of income by migrant Mexicans working in the United States has now approached $30 billion per year.[15]

Although some find employment in the formal sector, others fall prey to the vicissitudes of the criminal sector: prostitution, drug trafficking, and child labor. Most never find full-time wage employment and instead join the burgeoning informal or extralegal sector of the economy, working in literally millions of small, unregistered enterprises. In fact, Hernando de Soto, the well-known Peruvian economist, estimates that the informal sector accounts for 40–70 percent of total economic activity in developing countries. Because corrupt governments and bureaucratic red tape make official registration of small businesses by the poor prohibitively expensive, the informal economy has become the fastest-growing sector in much of the developing world.[16]

A growing number in the traditional economy have simply become permanent refugees. In China, for example, an estimated 120 million people roam from city to city, landless and jobless, driven from their villages by deforestation, soil erosion, droughts, and floods. Worldwide, the number of such environmental refugees from the traditional economy could be as high as 500 million people, and the figure is growing.[17]

The result is that, although humanity as a whole is clearly better off than it was a hundred years ago (even the poorest of the poor have better access to education, health care, and food than they did back then), inequity has grown, and the poor—particularly those in the traditional economy—generally face a bleak future. Either they can leave their families in search of potential wage employment in the cities, or they can remain to face an increasingly difficult economic and environmental situation at home. In the Middle East, the situation is particularly explosive: As we have seen, when religious extremism and a growing sense of humiliation are combined with widespread joblessness and hopelessness, the result is terrorism.

Nature's Economy

The third economy is *nature's economy*, which consists of the natural systems and resources that support the money and the traditional economies. In fact, the money and traditional economies are actually *embedded* in nature's economy because the former could not exist without the latter. Nonrenewable resources such as oil, metals, and other minerals are finite. Renewable resources such as soils, fisheries, and forests will replenish themselves—as long as their use does not exceed critical thresholds.

Technological innovations have created substitutes for many commonly used nonrenewable resources; for example, optical fiber now replaces copper wire. And in the developed economies, demand for some nonrenewable materials might actually diminish in the decades ahead because of reuse and recycling. Ironically, the greatest threat to sustainable development today is depletion of the world's *renewable* resources.

Indeed, as we begin the twenty-first century, the money and traditional economies are slowly destroying their own support system.[18] Increasing demands of the two economies are surpassing the sustainable yields of the ecosystems that underpin them. For example, one-third of the world's cropland is losing topsoil at a rate that is undermining its long-term productivity, fully half of the world's rangeland is overgrazed and deteriorating into desert, and the world's forests have shrunk by about half since the dawn of agriculture and are continuing to shrink. Water tables are falling under large expanses of the three leading food-producing countries—China, India, and the U.S. In China, for example, the combination of land clearing, overplowing, and overgrazing to satisfy rapidly expanding food demand is creating a dust bowl like the U.S. Dust Bowl of the 1930s, but on a much larger scale. Insufficient fresh water may prove to be the most vexing problem in the developing world over the next decade, as agricultural, commercial, and residential uses increase.[19]

Existing crop varieties are no longer responding to increased use of pesticides and fertilizer. As a consequence, per capita world production of both grain and meat peaked and began to decline during the 1980s.[20] Meanwhile, the world's 18 major oceanic fisheries have reached or exceeded their maximum sustainable yields. Some even believe that the great North Atlantic Cod fishery could go extinct within the decade. Furthermore, there is now international scientific consensus that human activity, driven by carbon emissions from fossil fuel use, is having a direct effect on the Earth's climate system.[21] For the past two decades, natural disasters have been on the increase, with property damage worldwide rising roughly 10 percent per year. And in the year 2000, open water was discovered at the North Pole, stunning many in the scientific community.[22]

By some estimates, humankind now uses more than 40 percent of the planet's net primary productivity, the total amount of the sun's energy fixed by green plants. As a result, loss of biodiversity is already a significant problem, especially in the tropics where the vast majority of life forms exist.[23] This biological impoverishment is the result of habitat destruction, pollution, climate alteration, and hunting. If, as projected, the human population increases from 6.5 billion to perhaps 10 billion over the next 50 years, we may ultimately drive the majority of remaining species into extinction. In short, nature's economy is in retreat on a global scale.

Collision Course

The interdependence of the three economic spheres is plain. In fact, the three economies have become worlds in collision, creating the major social and environmental challenges facing the planet, but also opening up business opportunities of vast proportions (see Exhibit 2.1). Consider, for example, that the average American today consumes 17 times more than his or her Mexican counterpart and hundreds of times more than the average Ethiopian.[24] The levels of material and energy used in the United States require massive quantities of raw materials and commodities, sourced increasingly from the traditional economy and produced in emerging economies.

Exhibit 2.1
Worlds in Collision: The Business Opportunity

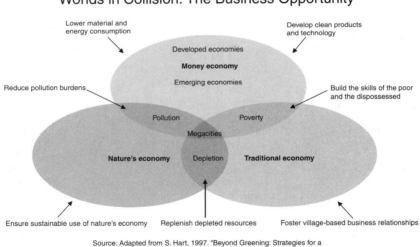

Source: Adapted from S. Hart, 1997. "Beyond Greening: Strategies for a Sustainable World." *Harvard Business Review*, January-February (1997): 66-76.

In the traditional economy, massive infrastructure development projects (dams, irrigation projects, mining operations, highways, and power stations), often aided by agencies, banks, and corporations in the developed countries, have provided access to raw materials. Unfortunately, such development has often had devastating

consequences for nature's economy and has tended to strengthen existing, often corrupt, political and economic elites, with little benefit to
those in the traditional economy. At the same time, such development
projects have contributed to a global glut of raw materials and, hence, to
a long-term fall in commodity prices. And as commodity prices have
fallen relative to the prices of manufactured goods, the currencies of
developing countries have weakened and their terms of trade have
become less favorable. Their purchasing power declines while their
already substantial debt load becomes even larger. The net effect of this
dynamic has been the transfer of vast amounts of wealth (an estimated
$40 billion per year since 1985) from developing to developed coun-
tries, producing a vicious cycle of resource exploitation and pollution to
service mounting debt.[25]

In the past, ignorance and isolation meant that those in the traditional and emerging economies were largely unaware of their plight.
Today, however, the digital revolution is bringing information—and
ideas—to growing numbers of the world's poor. Such knowledge is
potentially empowering, as we will see, creating the potential to reform
corrupt regimes, solve environmental problems, and spur more equi-
table forms of development.[26] However, the global information economy also possesses a dark side: It facilitates the efforts of nihilists,
anarchists, terrorists, and others bent on derailing the evolution of a
planetary civilization.

New Lenses on the Global Market

The growing interdependence among the three economies has defined
the major social and environmental challenges of our time. But as
Exhibit 2.1 also makes clear, the worlds in collision have also created
new opportunities for those companies with the capacity to understand
and address these challenges. Indeed, there are business opportunities in
each of the three economies, as well as at the intersection points. In the

money economy, there is significant need for lower material and energy consumption and the development of clean products and technologies. In the traditional economy, the ability to foster village-based businesses to understand and serve the needs of those at the base of the economic pyramid is of paramount importance. In nature's economy, ensuring sustainable use of natural capital offers significant opportunities for the future. The collision points are also pregnant with opportunity: Reducing waste and pollution, replenishing depleted resources, and building the skills of the poor and the dispossessed are all crucial for achieving a more sustainable world. They also represent significant business opportunities.

As my colleague Mark Milstein and I have argued, however, managers, particularly in multinational corporations, are more accustomed to viewing the global market as a single monolithic entity.[27] They focus almost exclusively on the money economy and customers who have achieved a certain level of affluence. They consider markets to be of value only to the extent that consumers have purchasing power comparable to that found in the United States, Western Europe, or Japan. Throughout human history, however, wherever there have been people, there have been markets. Indeed, markets are ubiquitous—they are not unique to the wealthy.[28] Thus, within any country or region, even the United States, there are *three* types of markets: developed, emerging, and traditional. The developed and emerging markets make up the money economy; traditional markets correspond to the traditional economy. All three are embedded in nature's economy. Not surprisingly, the sustainability challenges—and business opportunities—associated with each are dramatically different (see Exhibit 2.2).

In the developed, or consumer, market, about 800 million global customers have the purchasing power to afford virtually anything they want. A global supply chain and well-developed infrastructure allow for the rapid production and distribution of products and services, and consumption occurs at high levels. In the emerging market (well more than one billion people), rapid industrialization and urban migration are increasing demand for basic products and services. However, inadequate infrastructure and distribution hamper the ability of companies to effectively serve this rapidly growing market. Finally, in the traditional market, consisting of more than two-thirds of humanity, more than four billion people have been adversely affected by globalization, ignored by the world of commerce, and victimized by corruption. In most rural areas, there is virtually no infrastructure, credit and collateral are lacking, and legal protections are nonexistent; few companies, as a result, have dared to invest in what they perceive as a risky and potentially dangerous long-term proposition.

Exhibit 2.2
Major Challenges to Sustainability

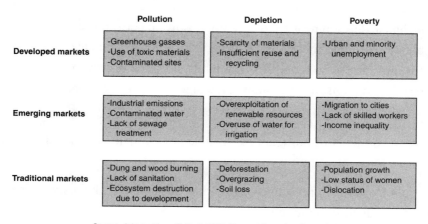

	Pollution	Depletion	Poverty
Developed markets	-Greenhouse gasses -Use of toxic materials -Contaminated sites	-Scarcity of materials -Insufficient reuse and recycling	-Urban and minority unemployment
Emerging markets	-Industrial emissions -Contaminated water -Lack of sewage treatment	-Overexploitation of renewable resources -Overuse of water for irrigation	-Migration to cities -Lack of skilled workers -Income inequality
Traditional markets	-Dung and wood burning -Lack of sanitation -Ecosystem destruction due to development	-Deforestation -Overgrazing -Soil loss	-Population growth -Low status of women -Dislocation

Source: Adapted from S. Hart, 1997. "Beyond Greening: Strategies for a Sustainable World." *Harvard Business Review*, January-February (1997): 66-76.

Given their distinctive characters, each market requires a different strategy to achieve a more sustainable form of development. To succeed in the developed (consumer) market, managers must focus on reducing the ecological footprint of their firms by reinventing products and processes. To meet the long-term needs of the emerging market, managers must avoid the collision between rapidly growing demand for products and the physical basis for supply or waste disposal. Finally, in

the traditional market, managers must recognize the opportunity presented by a massive group of potential customers whose real needs
remain poorly understood. Each of these is addressed in more detail in
the rest of the chapter.

Developed Markets: Reducing Corporate Footprint

In the consumer economy, many of the resource- and energy-intensive
industries—chemicals, automobiles, energy, and mining, to name a
few—leave very large corporate footprints. Product systems with large
footprints are usually based on mature technologies. As technologies
mature, they reach a point at which even large additional investments in
technical development yield only small gains in performance. The combination of large footprint and technological maturity creates openings
for innovation. To identify sustainability-related opportunities in the
developed (consumer) economy, managers should therefore ask these
questions:

- Are most of our technological advances incremental instead of
  breakthrough?

- Does our core technology hold us back from making significant
  reductions in footprint?

- Where can we remove material content from our products?

- How can our service content be dramatically increased?

- Can our waste be utilized productively in other processes?

DuPont CEO Chad Holliday recently commented: "The objective
for our industry ought to be sustainable growth. In the [twenty-first]
century, we are going to have to find ways to create value while
decreasing our environmental footprint."[29] In the late 1990s, I worked
with DuPont Vice President Paul Tebo and others to create a tool for

analyzing the corporate footprint by comparing the total pounds of materials consumed per annum in each business with shareholder value added (SVA) per pound. The analysis highlighted three distinct groups of businesses for DuPont (see Exhibit 2.3).

Small-footprint businesses, those using fewer materials and having a high SVA per pound, were seen as "differentiated" businesses; these included photopolymers, electronic materials, agricultural biotech, Lycra™, Tyvek™, Corian™, and auto finishes. Businesses with medium footprints and medium SVA per pound—Nylon and Polyester—were seen as "foundation" enterprises because they represented the traditional core of the company's business. Businesses with large footprints and low SVA per pound, such as the petroleum subsidiary Conoco, represented the company's least desired enterprises. DuPont sees the high earnings, cash flow, and intellectual content (R&D/capital) of the differentiated businesses as the models for the future. As a result, over the past few years, large-footprint businesses such as Conoco and even foundation (core) enterprises such as Nylon and Polyester have been divested or spun off in an effort to fuel future growth in the differentiated businesses and to reduce corporate footprint.

Exhibit 2.3
Reducing the Corporate Footprint at DuPont

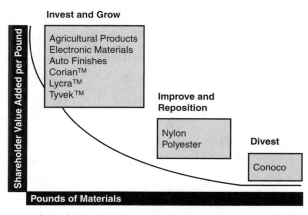

Source: S. Hart and M. Milstein, 1999. "Global Sustainability and the Creative Destruction of Industries." *Sloan Management Review*, 41(1) (1999): 23-33.

Collins & Aikman Floorcovering (now part of the Tandus Group) is another company that has premised its entire competitive strategy on footprint reduction. In the mid-1990s, the company became the first commercial carpet manufacturer in the world to convert old carpet and post-industrial PVC waste into carpet backing for a new product line.[30] Called ER3 (which stands for Environmentally Redesigned, Restructured, and Reused), this product actually possesses superior functionality (it is more stable and "cushy" than conventional backing made from virgin material) and is cheaper to produce (at least in part because much of the raw material is available in the form of "waste" from customer sites). The combination of lower cost and higher functionality has fueled the company's double-digit growth in both revenues and profits in an industry that is growing at only about 4 percent per year. Today the company no longer sells a virgin product in the carpet tile segment. Appropriately, the company's motto is "Mining buildings rather than resources."

Finally, Wisconsin-based SC Johnson Company, makers of Raid®, Glade®, and Windex®, among other household brands, has dramatically reduced its footprint—and realized substantial savings in the process.[31] As part of its campaign to reduce fossil fuel use and greenhouse gas emissions, the company partnered with a nearby landfill operator to access its methane potential. The company invested in a gas turbine unit and piped the methane gas from the nearby landfill to help power its Waxdale manufacturing facility, one of the company's major production sites. The 3200-kilowatt turbine with cogeneration capability (which utilizes the waste heat to make process steam) cut fossil fuel use in half at the facility while simultaneously saving the company more than $2 million per year. A second turbine together with the first would supply 100 percent of the average daily power needs at Waxdale. These two landfill gas projects alone have enabled the company to more than meet its aggressive goals for reduction in greenhouse gas emissions worldwide through 2005, a total of more than 50,000 tons of carbon dioxide per year.

Emerging Markets: Avoiding the Collision

Rapid urbanization and industrialization, together with increasing demand for products and services, are placing intense pressure on ecological and social systems in the emerging economies of the developing world. Technologies that previously fueled the development of the consumer market will be inadequate for meeting those future demands without exceeding nature's capacity for replenishment. Avoiding a collision between rapidly growing demand and a diminishing stock of material supply will, therefore, be the biggest challenge in emerging markets. To identify sustainability-related opportunities in emerging markets, managers should ask these questions:

- Is it environmentally feasible to triple or quadruple the size of our industry?

- What factors prevent our industry from achieving such growth?

- Can we meet growing consumer needs without depleting the natural systems on which we depend?

- Can we use emerging markets to develop "leapfrog" technologies?

- How can we meet growing needs without exacerbating urban problems?

More than one billion people have joined the ranks of the emerging market during the past 20 years. Paradoxically, this rapid "development" has resulted in burgeoning shantytowns, mountains of garbage, dead rivers, noxious air, and cesspools of toxic waste. These problems seriously jeopardize the public health and future growth prospects in many developing countries. Nonetheless, demand for products and services continues to rise.

In meeting growing demand, firms have replicated the strategies, products, and processes that were successful in the developed, consumer market. Given the scale and speed of development in the emerging market, however, a repeat performance of the consumer market is almost certain to lead to environmental and social meltdown. For example, if China came to consume oil at the current U.S. rate, it would need more than 80 million barrels per day—slightly more than the 74 million barrels per day the *world* now produces.[32] Sustainable development in the emerging market will, therefore, depend on firms' ability to meet rapidly growing demands without repeating the wasteful, outdated practices used in the consumer economy.

Because of the high rate of manufacturing growth in the emerging market, the capital stock in manufacturing is being rapidly replaced. In Asia, for example, the equipment stock of manufacturing plants doubles every six years.[33] Thus, firms can leapfrog to clean (closed-loop, zero-discharge) manufacturing technologies much more easily in the emerging market than in the developed market, where growth in demand is much slower. Technological leapfrogging will be essential if economic development is to occur at the rates required to lift people out of poverty.

Achieving sustainability in the emerging market is particularly challenging for industries that depend on renewable resources. For example, the global forest products industry must meet worldwide demand that is forecasted to grow 1 to 2 percent per year for the next several decades, even as the overall global supply of available timber declines. The industry, built primarily on the rapid harvesting of standing native forests, must find an alternative approach. Recognizing the collision course they are on, some companies have embarked on intensive agroforestry practices to ensure increased fiber supplies. Through high-yield practices, which rely on selective breeding, cloning, and careful site management, companies such as Aracruz Celulose have realized high returns while minimizing and containing environmental impact by producing high-quality wood and fiber on fewer continuously regenerated acres.

Similarly, the agricultural industry must supply the world's burgeoning population with food while water resources become more scarce, croplands less arable, climate less stable, and crops more homogenized and susceptible to mass failure. The existing model of commercial agriculture, heavily dependent on the intensive use of water, chemical pesticides, and fertilizers, is experiencing diminishing returns. Despite its controversial nature, the use of biotechnology to design crops that are resistant to pests, require less water and fertilizer, and are more nutritious may hold one of the keys to sustainable agriculture in the emerging markets.[34]

Fingerlakes Aquaculture, a startup company in Upstate New York, has based its entire strategy on avoiding the collision course.[35] Overfishing, combined with pressures from development and pollution, has strained wild fish stocks, leading to irregular supply, higher prices, and decreasing quality. As the limits of rangelands and fisheries are reached, there are only three options for increasing the supply of protein in the world: improve the efficiency of grain conversion into animal protein; shift from the less efficient forms of conversion, such as beef or pork, to more efficient ones, such as farmed fish; or rely on ruminants to convert more roughage into either meat or milk.[36]

Fingerlakes Aquaculture incorporates the first two of these options directly into its strategy. The company has perfected a proprietary water filtration and recirculation technology that enables it to cost-effectively grow fish in a controlled indoor setting, which avoids the pollution problems associated with pond-based fish-farming operations. The company has focused its attention on the production of tilapia, a fish species from the tropics with a firm, mild-tasting white meat reminiscent of cod, haddock, flounder, and other species that are under stress in the wild. Given their omnivorous nature, tilapia can be raised on an inexpensive grain-fed diet (soymeal). Tilapia are also highly efficient converters of grain to protein: 1.2 pounds of feed produce a pound of fish (compare this to beef, which requires 6 pounds of feed for every pound of meat). Furthermore, the company, which is about to launch its first commercial-scale production operation, believes that it can produce tilapia on a cost per pound basis competitive with the cost of Central and South American producers. If successful, this approach could revolutionize the industry—and help to reinvent the protein economy in the process.

Traditional Markets: Understanding Real Needs

Unlike either the developed or the emerging markets, the traditional market is dominated by the poverty and isolation found in the rural villages of the developing world, particularly those ravaged by resource extraction, cultural disruption, and attendant population growth. As we have seen, more than four billion people at the base of the economic pyramid are subsistence oriented and satisfy their basic needs directly from nature: They participate only sparingly in the money or formal economy. Demographers generally agree that as the world's population approaches 8 billion to 10 billion during the next few decades, most of the growth will occur in the traditional markets. Because vibrant small communities in rural areas stem the pressures for mass migration and accompanying social, political, and environmental breakdown, focusing on the traditional market is both the key to sustainable development and an unprecedented business opportunity for visionary firms. Managers can identify sustainability-related opportunities in the traditional market by asking these questions:

- Can our existing products and services be modified to meet the needs of the poor?

- Can we apply state-of-the-art sustainable technology to meet the needs of those at the base of the economic pyramid?

- Have we overlooked market vacuums, where needs are fundamentally unmet?

- Are we blinded by our current business model?

- Can we build a customer base that can become more substantial over time?

Companies need to focus on developing technologies, products, and services geared specifically to the needs of those in the traditional market. Managers must understand four factors:

- Deep listening and mutual learning are necessary if products and services are to meet real needs.

- Significant profits can be realized by meeting the needs of the poor and disenfranchised. Conventional wisdom holds that the poor do not make good customers, given their lack of money and education.

- Meeting those needs offers the opportunity to apply state-of-the-art (sustainable) technology in fundamentally new and disruptive ways. Simply transplanting business models from the consumer or even emerging markets will not work.

- Business models for the traditional market must leverage local talent, create employment opportunities, and build capacity in the local community.

Companies that recognize the business opportunity of the traditional market clearly understand and cater to the real needs of the poor. For example, more than one billion people worldwide still lack access to safe drinking water. Another 2.4 billion have no access to proper sanitation. As a result, approximately four billion cases of diarrheal illness associated with contaminated water cause nearly three million deaths annually, mostly among poor children under the age of five.[37] This is the equivalent of 20 loaded jumbo jets plunging to Earth each day—an unprecedented human tragedy. For the traditional market, then, access to clean water and improved sanitation are crucial elements of development and poverty alleviation. No one argues this point. The question is how to make the availability of clean water a reality.

Centralized water treatment and distribution systems are expensive and take years to complete. With population growing most rapidly in poor rural areas, providing water to the masses through infrastructure becomes increasingly untenable. Fortunately, other approaches exist: In-home (point-of-use) treatment of water allows individuals to control their own drinking water supply. Several companies have begun to focus commercial attention on this exciting—and sorely needed—opportunity. For example, Procter & Gamble is pioneering the development of a combined chemical treatment technology called *PuR*. This technology, which is equivalent to a water treatment plant in an affordable sachet packet, has been field tested in Nicaragua and the Philippines by the U.S. Centers for Disease Control. The product, specifically designed for the low-income market, has demonstrated significant reductions in diarrheal disease and is being rolled out in test markets in cooperation with CDC and several NGOs.

Perhaps even more significant, KX Industries, using nanotechnology, has created a revolutionary new water filter that cheaply and effectively produces microbiologically and chemically purified water from virtually any water source, regardless of its contamination level.[38] Using an easy-to-use gravity flow system consisting of a dispenser with upper and lower reservoirs separated by a replaceable filter "ticket," the microbiological (MB) filter can quickly transform contaminated water into pure drinking water at a cost of less than $10 per family per year. The MB dispenser can be easily produced at local manufacturing plants, creating much needed wage employment. Village-based distribution of replacement filter "tickets" can also help to create thousands of microentrepreneurs. KX estimates that even at a price of $8 per family per year, the market for the MB filter in the developing world is still in excess of $5 billion annually. Indeed, for about $500 million, a fraction of the billions of dollars earmarked for relief from AIDS, one could substantially solve the water-borne disease problem in Africa by providing the dispenser and filter tickets to the entire at-risk population.

As the P&G and KX Industries examples make clear, companies that look at poorer areas as dumping grounds for outdated technologies or dirty manufacturing facilities fail to identify market vacuums with minimal competition. Increasing numbers of telecommunication companies, for example, have recognized the benefit of avoiding prohibitively expensive landlines. Through satellite, cellular, and radio systems, they are reaching previously unserved rural areas with telecommunications comparable to those found in urban areas. Such wireless systems erase differences among regions and nations in their access to information, allowing smaller-scale economic development that reduces pressures on people to migrate to cities.

Firms succeed in the traditional market because their managers recognize the benefits of developing markets and building future customer bases. Daewoo, for example, realizing the limits of competing head on with U.S., Japanese, and European firms in overcrowded, technology-intensive markets in the consumer market, is relocating much of its industrial base to Burma, Iran, Uzbekistan, Russia, China, Vietnam, Brazil, and Tatarstan, where it can make long-term investments in economic infrastructure. Daewoo enters poor regions as a long-term development partner, offering skills in infrastructure planning, environmental management, and manufacturing. When hard currency is scarce, the company accepts barter. Uzbekistan, for example, is paying for its half of a joint venture factory with cotton, which Daewoo's trading arm sells on the world market. By using first mover advantage to build relationships, Daewoo is implementing a long-range growth strategy that caters to the world's poorest regions.

The Value Proposition

Recognizing global sustainability as a catalyst for new business development will prove increasingly important to corporate survival in the twenty-first century—the proverbial crossroads to the future. Understanding the broad global dynamics associated with the three economies outlined in this chapter is an important first step in identifying potentially innovative new strategies. To capture sustainable opportunities, however, managers must rethink their prevailing views about strategy, technology, and markets. Attention focused through the three lenses—developed, emerging, and traditional markets—should help in this regard.

Along with having such awareness and foresight, however, it is crucial to understand how sustainability-related business strategies can benefit a firm's economic and competitive position. Indeed, unless they see an avenue for value creation, it is unlikely that senior managers will commit the resources necessary to pursue such strategies. In the next chapter, a framework is developed showing how the challenges associated with global sustainability can help to identify distinctive strategies that contribute to a more sustainable world while simultaneously driving shareholder value.

Notes

1. See, for example, Paul Ehrlich, The *Population Bomb* (New York: Ballantine, 1968).
2. This example is borrowed from John McMillan, *Reinventing the Bazaar* (New York: W.W. Norton, 2002).
3. Erik Drexler, *Engines of Creation* (Garden City, NY: Anchor Press, 1986).
4. See Janine Benyus, *Biomimicry: Innovation Inspired by Nature* (New York: Morrow, 1997).
5. Diane Coyle, *Paradoxes of Prosperity* (New York: Texere Publishing, 2001).
6. This section draws from Stuart Hart, "Beyond Greening: Strategies for a Sustainable World," *Harvard Business Review* 75(1) (1997): 66–76.

7. See Paul Hawken, Amory Lovins, and Hunter Lovins, *Natural Capitalism: Creating the Next Industrial Revolution* (Boston: Little Brown & Company, 1999).

8. G. Daily, *Nature's Services* (Washington, D.C.: Island Press, 1997).

9. Mathis Wackernagel and William Rees, *Our Ecological Footprint* (Gabriola Island, B.C.: New Society Publishers, 1996).

10. Allen Hammond, *Which World?* (Washington, D.C.: Island Press, 1998).

11. Ibid.

12. Ibid.

13. Donella Meadows, Dennis Meadows, and Jorgen Randers, *Beyond the Limits* (Post Mills, VT: Chelsea Green Publishing, 1992).

14. See Helena Norberg-Hodge, *Ancient Futures* (San Francisco: Sierra Club Books, 1991), for a compelling description of how an ancient culture in the Himalayas (the Ladakh) was disrupted fundamentally by the forces of "development."

15. Personal communication, Professor Nicholas Guttierez, EGADE Business School, Tec de Monterrey, Mexico.

16. Hernando De Soto, *The Mystery of Capital* (New York: Basic Books, 2000).

17. Allen Hammond, *Which World?*

18. This section is drawn from Lester Brown, *Eco-Economy* (New York: W.W. Norton, 2001).

19. Jennifer Reck and Stuart Hart, *Water for the Masses* (Chapel Hill, NC: Center for Sustainable Enterprise, 2004).

20. Erik Simanis and Stuart Hart, *Monsanto Company (A): Quest for Sustainability* (Washington, D.C.: World Resources Institute, 2000).

21. National Research Council, *Our Common Journey* (Washington, D.C.: National Academy Press, 1999).

22. Lester Brown, *Eco-Economy*.

23. National Research Council, *Our Common Journey*.

24. Peter Menzel, *Material World: A Global Family Portrait* (San Francisco: Sierra Club Books, 1999).

25. Wouter Van Dieren, *Taking Nature into Account* (New York: Springer-Verlag, 1995).

26. Diane Coyle, *Paradoxes of Prosperity*.

27. This section is excerpted from Stuart Hart and Mark Milstein, "Global Sustainability and the Creative Destruction of Industries," *Sloan Management Review* 41(1) (1999): 23–33.

28. John McMillan, *Reinventing the Bazaar*.

29. Remarks by Chad Holliday, Chemical Industry Conference, Washington, D.C., 9 November 1998.

30. John Buffington, Stuart Hart, and Mark Milstein, *Tandus 2010: Race to Sustainability* (Chapel Hill, NC: Center for Sustainable Enterprise, 2003).

31. This description is based upon a presentation made by Scott Johnson of SC Johnson in April 2004 at Cornell's Society of Engineering Conference.

32. Lester Brown, *Eco-Economy*.

33. U.S. Asia Environmental Partnership, personal communication, April 1998.

34. Erik Simanis and Stuart Hart, *Monsanto Company (A): Quest for Sustainability*.

35. Personal communication with Paul Sellow, CEO of Fingerlakes Aquaculture, May 2004.

36. Lester Brown, *Eco-Economy*.

37. Jennifer Reck and Stuart Hart, *Water for the Masses*.

38. The description of this technology is excepted from Kevin McGovern, *Microbiological Water Filtration Technology (MB) Can Defeat One of the World's Greatest Killers: Water-Born Diseases* (Orange CT: KX Industries, 2004).

3

THE SUSTAINABLE
VALUE PORTFOLIO

Some years ago, William Ruckelshaus, former EPA administrator and CEO of Browning Ferris, made the following statement: "Sustainability is as foreign a concept to managers in capitalist societies as profits are to managers in the former Soviet Union." While intended to be at least partially tongue-in-cheek, I believe that this statement showed considerable insight. There can be little doubt that *sustainability* is one of the most frequently used but least understood terms of our time; it is right up there with the term *strategy* when it comes to overuse and lack of meaning. (I say that as a professor of both strategy and sustainability!) Indeed, it is with some regularity that I find myself engaged in a discussion with someone about sustainability, only to discover several minutes into the conversation that he is talking about something completely different from me.

This lack of precision in definition is often used by businesspeople to dismiss sustainability from consideration. I would be a rich man if I only had a nickel for every time I heard a manager say something like "Until you can give me a clear definition of 'sustainability,' I'm not inclined to spend much time focusing on it in my business." To be sure, sustainability's ambiguous and multidimensional nature can be maddening at times, yet it is also one of its greatest attractions from a business perspective. A smart strategist gravitates toward ill-defined and ambiguous opportunities. That is because once everything has been defined and reduced to standard operating procedure, there is no money left to be made.

Yet, it is not possible to design a coherent strategy (there is that term again) without some broad guideposts, conceptual categories, and frameworks to work with. Without some broad agreement on constructs, we end up talking past each other. Accordingly, this chapter provides a business-oriented way of thinking about sustainability that organizes and rationalizes the many terms, issues, and communities of practice that are floating around out there. More important, the chapter seeks to connect these key dimensions of sustainability to drivers of shareholder value and financial performance. To this end, my colleague Mark Milstein and I have developed a sustainable value framework that directly links the societal challenges of global sustainability to the creation of shareholder value by the firm.[1] The framework shows how the global challenges associated with sustainability, viewed through the appropriate set of business lenses, can help to identify strategies and practices that contribute to a more sustainable world while simultaneously driving shareholder value. This "win-win" approach we define as the creation of sustainable value by the firm.

Sustainability Buzzwords

As the first two chapters suggest, the terms *sustainability* and *sustainable enterprise* encompass a mind-numbing range of ideas, issues, concepts, and practices. In an effort to map the conceptual territory, Mark

Milstein and I brainstormed a lengthy (but I'm sure not exhaustive) list of buzzwords from the domain of sustainability. These are listed, in no particular order, in Exhibit 3.1. A quick scan of the exhibit will, no doubt, produce some familiar monikers (such as *corporate social responsibility*), but also some mysterious acronyms and labels (such as *B24B*). That is because the sustainability space is occupied by distinct and sometimes competing tribes of advocates, practitioners, and theoreticians. Further examination of the list will no doubt begin to produce frustration. You might be asking yourself, "How do I organize all of this stuff in any way that is useful or meaningful from a business point of view?"

Exhibit 3.1
Sustainability Buzzwords

- Environmental Management
- Corporate Social Responsibility
- Greening
- Industrial Ecology
- Stakeholder Management
- Life-Cycle Management
- Pollution Prevention (P2)
- Sustainable Development
- Design for Environment (DfE)
- Green Design
- Urban Reinvestment
- Brownfield Redevelopment
- ISO 14001
- Waste Reduction
- Closed Loops
- Resource Productivity
- Sustainable Technology
- Radical Transactiveness
- Systems Thinking
- Corporate Governance

- Clean Technology
- Eco-efficiency
- Eco-effectiveness
- Biomimicry
- Triple Bottom Line
- Inclusive Capitalism
- Base of the Pyramid
- Community Capitalism
- Corporate Citizenship
- Voluntary Regulation
- Civic Entrepreneurship
- Full Cost Accounting
- EMS
- Risk Management
- Leapfrog Technology
- Cradle to Cradle
- Restorative Technology
- B24B
- Take-Back
- Transparency

Fortunately, we were able to import one of the most important analytical tools from the field of strategy to help make sense of this blooming, buzzing confusion: the 2×2 matrix. As anyone who has attended business school knows, the 2×2 matrix is what defines the field of strategy! In all seriousness, two dimensions combined in a framework help to provide conceptual clarity and enable one to cluster related sustainability buzzwords and practices. The framework also helps to organize the parameters that are important to firm performance and the creation of shareholder value (see Exhibit 3.2).

Exhibit 3.2
Shareholder Value Model

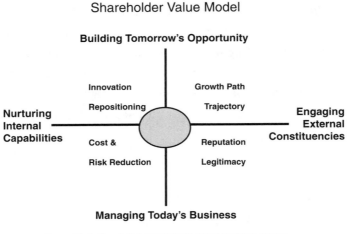

Source: Adapted from S. Hart and M. Milstein, 2003. "Creating Sustainable Value." *Academy of Management Executive*, 17(2) (2003): 56-69.

Elements of Shareholder Value

The vertical axis of Exhibit 3.2 reflects the firm's need to manage today's business while simultaneously creating tomorrow's technology and markets. This dimension captures the tension created by the need to realize short-term results while also fulfilling expectations for future growth. The horizontal axis reflects the firm's need to nurture and protect internal organizational skills, technologies, and capabilities while simultaneously infusing the firm with new perspectives and knowledge from outside stakeholders. This dimension reflects the tension created by the need to buffer the technical core so that it can operate without distraction, while at the same time remaining open to fresh perspectives and new, disruptive models and technologies.

Juxtaposing these two dimensions produces a matrix with four distinct dimensions of performance crucial to generating shareholder value—and understanding sustainability in terms relevant to the business. The lower-left quadrant focuses on those aspects of performance that are primarily internal and near-term in nature: cost and risk reduction. Quarterly earnings growth and reduction in exposure to liabilities and other potential losses are important drivers of wealth creation. Clearly, unless the firm can operate efficiently and reduce its risk commensurate with returns, shareholder value will be eroded.

The lower-right quadrant also focuses on performance dimensions that are near term in nature but includes salient stakeholders external to the firm: suppliers and customers in the immediate value chain, as well as regulators, communities, NGOs, and the media. Unless it respects these stakeholders' interests, the firm's right to operate might be called into question. But if it uses creativity to include their interests, the firm can differentiate itself, enhance its reputation, and establish the legitimacy it needs to preserve and increase shareholder value.

Shifting to the upper-left quadrant of the model, the firm must not only perform efficiently in today's businesses, but it should also be constantly mindful of generating the products and services of the future. This means developing or acquiring the skills, competencies, and technologies that reposition the firm for future growth. Without such a focus on innovation, it will be difficult for the firm to create the new product and service flow to ensure that it prospers well into the future. The creation of shareholder value thus depends upon the firm's ability to creatively destroy its current capabilities in favor of the innovations of tomorrow.

Finally, the upper-right quadrant focuses on identifying the needs that will define the growth markets of the future. Growth requires the firm to either offer new products to existing customers or tap into previously unserved markets. A convincing articulation of how and where the firm plans to grow in the future is crucial to the generation of shareholder value. The growth trajectory therefore provides guidance and direction for new technology and product development.

Firms must perform well in all four quadrants of the model if they are to continuously generate shareholder value over time.[2] Performing within only one or two quadrants is a prescription for suboptimal performance and even failure. Firms such as Kodak and Xerox, which failed to adequately invest in digital technology, illustrate how overemphasis on today's business (to the exclusion of tomorrow's technology and markets) might generate wealth for a time but will eventually erode shareholder value as competitors enter with superior products and services. The recent experience of many Internet companies also demonstrates how preoccupation with tomorrow's opportunity to the exclusion of performance today might be exciting and challenging, but short-lived.[3] Finally, companies such as Monsanto, which failed to adequately address stakeholder concerns over genetically modified food, show that overemphasis on the internal aspects of the firm might bring short-term results but will ultimately blind the firm to the constituencies and perspectives that are so important to both maintaining legitimacy and generating imaginative new ideas about how the firm might compete in the future.

The Buzzword Sort

Just as the creation of sustained shareholder value requires performance on multiple dimensions, the societal challenges associated with sustainable development are also multidimensional. Accordingly, we can use the shareholder value model described earlier to cluster and organize the buzzwords enumerated in the previous section (see Exhibit 3.3).[4] This produces four distinct categories or constructs associated with the four quadrants of the framework. Each captures a conceptually distinct aspect of sustainability and connects to firm performance and shareholder value in a distinct manner. Understanding these conceptual distinctions is key to creating a more disciplined understanding of sustainability to transcend the current rhetoric that still plagues the field.

The lower-left quadrant is populated with the assortment of buzzwords that have to do with resource efficiency and pollution prevention—doing more with less. They enable the firm to squeeze more saleable product out of each pound of raw material that it buys. Recognizing that increasing industrialization, with its associated material consumption, pollution, and waste generation, is a key sustainability driver, the items in the lower-left quadrant are all geared toward the reduction of the waste and emissions associated with firms' current operations.

Exhibit 3.3
The Buzzword Sort

	Tomorrow	
• Eco-effectiveness • Biomimicry • Leapfrog Technology • Sustainable Technology • Knowledge & Service Intensity • Cradle to Cradle • Closed Loops • Restorative Technology • Systems Thinking		• Sustainable Development • Base of the Pyramid • Urban Reinvestment • Brownfield Redevelopment • Inclusive Capitalism • Community Capitalism • Civic Entrepreneurship • Radical Transactiveness • B24B
Internal		**External**
• EMS • Greening • Pollution Prevention (P2) • Eco-efficiency • Risk Management • Environmental Management • ISO 14001 • Waste Reduction • Resource Productivity		• Corporate Social Responsibility • Industrial Ecology • Stakeholder Management • Life-Cycle Management • Design for Environment (DfE) • Green Design • Corporate Citizenship • Full Cost Accounting • Take-Back • Transparency
	Today	

The lower-right quadrant is composed of buzzwords that focus on stakeholder engagement, transparency, and life-cycle management. These seemingly diverse items cluster together because they all challenge companies to access voices from beyond their immediate operational control. As we have seen, Internet-connected coalitions of NGOs are making it increasingly difficult for governments, corporations, or any large institutions to operate in secrecy.[5] Driven by the proliferation and interconnection of civil society stakeholders, the items in this quadrant help firms incorporate voices from the entire product lifecycle;

this means more effective stakeholder engagement, new forms of governance, and a proactive approach to corporate social responsibility. Items in the lower-right quadrant thus challenge firms to operate in a transparent, responsive manner due to an increasingly well-informed, active stakeholder base.

The upper-left quadrant is populated by buzzwords that emphasize the development of new, inherently clean technologies and capabilities (through either internal development or acquisition). Specifically, this quadrant focuses on the emerging technologies (genomics, biomimicry, nanotechnology, information technology, and renewable energy) that could make many of today's energy- and material-intensive industries obsolete. New capability development in clean technology thus constitutes the key dimension of the upper-left quadrant.

Finally, the upper-right quadrant consists of the set of buzzwords that address the increases in population, poverty, and inequity associated with globalization. Whether we are dealing with disinvestment in urban cores, brownfield redevelopment, or the four billion poor at the base of the pyramid (B24B means "business to four billion"), this quadrant focuses on those who have been underserved or even exploited by capitalism to date. Social development and wealth creation on a massive scale, especially among the world's poorest, is thus the key aspect of the upper-right quadrant.

In sum, global sustainability is a complex, multidimensional concept that cannot be addressed by any single corporate action. Creating sustainable value requires that firms address each of the four quadrants—and be clear about how the strategies associated with each will help the firm build shareholder value. First, firms can create value by reducing the level of material consumption and pollution associated with rapid industrialization. Second, they can create value by operating at greater levels of transparency and responsiveness, as driven by civil society. Third, they can create value through the development of new, disruptive technologies that hold the potential to greatly shrink the size of the human footprint on the planet. Finally, firms can create value by meeting the needs of those at the base of the world income pyramid in a way that facilitates inclusive wealth creation and distribution.

Connecting the Dots: The Sustainable Value Portfolio[6]

When viewed through the appropriate set of business lenses, the sustainability framework discussed previously presents opportunities for firms to improve performance in all four quadrants of the shareholder value model, as illustrated in Exhibit 3.4. Thinking systematically, through the full range of challenges and opportunities associated with sustainability, is the first important step managers can take toward the creation of sustainable value. Each of the four quadrants of the framework is explored in greater depth next.

Exhibit 3.4
The Sustainable Value Framework

Source: Adapted from S. Hart and M. Milstein, 2003. "Creating Sustainable Value." *Academy of Management Executive*, 17(2) (2003): 56-69.

Growing Profits and Reducing Risk Through Pollution Prevention

Material consumption, waste, and pollution present an opportunity for firms to lower cost and risk by developing skills and capabilities in pollution prevention and eco-efficiency.[7] Pollution prevention is focused on reducing waste and emissions from current operations. Less waste means better utilization of inputs, resulting in lower costs for raw materials and waste disposal. Effective pollution prevention also requires extensive employee involvement, continuous improvement, and quality management capability.

Programs that reduce waste and emissions through eco-efficiency have been widely adopted by firms over the past decade and include such notable cases as Dow Chemical's Waste Reduction Always Pays (WRAP) and Chevron's Save Money and Reduce Toxics (SMART). Pollution-prevention programs have proliferated at the industry level and receive a great deal of attention from regulatory bodies in the United States and Europe as potential alternatives to command-and-control regulation.[8] The well-publicized results of such pioneering programs as 3M's Pollution Prevention Pays (3P) illustrate the direct, bottom-line benefits of pollution prevention. Indeed, between 1975 and 1990, 3M reduced its total pollution by more than 530,000 tons (a 50 percent reduction in total emissions) and, according to company sources, saved more than $500 million through lower raw material, compliance, disposal, and liability costs. In 1990, 3M embarked on 3P+, which sought to reduce the remaining waste and emissions by 90 percent, with the ultimate goal being zero pollution.[9]

During the 1990s, DuPont's $1 billion Lycra business helped to further underscore the potentially sizeable financial payoff associated with pollution prevention.[10] Between 1991 and 1995, more than 50 million pounds of waste were eliminated from the business's nine plants worldwide. This saved roughly $5 million in compliance, liability, and waste disposal costs. However, a more thorough accounting revealed that yield improvements attributable to the pollution-prevention program increased process efficiency and reduced material costs by $45 million. Additional revenue associated with saleable by-product (which previously was waste) totaled $100 million. Furthermore, the business avoided making new capital investments in plant and facility as a result of greater up-time and faster cycle time in the existing capacity; this, they estimated, was worth another $100 million. Without even estimating the higher productivity of workers due to healthier working conditions and higher morale, these cost savings totaled a whopping $250 million for the business, a major contribution to the business's bottom line.

Evidence thus clearly shows that pollution-prevention and waste-reduction strategies actually do reduce cost and increase profits.[11] Pollution prevention provides managers with the clearest, fastest way to increase shareholder value by growing the bottom line for existing businesses through reductions in cost and liability.

Enhancing Reputation and Legitimacy Through Product Stewardship

Whereas pollution prevention focuses on internal operations, product stewardship extends beyond organizational boundaries to include the entire product life cycle, from raw material access through production processes, to product use and disposal of spent products.[12] Product stewardship integrates the voice of the stakeholder into business processes by allowing the firm to interact with external parties such as suppliers, customers, regulators, communities, NGOs, and the media. It thus offers a way to both lower environmental impacts across the value chain and enhance the firm's legitimacy and reputation by engaging stakeholders in the conduct of ongoing operations. Product stewardship enhances outsiders' confidence in the firm's intentions and activities, helping to enhance corporate reputation and encouraging other firms to follow suit.

Firms can take many actions to increase shareholder value through product stewardship. Cause-related marketing appeals to consumers' desires to purchase products that have positive social and environmental benefits.[13] Life-cycle management extends the value chain beyond traditional limits by including in the firm's responsibility the costs and benefits of products from raw materials to production and ultimately to disposal by consumers.[14] SC Johnson, for example, has developed an approach called Greenlist™ that it uses in product development. By rating raw materials in terms of their environmental footprints, the company is able to facilitate the design of products that minimize environmental impact across the entire product life cycle.

Dofasco, one of the few profitable steel companies in North America, has hinged its strategy on product stewardship. By focusing on the production of ultralight steel auto bodies for the auto industry, the company has enabled its customers (the auto companies) to produce lighterweight and less costly vehicles that also realize better gas mileage. Because many of Dofasco's products also make use of scrap steel, the company has been able to boost its reputation—and its sales— through product stewardship.[15]

Companies such as Shell have increased the use of stakeholder engagement through town hall–style meetings, facilitated dialogues, Internet-based comment boxes, and other tools designed to provide venues for stakeholders to voice their views about a firm's operations. In fact, an increasingly active NGO community has led firms to pursue more collaborative approaches to business management. Together with industry, for example, European governments are pioneering take-back laws for electronic and appliances manufacturers, effectively closing the loop on the product life cycle.[16]

Nike serves as a recent salient example of the value of product stewardship. Faced with growing backlash against its labor and environmental practices, in the late 1990s, the company turned to product stewardship strategies to recover its reputation and preserve its right to operate. The company enacted a worldwide monitoring program for all contract factories, using both internal and third-party auditors such as PriceWaterhouseCoopers. Nike also became a charter member of the Fair Labor Association (FLA), a nonprofit group that evolved out of an antisweatshop coalition of unions, human rights groups, and businesses. Nike helped found the Global Alliance, a partnership among the International Youth Foundation, the MacArthur Foundation, and the World Bank, dedicated to improving workers' lives in emerging economies.[17]

Aside from taking action on the labor (social) front, Nike took action environmentally. Its footwear designers started evaluating their new prototypes against a product stewardship scorecard, using life-cycle analysis. Nike also launched the Reuse a Shoe Project to recycle old, unwanted footwear. The company's retailers collected shoes and shipped them back to the company, which ground and separated the materials. Through partnerships with sports surfacing companies, the outsole rubber and midsole foam were turned into artificial athletic surfaces. Profits from this business generated income for the Nike Foundation and funded donations of sport surfaces made of the recycled material.

As the Nike case makes clear, firms can use product stewardship to demonstrate that stakeholder voices and opinions matter and can affect company behavior. As with pollution prevention, product stewardship is centered on improving existing products and services. As a consequence, changes are immediate and value is quickly realized in the form of improved community relations, legitimacy, and brand reputation.

Accelerating Innovation and Repositioning Through Clean Technology

Clean technology refers not to the incremental improvement associated with pollution prevention, but to innovations that leapfrog standard routines and knowledge. The rapid emergence of disruptive technologies such as genomics, biomimicry, information technology, nanotechnology, and renewable energy presents the opportunity for firms—especially those heavily dependent upon fossil fuels, natural resources, and toxic materials—to reposition their internal competencies around more sustainable technologies. Thus, rather than simply seeking to reduce the negative impacts of their operations, firms can strive to solve social and environmental problems through the internal development or acquisition of new capabilities that address the sustainability challenge directly.[18]

A growing number of firms have begun to develop the next generation of clean technologies to drive future economic growth. BP and Shell are ramping up investments in solar, wind, and other renewable technologies that might ultimately replace their core petroleum businesses. In the automotive sector, Toyota and Honda have already entered the market with hybrid power systems in their vehicles, which dramatically increase fuel efficiency. They also launched a market experiment in fuel-cell vehicles in Japan at the end of 2002. Whereas many car makers talk of a transition to alternative power taking 20–30 years, GM, Toyota, and Honda are committed to making it a commercial reality within a decade.

Firms such as General Electric, Honeywell, and United Technologies are investing in the development of small-scale, widely distributed energy systems that could make centralized coal-fired and nuclear power plants obsolete. Finally, firms such as Cargill and Dow are exploring the development of biologically based polymers to enable renewable feedstocks such as corn to replace petrochemical inputs in the manufacturing of plastics. Each of these cases is notable for the firm's willingness to disrupt the very core technologies upon which its businesses currently depend.

Bold strategies in clean technology continue to be less common among large, established corporations than are activities in pollution prevention or product stewardship. Entrenched corporate mindsets and standard operating procedures inhibit the creation of structures that can catalyze innovation. The risks associated with such investments stand in stark contrast to the risk-reducing efforts associated with the pollution-prevention programs discussed previously. However, it is likely that future economic growth will be driven by those firms that are able to develop disruptive technologies that address society's needs. Firms that fail to lead the development and commercialization of such technologies are unlikely to be a part of tomorrow's economy.[19]

Crystallizing the Firm's Growth Path and Trajectory Through Sustainability Vision

Too many corporate clean technology initiatives have floundered because the resulting technologies have stumbled in the marketplace— witness GM's failed effort to develop an electric car during the 1990s. To succeed, therefore, it is crucial to develop a vision not only for what needs the company is trying to address and how they relate to sustainability, but also *where* the most appropriate markets can be found. The unmet needs of those at the base of the economic pyramid may present the best opportunity for firms to define a compelling trajectory for future growth. A more inclusive form of capitalism, characterized by collaboration with stakeholders previously overlooked or ignored by firms (such as radical environmentalists, shantytown dwellers, or the rural poor in developing countries), can help open new pathways for growth in previously unserved markets.

The case of the Grameen Bank in Bangladesh demonstrates how a vision aimed at those who had been bypassed by the financial system, opened a totally new pathway for business growth.[20] Nearly 30 years ago, Muhammad Yunus then a professor of economics at Chittagong University in Bangladesh, conceived of the idea of a bank focused on offering "microcredit" loans to the poorest of the poor. This business concept was developed as a direct result of personal interactions that he had with poor people in rural villages and shantytowns. Most bankers assumed that laziness or lack of skill were the reasons that so many lived in abject poverty. As a result, they focused their attention on more affluent customers. But Yunus was personally motivated to understand what the poor felt they needed to change their lives for the better. Much to his surprise, he discovered, by traveling through villages and through extended personal interaction, that they were, for the most part, energetic and motivated and knew exactly what they needed to move forward. In almost every case, this involved gaining access to small amounts of credit to launch or expand small enterprises. Grameen Bank was established to serve this need.

To succeed, it was necessary for Grameen to turn most of the established assumptions about banking (loan size, need for collateral, contractual enforcement) upside down. Conventional banking is based on the priciple that the more you have, the more you can get. Grameen Bank started with the belief that credit should be accepted as a human right. By focusing on making very small loans to poor women based upon a "peer lending" model, a system was built where those who posssessed the *least* get the highest priority. Small groups of loan recipients ensure that everyone behaves in a responsible way and no one gets into repayment trouble. The bank's sales and service people visit villages frequently, getting to know the women who have the loans and the projects in which they are supposed to invest. In this way, lending due diligence is accomplished through trust-based interaction and exchange rather than mountains of paperwork and legal documentation characteristic of conventional banks. In fact, the individual loan amounts are often smaller than the document-processing charges of most financial institutions.

By 2004, Grameen was lending in excess of $445 million each year to more than 3.8 million poor customers in more than 46,000 villages throughout Bangladesh. Even more amazing, it has achieved a 98.9 percent repayment rate, the highest of any bank on the Indian subcontinent, and indeed much higher even compared to North American and European banks in the United States.[21] The competitive imagination of Yunus and the Grameen Bank has led to a global explosion of institutional interest in microlending over the past decade, including the recent entry of financial giants such as Citigroup.

Increasingly, MNCs are recognizing that the voices of the poor and disenfranchised can be a source of creativity and innovation. Recognizing that information poverty may be the single biggest roadblock to sustainable development, Hewlett-Packard, for example, has begun to focus attention on the needs of the isolated and disconnected through its World e-Inclusion initiative. HP created an "i-community," a living laboratory, in rural India with the express purpose of coming to understand the particular needs of the rural poor. The firm has quickly realized that this is not unoccupied space: Local companies such as N-Logue and Tarahaat are also developing information technology and business models to serve this enormous potential market. Through shared access (for example, Internet kiosks), wireless infrastructure, and R&D focused on cost reduction, these companies are dramatically reducing the cost of being connected.

Despite the efforts of organizations such as Grameen and HP, however, most companies continue to mistakenly assume that poor markets possess no value opportunities and have yet to try to understand the possibilities of serving the markets they are used to ignoring. Firms that do take the time appear to recognize that those at the base of the pyramid lack attention and capital, not ingenuity and aspiration. Thus, these firms have the potential to unlock future markets of immense scale and scope.

Charting the Sustainable Value Portfolio

By now, the core dimensions of sustainability and their linkages to firm performance and value creation should be clear: Firms are

challenged to minimize waste from current operations (pollution prevention), while simultaneously acquiring or developing more sustainable technologies and skill sets (clean technology). Firms are also
challenged to engage in extensive interaction and dialogue with external stakeholders, regarding both current offerings (product stewardship)
and economically sound new solutions to social and environmental
problems for the future (sustainability vision).

Taken together, as a portfolio, these strategies and practices hold
the potential to reduce cost and risk, enhance reputation and legitimacy,
accelerate innovation and repositioning, and crystallize growth path and
trajectory, all of which are crucial to the creation of shareholder value.
The challenge for the firm is to decide which actions and initiatives to
pursue and how best to manage them. Companies can begin by taking
stock of each component of what I call their *sustainable value portfolio*
(see Exhibit 3.5). This simple diagnostic tool can help any company
determine whether its strategy has the potential to truly create sustainable value.

Exhibit 3.5
The Sustainable Value Portfolio

	Clean Technology	**Sustainability Vision**
Tomorrow	Is the sustainability of our products limited by our existing competency base? Is there potential to realize major improvements through new disruptive technology?	Does our corporate vision direct us toward the solution of social and environmental problems? Does our vision focus us on serving the unmet needs at the base of the economic pyramid?
Today	**Pollution Prevention** Where are the most significant waste and emission streams from our current operations? Can we lower costs and risks by eliminating waste at the source or by using it as useful input?	**Product Stewardship** What are the implications for product design and development if we assume responsibility for a product's entire life cycle? Can we build reputation and legitimacy by engaging a broader range of stakeholders?
	Internal	**External**

Source: Adapted from S. Hart, 1997. "Beyond Greening: Strategies for a
Sustainable World." *Harvard Business Review*, January-February (1997): 66-76.

First, assess your company's (or your business unit's) capability in each of the four quadrants by answering the questions in Exhibit 3.5. Then rate your capability on the following scale for each quadrant: 1: nonexistent, 2: emerging, 3: established, or 4: institutionalized. Unbalanced portfolios spell missed opportunity and vulnerability: A bottom-heavy portfolio suggests a good position today but future vulnerability. A top-heavy portfolio indicates a vision of sustainability without the operational or analytical skills needed to implement it. A portfolio skewed to the left side of the chart indicates an inward focus that could lead to myopia and might ignore important perspectives from external constituencies. Finally, a portfolio skewed to the right side, although highly open and public, runs the risk of being labeled "greenwash" because the underlying plant operations and core technology still cause significant harm.

Programs in pollution prevention and product stewardship are well institutionalized within most MNCs today and have saved hundreds of millions of dollars over the past decade. U.S.-based companies have been especially focused on the efficiency gains and cost savings associated with pollution prevention. Highly publicized crises at companies such as Monsanto and Nike that failed to successfully engage the views of stakeholders have also caused growing numbers of firms to explore strategies for product stewardship. European companies have been particularly active in engaging in more stakeholder dialogue, extending producer responsibility for products, and adopting more inclusive forms of corporate governance. Research and consulting experience, however, suggest that few firms seem to recognize, let alone exploit, the full range of sustainable business opportunities available.[22] Most focus their time and attention primarily on the bottom half of the matrix: short-term solutions tied to existing products and stakeholder groups.

The Road to Sustainability

Consider the auto industry. During the 1970s, government regulation and dirty tailpipe emissions forced the industry to focus on pollution control. In the 1980s, the industry began to tackle pollution prevention. Initiatives such as the Corporate Average Fuel Efficiency requirement and the Toxic Release Inventory led auto companies to examine their product designs and manufacturing processes to improve fuel economy and lower emissions from their plants. The 1990s witnessed the first signs of product stewardship. In Germany, the 1990 "take-back" law required auto manufacturers to take responsibility for their vehicles at the end of their useful lives. Innovators such as BMW influenced the design of new cars with "design for disassembly" efforts. Industry-led consortia such as the Partnership for a New Generation of Vehicles were driven largely by the product stewardship logic of lowering the environmental impact of automobiles throughout their life cycles.

Early attempts to promote clean technology were driven by initiatives such as California's Zero-Emission Vehicle Law and the U.N. Climate Change Convention, which seeks to limit greenhouse gas emissions on a global scale. But early efforts by industry incumbents were either incremental—for example, the development of natural gas vehicles—or defensive in nature. Electric vehicle programs, for instance, were used primarily to demonstrate the infeasibility of the California law rather than to lead the industry to fundamentally cleaner technology. It came as no surprise that there was little demand for GM's Impact, an electric vehicle that featured 2,000 pounds of batteries, a range of less than 100 miles, and a price tag double that of other vehicles in its class. Similarly, the issue of climate change, perhaps the single biggest threat to the internal combustion engine as we know it, was addressed primarily through stakeholder dialogue and the establishment of incremental reduction goals for greenhouse gas emissions. These initiatives, while laudable as far as they went, were motivated primarily by a desire to maintain legitimacy and the right to operate in the face of a product fleet that was becoming increasingly dominated by behemoth, gas-guzzling SUVs and oversize pickup trucks.

The early 2000s saw the introduction of the first serious new product entries containing alternative power plants. Hybrid-electric vehicles such as the Prius and the Civic, from Toyota and Honda, respectively, were introduced at competitive prices with fuel efficiencies double or triple that of the fleet average. Despite clear signals of consumer acceptance, however, production capacity lagged far behind demand and, as of 2004, was still restricted to vehicles at the low end of the market, where conventional cars were already quite fuel-efficient. There were no hybrid options in the large car, minivan, SUV, or pickup truck segments, which were, by far, the most polluting and least energy-efficient. Hybrid minivans and small SUVs were due out in the 2005 model year.

The advent of the new century also saw a rush by car companies into hydrogen fuel cell development programs. Some automakers (such as Ford) sought joint ventures with existing fuel cell companies; others (such as GM) initiated their own programs of technology development. Most targeted the United States as the entry market for this revolutionary new technology. Unfortunately, because there are no alternative fuels for sale to consumers in the United States, it will be necessary to outfit these fuel-cell vehicles with expensive gasoline reformers well into the future. Converting gasoline into hydrogen does not solve the problem of fossil fuel dependence or greenhouse gas emissions.

Indeed, it is staggering that none of the large auto companies has connected the challenge of clean technology development to its strategies for emerging markets (such as China and India, where there will be massive transportation needs in the coming decades). Consider the impact of automobiles on China alone. In the mid-1990s, there were fewer than one million cars on the road in China. However, with a population of more than 1 billion, it would take less than 30 percent market penetration to equal the current size of the U.S. car market (12 million to 15 million units per year). Ultimately, China might demand 50 million or more units annually. Because China's energy and transportation infrastructures are still being defined, there is an opportunity to leapfrog to clean technology, yielding important environmental, public health, and competitive benefits.

Assume for a moment that auto companies succeed in creating a commercially viable next generation of renewable (and affordable) vehicles using emerging markets as the incubator. Now try to envision a transportation infrastructure capable of accommodating so many vehicles. How long will it take before gridlock and traffic jams force the auto industry to a halt? Sustainability will require new transportation solutions for the needs of emerging economies with huge populations. This might feature entirely new products and services designed to make smaller cities and villages more economically viable so that mass migration to megacities becomes unnecessary and even undesirable. Will the giants in the auto industry be prepared for such radical change, or will they leave the field to new ventures that are not encumbered by the competencies of the past?

In summary, although the auto industry has made progress, most companies fall far short of creating truly sustainable value. While most have succeeded in implementing some version of pollution prevention and product stewardship, few have ventured very far beyond the safe confines of the current technology and business model. Initiatives in the clean technology and sustainability vision quadrants have been fragmentary, at best, leaving open a future opportunity of potentially vast proportions.

Pursuing the White Space

As the case of the auto industry suggests, relatively few firms have begun to explore seriously the opportunities associated with the upper half of the sustainable value portfolio, the portion focused on building new capabilities and markets. Indeed, most clean technologies today are being developed and commercialized by small, often undercapitalized, new ventures, not by the MNCs that possess the financial resources for doing so successfully. Similarly, most business experiments at the base of the economic pyramid have been initiated by NGOs or small local firms, while MNCs' emerging market plays have been limited largely to the elites or emerging middle classes in the developing world. Given that pursuit of clean technology and markets at the base of the pyramid is disruptive in character, perhaps we should not be surprised that large firms have not actively blazed these trails.

Yet, it need not be this way. Just as particular competencies (for example, quality management, continuous improvement, boundary-spanning capability) predispose some companies to be more effective than others in implementing pollution prevention and product steward-ship, some MNCs will be better positioned than others to pursue clean technologies and markets at the base of the pyramid—those with demonstrated ability in acquiring new skills, working with unconventional partners, incubating disruptive innovations, shedding obsolete businesses, and creatively destroying existing product portfolios, to name just a few. Incumbent firms with these skill sets possess a potentially powerful first-mover advantage.

The opportunity to create sustainable value—shareholder wealth that simultaneously drives us toward a more sustainable world—is huge but yet to be fully exploited. The sustainable value portfolio outlined in this chapter shows the nature and magnitude of the opportunities in sustainable business development and connects them to ways for the firm to create value. The strategies associated with the four quadrants also enable a sustainable competitive advantage because they cannot be easily or quickly copied by competitors. The framework's simplicity, however, should not be mistaken for ease of execution: Understanding the connections is not the same thing as successfully implementing the necessary strategies and practices. This task is very challenging and complex indeed. Only a few firms will be able to successfully carry out activities in all four quadrants simultaneously, especially those in the upper part of the portfolio that require the greatest efforts in terms of vision, creativity, and patience.

Stagnant economic growth and stale business models will present formidable challenges to corporations in the years ahead. Focusing on incremental improvements to existing products and businesses is an important step, but it neglects the vastly larger opportunities associated with clean technology and the underserved markets at the base of the economic pyramid. Indeed, addressing the full range of sustainability challenges by moving "beyond greening" can help to create shareholder value and could represent one of the most underappreciated avenues for profitable growth in the future. It is to this prospect that we turn our attention in the next section of the book.

Notes

1. The discussion of the sustainable value framework in this chapter is excerpted from Stuart Hart and Mark Milstein, "Creating Sustainable Value," *Academy of Management Executive* 17(2) (2003): 56–69.

2. This idea is similar to the balanced scorecard (see Robert Kaplan and David Norton, "The Balanced Scorecard—Measures That Drive Performance," *Harvard Business Review* 72(1) (1992): 71–79) and other tools that emphasize the need to balance a portfolio of actions to drive firm value over time.

3. The experiences of Enron and the numerous dot-bombs of the tech wreck serve as the most recent illustrations that, although it can be very glamorous to be viewed as on the cutting edge of the business world, bankruptcy provides a particularly ineffective platform from which to generate future growth.

4. Admittedly, the clustering of these terms represents our interpretation of where each belongs. Others may well take issue with our choice of placement.

5. Howard Rheingold, *Smart Mobs: The Next Social Revolution* (Cambridge, MA: Perseus Publishing, 2002).

6. The four strategies developed in this section were first articulated in: Stuart Hart, "Beyond Greening: Strategies for a Sustainable World," *Harvard Business Review* 75(1) (1997): 66–76. I would also like to thank my colleagues at the Sustainable Enterprise Academy—in particular, Brian Kelly, David Wheeler,

Bryan Smith, John Ehrenfeld, Chris Galea, Art Hanson, David Bell, Nigel Roome, Jim Leslie, and Pat Delbridge—for helping us to clarify our thinking regarding how the drivers of sustainability, viewed through the proper set of business lenses, influence shareholder value.

7. The most comprehensive treatment of eco-efficiency was done by the World Business Council for Sustainable Development in Livio DeSimone and Frank Popoff, *Eco-efficiency: The Business Link to Sustainable Development.* (Cambridge: MIT Press, 1997).

8. See Alfred Marcus, *Reinventing Environmental Regulation* (Washington, D.C.: Resources for the Future Press, 2002).

9. 3M Company, *Pollution Prevention Pays,* 1992 videotape.

10. Personal communication, Paul Tebo, Executive VP, DuPont, April 1998.

11. See, for example, Petra Christmann, "Effects of 'Best Practices' of Environmental Management on Cost Advantage: The Role of Complementary Assets," *Academy of Management Journal* 43(4) (1998): 663–680; and Sanjay Sharma, and Harrie Vredenburg, "Proactive Corporate Environmental Strategy and the Development of Competitively Valuable Organizational Capabilities," *Strategic Management Journal* 19(8) (1998): 729–753.

12. See, for example, Ulrich Steger, "Managerial Issues in Closing the Loop," *Business Strategy and the Environment* 5(4) (1996): 252–268.

13. Steve Hoeffler and Ken Keller, "Building Brand Equity Through Corporate Societal Marketing," *Journal of Public Policy and Marketing* 21(1) (2002): 78–89.

14. Joseph Fiksel, *Design for Environment: Creating Eco-efficient Products and Processes* (New York: McGraw-Hill, 1995).

15. Personal communication, Don Pether, CEO of Dofasco, Inc., November 2003.

16. See, Proposal for a Directive of the European Parliament and of the Council on Waste Electrical and Electronic Equipment and on the Restriction of the Use of Certain Hazardous Substances in Electrical and Electronic Equipment, COM #(2000)347, available at http://europa.eu.int/comm/environment/docum/00347_en.htm.

17. The Nike example is drawn from Heather McDonald, Ted London, and Stuart Hart, *Expanding the Playing Field: Nike's World Shoe Project* (Washington, D.C.: World Resources Institute, 2002).

18. William McDonough and Michael Braungart, *Cradle to Cradle* (New York: North Point Press, 2002).

19. Gary Hamel, *Leading the Revolution* (Boston: Harvard Business School Press, 2000); Clay Christensen, Thomas Craig, and Stuart Hart, "The Great Disruption," *Foreign Affairs* 80(2) (2001): 80–95; and Robert Foster and Sarah Kaplan, *Creative Destruction* (New York: Currency Books, 2001).

20. Alex Counts, *Give Us Credit* (New York: Times Books, 1996).

21. Muhammad Yunus, *Grameen Bank at a Glance* (Dhaka: Grameen Bank, 2004).

22. Stuart Hart and Mark Milstein, "Global Sustainability and the Creative Destruction of Industries," *Sloan Management Review* 41(1) (1999): 23–33; Stuart Hart and Clay Christensen, "The Great Leap: Driving Innovation from the Base of the Pyramid," *Sloan Management Review* 44(1) (2002): 51–56; and C. K. Prahalad and Stuart Hart, "The Fortune at the Bottom of the Pyramid," *Strategy+Business* 26 (2002): 54–67.

Part Two
BEYOND GREENING

4

CREATIVE DESTRUCTION
AND SUSTAINABILITY

More than 50 years ago, economist Joseph Schumpeter described the dynamic pattern in which innovative upstarts unseat established firms as "creative destruction."[1] Whereas most twentieth-century economists focused on competition under conditions of static equilibrium, Schumpeter insisted that *disequilibrium* was the driving force of capitalism. There is now little doubt that the economy is driven by firms that are able to capitalize on the "new combinations" described by Schumpeter: Coal Age technologies gave way to Oil Age technologies that are now giving way to Information Age technologies. With each change, the technological and economic infrastructure of society experiences dramatic transformation, with new institutions, enterprises, and geographic patterns of development.

Not surprisingly, the notion of creative destruction makes many managers uncomfortable—and it should. Frequently, incumbent firms either have discounted the significance of emerging technology or have reacted to changes by becoming more committed to existing products and markets. Incumbents that survive episodes of creative destruction do so because they display more foresight than their peers; they invest and form partnerships to acquire new competencies and experiment in new, untested markets.[2] They are not held hostage by their current technology or market position.[3]

Mark Milstein and I have argued that the emerging challenges associated with global sustainability are, in reality, catalysts for a new round of creative destruction that offers unprecedented business opportunities.[4] Today's corporations can seize the opportunity for sustainable development, but to do so, they must look beyond the incremental improvements associated with pollution prevention and product stewardship in the current business. Instead, companies must make obsolete the very technologies and product systems upon which they currently depend.[5]

Continuous Improvement Versus Creative Destruction

Episodes of creative destruction are usually driven by waves of scientific and technological discovery or major periods of sociopolitical change. We are now in the early stages of such a revolution—the transformation toward a sustainable global enterprise. Most existing large corporations evolved in an era of abundant raw materials, cheap energy, and seemingly limitless sinks for waste disposal. During the past few decades, however, it has become increasingly clear that many of the technologies developed during this period are unsustainable. Indeed, the specters of toxic contamination, depleted forests and fisheries, eroded soils, loss of biodiversity, global climate change, burgeoning populations, and a widening gap between rich and poor are explicit signals that companies must take more seriously the social and environmental impacts of their technologies and businesses.

In fact, only by replacing many of today's unsustainable technologies with those that are inherently clean, renewable, and nontoxic can we make rapid progress toward a more sustainable world. Just as nature enables some species to out-compete others through a process of natural selection and succession, so the sustainability revolution will enable those firms with more sustainable strategies to outperform—and, ultimately, replace—those with outmoded strategies and damaging technologies. No amount of greening will save firms from the gales of creative destruction that are likely to ensue in the coming decades. In short, most truly sustainable technologies are likely to be disruptive—but not all disruptive technologies will be sustainable. Learning the difference could hold the key to long-term survival.

Greening = Continuous Improvement

Strategies for greening generally serve to incrementally improve the performance of existing products and processes (see Exhibit 4.1). Initiatives in pollution prevention and product stewardship solidify incumbents' competitive positions by rewriting the rules of the game in their favor. Greening perpetuates the current industry structure; it fosters continuous improvement rather than reinvention or fundamental innovation. In the long run, however, the dynamics of creative destruction will work against firms that rely only on incremental improvements and fail to change the fundamental manner in which they provide products, processes, and services.

Exhibit 4.1
Continuous Improvement Versus
Creative Destruction

Strategies for Greening	Strategies for Beyond Greening
Focus on Existing:	*Focus on Emerging:*
Products	Technologies
Processes	Markets
Suppliers	Partners
Customers	Needs
Shareholders	Stakeholders
Characteristics:	*Characteristics:*
Incremental	Discontinuous
Continuous improvement	Creative destruction
Rationalizes industry	Restructures industry
Example: Responsible care	Example: Biotech revolution

Source: Adapted from S. Hart and M. Milstein, 1999. "Global Sustainability and
the Creative Destruction of Industries." *Sloan Management Review*, 41(1) (1999): 23-33.

An example of incremental innovation is the Chemical
Manufacturers Association's (CMA) Responsible Care program, which
helped rescue the industry from near oblivion but has not led its members to revolutionize practices. Following the Bhopal disaster in 1984
(in which 3,000 residents of Bhopal, India, died as a result of a toxic
chemical explosion at a Union Carbide plant), leading chemical
companies, including Dow, DuPont, and Monsanto, pressed for self-
regulation in the face of public hostility and calls for stricter regulatory
measures that threatened industry survival. In 1988, the CMA adopted
Responsible Care, a statement of environmental principles and codes of
management practices that included provisions for pollution prevention,
product stewardship, and community advisory panels. To strengthen the
program, the principles and codes were made mandatory for CMA
member companies, which make up 90 percent of the chemical capacity in the United States; noncompliance was grounds for expulsion from
the CMA. Since 1988, Responsible Care has transformed the chemical

industry's environmental behavior and helped to change the public's perception of the industry from shameless polluter to more responsible actor.

But although it has been successful in reestablishing the legitimacy of an industry under tremendous public pressure, Responsible Care has failed to address the fundamental underlying problems associated with the chemical industry: Many of its products and processes are highly toxic, resource-intensive, and inherently unsustainable. As an industry-level collaborative process, the Responsible Care program has fostered incremental improvement by forcing hundreds of smaller chemical firms to mimic the leaders in terms of environmental management and community involvement. This has left the leading firms such as DuPont and Dow in a stronger competitive position by helping to shore up support for their right to operate but, ironically, has reduced the likelihood of fundamental innovation by chemical company incumbents. Indeed, research now shows that the biggest gains in environmental performance occurred not within the Responsible Care firms, but among those firms that decided not to join.[6]

Beyond Greening = Creative Destruction

If we reflect on the generally accepted definition of sustainable development as the ability of the current generation to meet its needs without compromising the ability of future generations to meet theirs, we can see how most existing products and processes fail to meet this criterion.[7] Growing data suggests that today's extractive and material-intensive industries (for example, mining, energy, chemicals, forest products, agriculture, and transportation) are not sustainable. If the entire world were as material-intensive as North America, it would take more than three planet Earths to support the material requirements of the current world population.[8] We should therefore see global sustainability as a major disruptive force, with the power to radically transform the structure of many industries.

Visionary companies have an opportunity to drive the redefinition and redesign of their industries. Material- and energy-intensive industries will find global sustainability to be a competency-destroying challenge that calls for radical repositioning and new competency development. Information- and service-intensive industries will find global sustainability to be a competency-enhancing challenge that offers significant potential for substitution and leapfrogging over existing unsustainable technologies.

Unlike greening, which works through the existing supply chain to effect continuous improvement in the current business system, "beyond greening" strategies focus on *emerging* technologies, new markets, and unconventional partners and stakeholders. Such strategies are thus disruptive to current industry structure and raise the possibility of significant repositioning, enabling new players to establish leading positions as the process of creative destruction unfolds.

In the chemical industry, we can also see the early stages of creative destruction, as key incumbents begin to reposition themselves for the clean technology revolution. Consider the case of DuPont. In the late 1800s, the company transformed itself from a manufacturer of gunpowder and explosives into a chemical company focused on the production of synthetic materials using petroleum feedstocks. This strategy produced nearly a century of success, with such well-known blockbuster products as Nylon, Lycra, Teflon, Corian, and Kevlar.

In the late 1900s, DuPont embarked on its second major transformation—from an energy-intensive petrochemical company to a renewable resource company focused on sustainable growth.[9] To realize this transformation, the company has pursued a strategy of acquisition, divestiture, and internal technology development. Within the past decade, for example, DuPont has invested more than $15 billion in biotechnology, including the acquisition of Pioneer Hi-Bred, a major player in the agricultural biotech business. It has also divested resource- and energy-intensive businesses such as its oil subsidiary (Conoco) in the 1990s, and, most recently, its core Nylon and Lycra businesses in 2004.

In an effort to dramatically shrink its footprint, the company has set bold targets for 2010: to reduce greenhouse gas emissions by two-thirds while holding total energy use flat, and to increase its use of renewable resources to 10 percent of global energy needs. To hit such ambitious targets while continuing to grow as a company, the firm must reorient its technology base toward biology (for example, genomics and biomimicry), renewable energy (for example, fuel cells), and information (for example, knowledge-intensive rather than resource-intensive products). To accelerate this process, DuPont is seeding internal ventures focused on sustainable technology development and innovations aimed at the developing world.[10]

During the past decade, de-mergers, spin-offs, acquisitions, and significant new technology developments have structurally transformed the chemical industry. Monsanto, Hoechst, and Rhone-Poulenc have spun off their chemical businesses to concentrate on life sciences, food, pharmaceuticals, and biotechnology. ICI, Sandoz, and Ciba-Geigy have refocused on chemicals by spinning off their life sciences and biotechnology investments (for example, the creation of Zeneca and Novartis). Dow is ramping up significant investments in biotechnology. Other firms, such as Novo Nordisk, the fast-growing Danish pharmaceutical and biotechnology company, and Empresas La Moderna, an emerging life sciences powerhouse, are exploring "green chemistry" and finding biological substitutes for synthetic chemicals. In fact, many of the new technologies being developed by these firms will make existing petrochemically based products and applications obsolete.

Almost every energy- and material-intensive industry, from energy and automobiles to food and forest products, is experiencing similar changes. Every firm must strike a balance between the incremental change and continuous improvement associated with greening, and the disruptive innovation and creative destruction associated with beyond greening. In the past, competitive advantage was based largely upon lowering cost or gaining differentiation in existing industries and businesses. In the future, however, it appears that competitive advantage will depend more upon the capacity to generate disruptive innovation and creative destruction through competitive imagination. A growing body of scholarly work affirms Joseph Schumpeter's assertion over a half-century ago that "the problem that is usually being visualized is how capitalism administers existing [industrial] structures, whereas the relevant problem is how it creates and destroys them."[11] Disruption and innovation are more important to corporate success than it has ever been. [12]

In their book *Creative Destruction*, Foster and Kaplan demonstrate empirically that the base rate of the economy has been accelerating over the past 80 years, with dire consequences for industry incumbents: The turnover rate for the S&P 500 has increased from about 1.5 percent per year in the 1920s to nearly 10 percent today. This implies that the average number of years a firm spends on the Standard and Poor index has declined from 65 in the 1920s and 1930s (S&P 90) to 10 in the 1990s (S&P 500). By 2020, they state, "more than three-quarters of the S&P 500 will consist of companies we don't know today—new companies drawn into the maelstrom of economic activity from the periphery, springing from insights unrecognized today."[13]

To date, unfortunately, the lion's share of effort and activity in most companies has focused on greening—the continuous improvement of existing products and processes. Given the velocity of technological change and the growing significance of sustainability, this no longer appears to be a viable strategy: Creative destruction appears to hold the key not only to the growth industries of the future, but to corporate survival.

From Textile Dyes to Biomaterials

Burlington Chemical Company provides a vivid illustration of continuous improvement versus creative destruction.[14] Founded in the early 1950s in the heart of North Carolina's textile belt, Burlington focused on producing chemicals and dyes for the many textile companies in the region. The company grew steadily throughout the 1960s and '70s until the early 1980s, when the State of North Carolina passed a stringent new regulation requiring that fish be able to successfully reproduce in the effluent water coming from textile mills. This requirement presented a formidable challenge to the textile companies in the state. Recognizing that its customers' problems were its problems, too, Burlington seized the opportunity and began to focus on producing more environmentally friendly textile chemicals and dyes.

Led by Sam Moore, the grandson of the company's founder, Burlington's management team adopted the ideals of product stewardship and industrial ecology in 1983. This revolutionary approach led the company into a whole new line of textile chemical products that were low in toxicity, biodegradeable, and much more energy-efficient. Despite the textile industry's steady decline, by the early 1990s, Burlington had grown to more than $50 million in annual sales and employed more than 150 people. Product stewardship and design-for-environment had enabled the company to thrive in what was otherwise a highly cost-competitive, commodity business. Then came the passage of the North American Free Trade Agreement (NAFTA) in 1995.

With NAFTA, the slow decline of the textile industry in North Carolina turned into a mass exodus. Textile mills across the state shut down and moved to Mexico to take advantage of the dramatically lower labor costs there. Between 1995 and 2000, Burlington's revenues declined by more than 50 percent, and more than 60 percent of its customers went out of business. Even worse, the average selling price of its products dropped by more than half. Burlington was forced to lay off more than 100 of its employees. Fortunately, given the company's

strong focus on employee training and advanced technological compe-
tence, laid-off workers found jobs that paid at least as well within a few
months. It was clear, however, that if the company were to survive, it
would need new "lifeboat" businesses outside the textile industry. The
company's managers thus committed themselves to a strategy of "creative destruction."

Burlington's investment in product stewardship and industrial ecology during the 1980s paid off: After two failed attempts to sell its textile chemical and dyes business (one acquirer would have shut down the
operation, displacing the remaining workers), the firm succeeded in
selling it to a German company in 2003. Under the terms of the agreement, Burlington retained exclusive manufacturing rights, and the new
owner agreed to hire all Burlington's salespeople. The German firm
was then able to leverage Burlington's clean textile dye technology
throughout its extensive textile operations in Asia—a win-win, both
financially and environmentally.

During the same period, Burlington built manufacturing facilities to
focus on the development and production of new, bio-based lubricants,
catalysts, and additives. In 2000, it launched a new Luberos lubricants
division. The sale of the textile chemicals business freed assets with
which to expand the new vision, which is focused on bio-based sustainable chemistry for manufacturing and service industries. New products
include lubricants manufactured from used vegetable oils, soy-based
fabric softeners, and new cleaning systems for the transportation industry. By 2004, the company had begun to turn the corner, realizing a positive cash flow for the first time in six years and an improving balance
sheet. The new vision provided vast opportunities for future growth in
emerging industries, with tremendous upside potential. The company's
early commitment to industrial ecology had provided it the intellectual
and physical capital to make the leap into a whole new technology and
business space. In short, an early commitment to sustainability saved
the company.

Using Carbon Dioxide to Change the World

During the mid-1990s, an innovative new venture was spun out of the University of North Carolina at Chapel Hill. Spearheaded by chemistry professor Joe DeSimone, Micell Technologies and its research arm, the Kenan Center for the Utilization of Carbon Dioxide in Manufacturing, focused on the growing demand for green manufacturing methods. Creative destruction has been the company's stock and trade. Micell Technologies is dedicated to the vision that liquid (supercritical) carbon dioxide can reduce water-based waste streams and replace a significant amount of the 30 billion pounds of organic and halogenated solvents used and released each year. DuPont has already benefited directly from this work in the form of a new process for making Teflon in carbon dioxide in place of the current method, which is water- and solvent-intensive.

Micell is also seeking to revolutionize the semiconductor industry, in which chip fabrication currently uses massive quantities of both water and toxic solvents. Through its innovative technology, the company has developed applications that complete the most chemical- and water-intensive steps of the chip-production in a liquid carbon dioxide environment, eliminating the use of water and solvents for cleaning—and reducing the costs of production in the process. Ultimately, the company aims to creatively destroy the entire chip-fabrication process through its carbon dioxide–based approach, making the process a virtually closed system and eliminating entirely the need for expensive clean room technology.

One of Micell's most interesting business applications is in dry cleaning. Current dry cleaning technology uses a highly toxic chemical, perchloroethelene, as the cleaning agent. This chemical not only contaminates the sites where it is used (making virtually every dry cleaning shop a hazardous waste site), but it is also very hard on fabrics, shortening the useful life of clothing items. DeSimone and Micell have designed a set of soaps and surfactants that work especially well in a liquid carbon dioxide environment. Under pressure in a specially designed washing machine, carbon dioxide turns to a supercritical liquid; clothes are then "washed" with the specially designed surfactants. Upon completion of the process, the pressure is released, allowing the carbon dioxide to return to a gas; the surfactants are separated from the dirt and captured for reuse. The clean clothes are ready, without the need for any form of drying. The entire process is a closed system, eliminating all forms of waste, pollution, and emissions.

Micell's franchise operation, Hanger's Cleaners, is now being rolled out across North America. The clean and safe nature of the workplace, combined with the more sophisticated nature of the technology, enables Hangers to create jobs with a higher skill and wage base. There are now a handful of other carbon dioxide–based dry cleaning plays on the market. It is only a matter of time before the toxic dry cleaning sweatshops of today are relegated to the scrap heap of history.

Whole Systems Thinking

The cases of Burlington Chemical and Micell Technologies make it clear that managing for continuity and efficiency, through cost or differentiation advantages in existing industries and businesses, is no longer enough. In the future, competitive advantage will increasingly shift to the capacity for exploration, disruptive innovation, creative destruction, and corporate imagination.[15] This shift necessitates moving beyond the conventional modes of business analysis, those emphasizing comparison of existing alternatives so prevalent in business schools and firms today.

The logic of marginal analysis—the tracking of incremental changes in costs and benefits—holds that there is an optimum point beyond which it makes no sense to seek additional performance improvements in, say, quality or emissions reduction. Beyond a certain point, in other words, it costs more to achieve an additional increment of improvement than it is worth. Although this form of analysis makes implicit sense in a world of predetermined alternatives and incremental adjustments, it becomes self-defeating when the objective is disruptive change. To succeed in this space, a new logic is required, one based upon whole systems thinking.

In their encyclopedic treatise *Natural Capitalism*, Paul Hawken, Amory Lovins, and Hunter Lovins make a persuasive case for the logic of whole systems thinking in connection with sustainability.[16] They demonstrate how incremental thinking can blind us to the potential for leapfrog innovation. Using the familiar example of home construction, they show how component-based, marginal analysis leads us to design buildings that fail to realize their full potential. For example, the energy efficiency of buildings is usually determined after the basic structure and utilities have already been put in place by how much insulation is used, what grade of windows are installed, what types of appliances are purchased, and so on. Each of these decisions is made separately using marginal analysis: Additional insulation becomes "uneconomic" beyond a certain point because the initial capital cost will never be recouped through energy savings. This style of analysis has trained us to believe that the only way to realize more energy-efficient homes is to pay the additional cost required to install the necessary conservation technology. Incremental benefits must exceed incremental costs.

But what happens if we step outside the artificial cage imposed by component-based, marginal thinking? To do this, we must abandon the existing design conventions associated with home construction (which means we also have to set aside existing building codes, regulations, and industry best practices). We must start with a clean sheet and embrace the logic of whole systems thinking. When we do this, however, we can readily see that it is possible to "have your cake and eat it, too." That is, we can design superefficient houses and even cars that actually cost *less* to build than the original unimproved versions.

How is this possible? The fatal flaw of marginal analysis is its tacit acceptance of current designs and products as given. By accepting the world as it currently exists, we ensure that only incremental improvements are possible. Thus, in seeking a more energy-efficient home, we accept that the current convention (indeed, *requirement* in most localities in the United States) of having heating systems, ductwork, blowers, air compressors, and so on is necessary and appropriate. The aim is simply to reduce the extent of their use through add-on energy-conservation investments (it should be apparent that this is nothing more than a glorified form of end-of-pipe thinking).

But what if we question the very need for these expensive and potentially unnecessary pieces of capital equipment? What if we invest *more* in building a well-insulated, passively heated and cooled structure powered by solar energy so that we can eliminate the need for a conventional heating and cooling system altogether? Might this not produce a home of superior functionality, energy efficiency, and cost? Ample evidence demonstrates that, indeed, such a design philosophy can and does work. What holds it back is not technology, but rather restrictive rules, laws, and building codes, and the inertia associated with the current construction industry, particularly material suppliers and contractors, who only know how to build one way: the unsustainable way.

Although implementing the logic of whole systems thinking in a fragmented industry such as home construction is difficult, it may be easier to achieve in industries dominated by large incumbent players with the bargaining power to change the rules of the game. Thus, thinking like a disruptive innovator through the logic of whole systems thinking may hold the key to future growth for incumbents in industries currently mired in low-growth, commodity competition. It may also hold the key to moving us toward a more sustainable world. Consider the possibilities.

Reinventing the Wheels

Chapter 3, "The Sustainable Value Portfolio," analyzed the automobile industry's evolution over the past 50 years in terms of the sustainable value portfolio. It traced the industry's path from a strictly adversarial command-and-control approach, to the pollution-prevention and product stewardship initiatives of the 1980s and 1990s. By the early twenty-first century, all major car companies had initiated clean technology (fuel cell or alternative) vehicle programs. Unfortunately, all had continued to use the logic of component-based, incremental thinking in these clean technology initiatives, except one: General Motors.

Most fuel cell vehicle programs, like their hybrid vehicle cousins, still envisioned the product in conventional terms: a heavy metal chassis and body with thousands of component parts. Unfortunately, in the early twenty-first century, fuel cells were still many times more expensive to produce than internal-combustion engines. Thus, when a fuel cell (with an electric motor) is seen as a simple replacement for the internal-combustion engine, the result is an overpriced product that few consumers (save the ultragreen) would ever consider purchasing. GM had already been down this path with its overpriced and underperforming electric vehicle, the Impact, in the 1990s. With more than 2,000 pounds of batteries, it failed miserably, even in the regulation-driven California market, where a certain percentage of zero-emission vehicles was required by law. As Amory Lovins likes to say, "Optimizing one element in isolation pessimizes the whole system."[17]

In 2002, General Motors launched the AUTOnomy project, a bold $1 billion initiative to reinvent the automobile around hydrogen fuel cell technology. Unlike its competitors, GM has taken a clean-sheet approach not only to vehicle design, but to the entire manufacturing system. Rather than thinking of the fuel cell as a simple replacement for the engine, GM tried to imagine a different approach. Who said that fuel cells have to be boxlike contraptions that look like batteries or engines? Why couldn't the fuel cell be integrated into the design of the vehicle in a more functional way? Accordingly, the design team devised a way to build a fuel cell that doubles as the vehicle's chassis—a fuel cell "skateboard" with four small electric motors to power each of the four wheels independently (see Exhibit 4.2). This design not only delivers superior power and torque, especially at the low end, but it also allows the wheels to be controlled independently, enabling the vehicle to be driven sideways into a parallel parking place.

The skateboard forms the backbone for the product concept, which can then take on virtually any form or functionality. Body types and seating capacity can be modularly designed and installed on the skateboard in a way that allows for maximum flexibility. Want an SUV? Lease an SUV body and interior. Want a sedan? Switch to this body type as you see fit. What's more, GM has moved to radically simplify the vehicle's design. Apart from the electric motors and the wheels, there are virtually no moving parts: The steering and all the vehicle's functions are controlled electronically using wireless technology. This so-called Hy-wire approach has allowed GM engineers to reduce the number of component parts from thousands to hundreds, drastically simplifying the supply chain and cycle time of the product. Thus, by radically simplifying the design around a fuel cell that doubles as the vehicle's chassis, GM hopes to compensate for the higher cost of the fuel cell with much lower sourcing and production costs.[18] This is whole systems thinking at its best.

Yet conceptualizing and building the innovative new product is not enough. Commercialization strategy is also a crucial piece of the puzzle. Here it is not clear that GM, which is famous for creating impressive new technologies only to have them fail in the marketplace, has a compelling lead. GM's plan is to launch the AUTOnomy in the highly competitive United States market. Unfortunately, given the widespread availability of cheap gasoline in the U.S., it is highly unlikely that a hydrogen fuel infrastructure will be developed anytime soon, unless the federal government has a significant change of heart. Because fuel cells depend on hydrogen for fuel, the only way that GM can bring its product to market in the United States is to add an expensive piece of equipment that "reforms" gasoline into hydrogen to power the fuel cell. Thus, even though the vehicle would be powered by a fuel cell, it would use fossil fuels to supply hydrogen to the cell, effectively nullifying the alternative nature of the technology. In a carbon-constrained world with significant dependence on oil from the Middle East, this would not seem to be a very sustainable strategy.

Exhibit 4.2
GM's Autonomy

First driveable U.S. fuel cell

Ready for mass market in 2010

"Wireless" steering controls and fuel
cell "skateboard" mean more
flexible body design

Unfortunately, most car companies persist in viewing the developing world market as consisting only of the rich at the top of the pyramid. GM's China strategy consists largely of producing Buicks to compete against prestige brands such as Mercedes, BMW, and Lexus in a battle to win the business of China's wealthiest and most sophisticated consumers. But what if GM connected its recently announced joint venture to produce "minivehicles" in China to its billion-dollar strategy to produce fuel-cell vehicles in the United States? Might it be possible to invent a whole new product category while simultaneously incubating a renewable fuel infrastructure in China?

Technologies of Liberation

Since the dawn of the Industrial Revolution, Western economies have relied on the unsustainable use of raw materials and energy from lesser-developed countries to prosper: timber from South America, oil from the Middle East, minerals from Africa. Economies of scale ruled the day, with massive investments in power plants, pipelines, factories, dams, and highways to more efficiently serve the burgeoning consumption needs of those at the top of the economic pyramid. Industrial-era technologies (such as electricity, petrochemicals, and automobiles) were also closely associated with mass production, the assembly line, and centralized, bureaucratic organization, resulting in the rise of organized labor, worker alienation, and growing social stratification. As Diane Coyle points out in her book *Paradoxes of Prosperity*, society both shapes the dominant technology and is, in turn, shaped by it.[19]

As we enter the new century, the "dark satanic mills" of the Industrial Revolution are giving way to a new generation of technologies that promise to change dramatically the societal, economic, and environmental landscape. The information economy powered by the microchip has already begun to revolutionize society by democratizing access to information, empowering workers, and increasing productivity. In the coming years, bioscience, nanotechnology, new materials, wireless IT, solar, fuel cells, and other forms of distributed energy generation could also dramatically reduce the size of the human footprint on the planet.

Perhaps even more important, given their small scale and distributed nature, such "sustainable" technologies hold the potential to creatively destroy existing hierarchies, bypass corrupt governments and regimes, and usher in an entirely new age of capitalism that brings widely distributed benefits to the entire human community. And rather than depending upon national governments or paternalistic social engineers to design the future for the aspiring masses, these disruptive new technologies may be best brought forward through the power of capitalism—not the capitalism of the Industrial Revolution, which enriched a few at the expense of many, but rather a new, more dynamic form of global capitalism that will uproot established elites and unseat incumbents by creating opportunity at the base of the economic pyramid on a previously unimagined scale.

Eating Your Own Lunch

Joseph Schumpeter was skeptical of the ability and motivation of large, incumbent corporations to drive the process of creative destruction, but he did not dismiss them entirely. He thought that large investments in an installed asset base and misaligned managerial incentives would reduce incumbents' motivation to make their established positions obsolete. Yet he also recognized that, paradoxically, large corporations have financial, technical, and organizational resources that cannot be matched by small, entrepreneurial new entrants: "[I]t may happen that new combinations should be carried out by the same people who control the productive or commercial process which is to be displaced by the new."[20]

Clearly, incumbents in certain industries are *structurally* more likely than others to pursue the path of creative destruction. Industries characterized by high asset intensity and long asset life (for example, utilities, mining, oil, petrochemicals, and automobiles) may find it the most difficult to engage in the sort of self-disruption described in this chapter. Greening clearly presents the path of least resistance for these incumbents, given their heavy commitment to existing assets in the ground. Why? Fully depreciated assets are very profitable to run; shutting them down prematurely results in a significant performance penalty in the short term.

At the other end of the spectrum are service industries, retailers, and firms based on the emerging "technologies of liberation" described previously. Players in these industries are in a prime position to focus their strategic energy on disruption for sustainability. Because they are not wed to long-lived assets in the ground, firms in these industries can purposefully skip over emphasis on the incremental improvements to current technologies associated with greening. Between these two extremes are industries with intermediate levels of asset life and intensity—electronics, computers, information technology, and consumer products, for example. Incumbents in these industries are well positioned to pursue hybrid strategies of both continuous improvement and creative destruction, given their shorter technology life cycles and more rapid turnover of assets.

Industry structure thus determines, at least to some extent, the proclivity of incumbents to pursue beyond greening strategies. Although firms in asset-intensive industries may be the least likely to pursue this path, they paradoxically face the biggest threat if they ignore the challenge: For these firms, continued blind adherence to yesterday's technology could spell doom, not just a missed opportunity. It is therefore crucial that all firms, especially incumbents in pollution- and asset-intensive industries, begin to accelerate the process of creative destruction for sustainability.

To succeed at creative destruction, innovators—be they large corporations or entrepreneurial start-ups—will need to find the appropriate early markets for the sustainable technologies of the future. As we saw with the GM fuel cell case, forcing clean technologies into the established market at the top of the pyramid may not be the best course of action. Finding the early markets for clean technologies with the potential for creative destruction may instead require a fundamentally different approach. In this context, the base of the economic pyramid, where four billion people's needs are still unmet, may be the best place to incubate the technologies of the future.

Notes

1. Joseph Schumpeter. *The Theory of Economic Development* (Cambridge, MA: Harvard University Press, 1934).

2. Clayton Christensen, *The Innovator's Dilemma: When New Technologies Cause Great Firms to Fail* (Boston: Harvard Business School Press, 1997).

3. Ibid.

4. Portions of the next section are excepted from Stuart Hart and Mark Milstein, "Global Sustainability and the Creative Destruction of Industries," *Sloan Management Review* 41(1) (1999): 23–33.

5. Stuart Hart and Clayton Christensen, "The Great Leap: Driving Innovation from the Base of the Pyramid," *Sloan Management Review* 44(1) (2002): 51–56.

6. Andy King and Michael Lenox, "Exploring the Locus of Profitable Pollution Reduction," *Management Science* 47(2) (2002): 289–299.

7. World Commission on Environment and Development, *Our Common Future* (Oxford: Oxford University Press, 1987).

8. Mathis Wackernagel and William Rees, *Our Ecological Footprint* (Gabriola Island, B.C.: New Society Publishers, 1996).

9. Chad Holliday, "Sustainable Growth, the DuPont Way," *Harvard Business Review* 79(8) (2001):129–132.

10. The information about DuPont comes from personal communications with key executives, including Paul Tebo, Corporate Vice President for Safety, Health, and Environment; and Eduardo Wanick, President of DuPont Latin America.

11. Joseph Schumpeter, *Theory of Economic Development*.

12. See, for example, Richard Foster and Sarah Kaplan, *Creative Destruction* (New York: Doubleday, 2001); Gary Hamel and C. K. Prahalad, *Competing for the Future* (Boston: Harvard Business School Press, 1994); and Clayton Christensen, *The Innovator's Dilemma*.

13. Richard Foster and Sarah Kaplan, *Creative Destruction*.

14. Many thanks to Sam Moore, Chief Technologist for Burlington Chemical, for the information cited in this case.

15. James March, "Exploration and Exploitation in Organizational Learning," *Organization Science* 2(1) (1991): 71–87; Clayton Christensen, *The Innovator's Dilemma*; Stuart Hart and Mark Milstein, "Global Sustainability;" and Gary Hamel, *Leading the Revolution* (Boston: Harvard Business School Press, 2000).

16. Paul Hawken, Amory Lovins, and Hunter Lovins, *Natural Capitalism* (Boston: Little Brown and Co., 1999).

17. Ibid.

18. David Baum, "GM's Billion-Dollar Bet," Wired.com, www.wired.com/wired/archive/10.08/fuelcellcars.html, 2002.

19. D. Coyle, *Paradoxes of Prosperity* (New York: Texere Publishing, 2001).

20. Joseph Schumpeter, *Theory of Economic Development*, p. 66.

5

THE GREAT LEAP
DOWNWARD

I still vividly recall the conversation that started it all. It was the fall of 1997, and I had recently published an article in the *Harvard Business Review* (HBR) that examined the opportunity for the corporate sector to profitably pursue strategies for a more sustainable world. Global poverty, rising inequity, and environmental degradation in the Third World led the list of problems to be solved. The article, "Beyond Greening: Strategies for a Sustainable World," went on to win the McKinsey Award as the best article in HBR that year. My mentor and strategy colleague at Michigan, C. K. Prahalad, had just completed a draft manuscript with Ken Lieberthal that would ultimately appear in HBR in 1998 as "The End of Corporate Imperialism."[1] He shared a copy of the paper and asked for comments and suggestions.

I remember being absolutely struck by the complementary nature of our thinking. In the paper, Prahalad and Lieberthal make a compelling argument for both the challenge and opportunity of serving the emerging markets in China and India, especially the tier below the wealthiest consumers in these countries that most multinationals had been preoccupied with up to that point. In our ensuing discussion about the paper, I remember making the comment that serving the next tier down from the top was indeed important, but this still left unexamined (and unserved) the vast majority of humanity in the lowest tiers of the global economic pyramid. Neither government (including the multilaterals) nor the nonprofit sector had been particularly successful in addressing this mounting problem over the past half-century. Aid and philanthropy were clearly insufficient to solve the problem.

At that moment, it became apparent to both of us that what was missing (and critically needed) was a logic for why (and how) the corporate sector might focus attention on understanding and serving the four billion poorest people at the "bottom" of the economic pyramid (or the BOP, for short). We developed a working paper in 1998 that went through literally dozens of revisions over the next four years before it was published in January 2002 as "The Fortune at the Bottom of the Pyramid."[2] The concept of the BOP was born.

Significant momentum has now been established around this agenda, with literally dozens of colleagues from around the world now working actively in this arena.[3] In 2000, the Base of the Pyramid (BOP) Learning Laboratory was founded at UNC's Kenan-Flagler Business School.[4] The BOP Learning Lab is a consortium of corporations, NGOs, and academics interested in learning how to serve the needs of the poor in a way that is culturally appropriate, environmentally sustainable, and profitable.[5] Since the advent of the BOP Learning Lab, the World Resources Institute, the World Business Council for Sustainable Development, and the United Nations Development Program, among others, have launched major programs focused on the role of the private sector in alleviating poverty and catalyzing sustainable development. Over the past seven years, it has become apparent that the BOP offers both enormous opportunities and challenges for companies accustomed to serving the wealthy at the top of the economic pyramid.

On the Horns of a Dilemma

At the dawn of the twenty-first century, world commerce finds itself on the horns of a twin dilemma. First, with the unprecedented performance of stocks over much of the previous decade as a backdrop, shareholders now expect double-digit returns as a matter of course. For companies, this means not only delivering unswerving earnings performance, but also traveling an unrelenting trajectory of growth. Yet with the global economy still sleepwalking at an annual average rate of growth of 3–4 percent, how will companies generate the 10–20 percent growth in sales and earnings they require in the coming years? Indeed, the majority of large companies seem to be mired in saturated markets that have few significant growth opportunities.

Second, as we have seen, the rapid rise of global capitalism over the past decade has been accompanied by mounting concerns over environmental degradation, labor exploitation, cultural hegemony, and loss of local autonomy, particularly among developing nations. The antiglobalization demonstrations in Seattle, Davos, Prague, Genoa, and Cancun make it apparent that corporate expansion at the expense of the poor and the environment will encounter vigorous resistance. Must corporations' quest for future growth serve only to fan the flames of the antiglobalization movement?

Along with my colleague Clay Christensen at Harvard Business School, I have argued that there is a way out of this global "Catch-22":[6] The best way to both generate growth and satisfy social and environmental stakeholders is to focus on emerging markets. By this, we do not refer to incremental market expansion targeted at the wealthy few in the developing world. Instead, we argue that the best path will be through a

Great Leap Downward—to the base of the economic pyramid, where more than four billion people have been bypassed or damaged by globalization. It is here that companies will find the most exciting growth markets of the future—and the basis for a formidable sustainability vision. It is also here that the disruptive technologies needed to address the social and environmental challenges associated with economic growth can best be incubated and developed.

The Tip of the Iceberg

For much of the past half-century, multinational corporations have chosen to focus their attention exclusively at the top of the world economic pyramid, especially the very top where 75 million to 100 million highly affluent "Tier 1" consumers reside.[7] This is a cosmopolitan group, to be sure, composed of upper-income people in developed countries, especially the U.S., Western Europe, and Japan, and the few rich elites from the developing world.

With the fall of communism in the late 1980s, however, multinational corporations rushed into so-called "emerging markets"—the former Soviet Union and its allies, along with China, India, and Latin America—with the expectation that they would be the next great business bonanza. Unfortunately, by the early twenty-first century, corporate momentum in emerging markets had slowed considerably. The prospect for hundreds of millions of new middle-class consumers in the developing world had been vastly oversold. The Asian and Latin American financial crises put a damper on the rate of foreign direct investment (FDI). The events of September 11, 2001, further hastened the retreat.

With the benefit of hindsight, we can now see more clearly why most multinationals' global and emerging market strategies were failures: They were neither very global nor particularly oriented toward emerging markets. In the developing world, most FDI has targeted only the few "large market" countries, such as China, India, and Brazil. And even there, most MNC emerging market strategies have focused exclusively on the 800 million or so wealthy customers, ignoring the vast majority of people considered too poor to be viable customers (see Exhibit 5.1).

Exhibit 5.1
The Global Pyramid

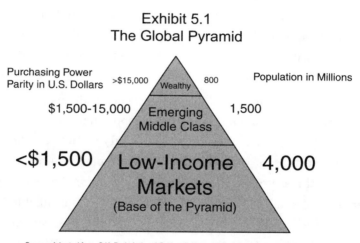

Purchasing Power Parity in U.S. Dollars

>$15,000   Wealthy   800   Population in Millions

$1,500-15,000   Emerging Middle Class   1,500

<$1,500   Low-Income Markets (Base of the Pyramid)   4,000

Source: Adapted from C.K. Prahalad and S. Hart (with assistance from Ted London), 2002. "The Fortune at the Bottom of the Pyramid." *Strategy+Business*, 26 (2002): 54-67.

Many reasons have been offered to justify and explain MNC preoccupation with the top of the economic pyramid in emerging economies. Some, for example, have suggested that such customers are more similar to American, European, and Japanese consumers, which MNCs are accustomed to serving, and thus present less "psychic distance" than do the impoverished inhabitants of shantytowns and rural villages. Others point to the lack of important institutions in the developing world (such as rule of law and intellectual property), which makes conventional MNC operations all but impossible.[8]

Not surprisingly, then, most MNC strategies have aimed to tailor existing products to fit the needs of the top of the pyramid in the developing world. The incremental product changes and modest cost reductions associated with this strategy, however, have not succeeded in making products and services available to the vast majority of those in the Third World. The net result is that the 4 billion to 5 billion people at the base of the economic pyramid—fully two-thirds of humanity—have been largely ignored by MNCs. They have been bypassed by globalization, their needs are being poorly met by local vendors, and they are increasingly the victims of corruption and active exploitation by predatory suppliers and intermediaries.[9] Much like the proverbial iceberg with only its tip in plain view, this huge segment of the global population—along with its massive potential market—has remained largely invisible to the corporate sector.

With stagnation in the established markets of the world economy and rising antiglobalization sentiments, the opportunities for serving the base of the pyramid are becoming increasingly attractive. Concealed below the surface of the purchasing power parity numbers is an immense and fast-growing economic system that includes a thriving community of small enterprises, barter exchanges, sustainable livelihoods activities, and subsistence farming.[10] Indeed, it is estimated that well over half of the total economic activity in the developing world takes place outside the formal economy, in the so-called informal or extralegal sector.[11]

The base of the pyramid is also rich in assets, although most are unregistered and, therefore, remain invisible. In his book *The Mystery of Capital*, Hernando de Soto estimates that there are well over $9 *trillion* unregistered assets (houses, equipment, and so on) in the rural villages and urban slums of the world.[12] Because the poor typically do not hold legal title to these assets, they remain trapped and underleveraged, protected only by the informal property systems enforced by local strongmen.

Unlike the "underground" economy at the top of the pyramid, which is driven by the desire to avoid paying income taxes (just ask your waiter or carpenter), the informal sector at the base of the pyramid exists because of the difficulty and expense of becoming legally registered due to corruption and archaic rules. It has been estimated, for example, that it takes thousands of dollars, several hundred steps, and more than a year of effort to officially register a business in most developing countries today.[13] Small wonder, then, why the extralegal sector is thriving while the formal economies in many developing countries today show little or even negative growth. The challenge is to connect the informal and formal economies in a productive and mutually beneficial partnership.

In short, the emerging market opportunity may be much larger than previously thought. However, the new untapped source of promise is not the wealthy few in the developing world, or even the rising middle-class consumers—it is the billions of aspiring poor who are seeking to join the market economy for the first time. The Great Leap Downward thus calls for disruptive innovation on a massive scale—and the creation of entirely new, more sustainable industries in the process.[14] Like Mao Zedung's Great Leap Forward in China, which ended up taking the country *backward* during the Cultural Revolution, the Great Leap Downward may ultimately incubate more sustainable ways of living for people at the *top* of the pyramid.

Creative Creation

As Clay Christensen so eloquently explains in his path-breaking book *The Innovator's Dilemma*, disruptive innovations are products and services that initially aren't as good as those that historically have been used by customers in mainstream markets and that, therefore, can take root only in new or less-demanding applications among nontraditional customers.[15] Examples include transistor radios, small cars, personal computers, solar energy, and online investing; in each case, the initial offering was seen as different—even strange—from the standpoint of the mainstream market. Recall that transistor radios were initially adopted by teenagers, small cars by the cost-conscious, personal computers by artists and academics, solar energy by "greens," and online investing by the Internet-savvy.

Well-managed companies are pressured to invest in innovations that target markets large enough to sustain corporate growth rates and enhance overall profit margins. To them, pursuing disruptive innovations seems irrational. This allows disruptive innovators to incubate their businesses in the safety of markets that resource-rich competitors are motivated to ignore and then to grow up-market by attacking a sequence of market tiers that are the least attractive investment options facing the leaders.

Disruptive innovations typically enable a larger population of less-skilled or less-wealthy people to begin doing for themselves things that historically could be done only through skilled intermediaries or by the wealthy. Disruptions have thus been a fundamental mechanism for creating new growth businesses and improving our standard of living. Joseph Schumpeter's notion of creative destruction tells only half the story: In reality, before a disruptive innovation destroys industry leaders and incumbent technologies, a long and fruitful period of "creative creation" typically occurs. Indeed, the social good is well served through disruption, which has, over the decades, created millions of jobs, generated hundreds of billions of dollars in revenues and market capitalization, and raised standards of living by making available cheap, high-quality products. We have gained more through creative creation than we have lost through creative destruction.

For example, until the late 1970s, only employees of large companies and universities had access to computers—and that access could be had only by giving punched cards to the expert in the mainframe center who ran the job. Minicomputer makers such as Digital Equipment listened diligently to their customers, and their customers told them that the nascent technology of personal computing was a waste of time. It was a quirky new gadget only for artists, kids, and hippies, not something intended for the sophisticated technologists in large corporations and universities that controlled access to computing. Not surprisingly, the early market for PCs, led by upstarts such as Apple, was to be found among artists, academics, and other members of the counterculture.

But as PC technology evolved and developed, its performance improved, even on dimensions that were important to the mainstream market. Gradually, PCs began eating into the lower end of the mini-computer market. When companies such as IBM and Compaq entered the business, they were able to make computing accessible to a much larger population of average—and, ultimately, lower-income—non–computer scientists and nonprogrammers. Now that the masses could use computers without the level of training of experts, the technological progress and industry growth that followed enabled average people to do many more things than had been possible on mainframes run by experts.

Because computers and a host of other industries (such as automobiles, consumer electronics, and financial services) were disrupted, extraordinary waves of growth occurred. In each instance, we enjoyed higher quality, lower cost, and greater convenience. Those who are better off today include many more people than those few who could afford it before the disruptions. Disruptive innovators have generated hundreds of billions of dollars in revenues and market capitalization, and created tens of millions of jobs in the process. And yet firms have achieved all this, as the left side of Exhibit 5.2 suggests, by dipping only slightly down from the peak of the population pyramid—by going from the wealthiest and highest skilled of those living in developed countries into the tiers of lower skills and income in those same developed countries.

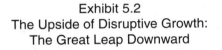

Exhibit 5.2
The Upside of Disruptive Growth:
The Great Leap Downward

Major waves of growth historically have been created through forays to the bottom of developed markets.

Great leaps downward have a much greater upside than disruptions that begin and end in developed markets.

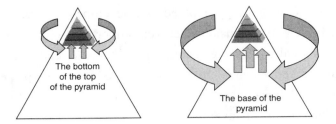

Source: Adapted from S. Hart and C. Christensen, 2002. "The Great Leap: Driving Innovation from the Base of the Pyramid." *Sloan Management Review*, 44 (1) (2002): 51-56.

The disruptive technologies that were developed to reach just down to these tiers cannot be easily deployed toward even lower-income consumers—it is very difficult to remove cost from a business model aimed at higher-income customers without affecting its quality or integrity. But new waves of disruptive technology deployed by companies making a Great Leap Downward can have extraordinary potential to generate growth because they have even more upside once they have taken root. Indeed, the low-cost structure needed to serve the base of the pyramid presents the opportunity to add cost and features to products and move up-market to tiers of higher income and affluence. In short, the farther down the income pyramid the technology is that we initially target, the more upside growth potential exists over the life of the innovation.

Driving Innovation from the Base of the Pyramid

As Clay Christensen and I have argued, the base of the pyramid is the ideal target market for new disruptive technologies for at least two reasons.[16] The first is that business models forged in low-income markets can travel profitably to more places than can business models defined in high-income markets. Honda's success with motorcycles provides an example. In the 1950s, Honda began selling motorized bicycles to small distributors in the crowded and impoverished Japanese cities that were rebuilding from the ruin of World War II. The company developed a business model that could make money selling at very low price points. When Honda entered the United States market in the early 1960s with its disruptive Supercub, the product's simplicity and low price point enabled a much larger population—people who lacked the money or boldness to own Harleys—to buy and use motorcycles. Honda's base in impoverished Japan gave it a huge competitive advantage in disrupting the American motorcycle makers because it could make money at prices that were unattractive to the established leaders.

Toyota and Sony followed the same recipe and enjoyed decades of success while taking on the market leaders in developed countries. In fact, the industries that constituted the engine of Japan's economic miracle from the 1960s to the 1980s all followed the disruptive strategy of attacking markets that established competitors wanted to avoid because their likely revenue and profits were unattractive to them. Disruption was the nation's strategy for economic development. The reason Japan's economy has suffered from no growth for a decade or more is that its institutions will not permit new waves of disruptive innovation to be launched against today's multinational giants, the very companies that were yesterday's disrupters.[17]

In addition to having more adaptable business models, disruptive innovators compete against nonconsumption—that is, they offer a product or service to people who otherwise would be left out entirely or would remain poorly served by existing products. That is the second reason the base of the pyramid offers better markets for new growth businesses. When companies searching for growth fight against capable competitors to win the business of savvy customers in established markets, the barriers to success are formidable. When they bring a disruptive product to customers who have been poorly served or even actively exploited, the customers are delighted to have simple products with modest functionality.

Consider a Chinese company called Galanz, which has achieved extraordinary growth through a Great Leap Downward.[18] In 1992, Galanz decided to enter the market for microwave ovens, even though the firm was a textile and garment manufacturer at the time. The global market for microwaves was mature and shrinking, and it was hard to differentiate products because most of them were good enough to do what people wanted them to do. Manufacturing had migrated to countries where labor costs were low, and consumption was concentrated in developed countries. In China, only 2 percent of all households owned a microwave oven. Most families did not have kitchens large enough to accommodate the available models, which had been designed to fit into homes in the West.

Rather than pursue the obvious strategy of using inexpensive Chinese labor to make lower-cost ovens for export, Galanz's founder Qingde Liang chose to compete against nonconsumption in the domestic market. Galanz developed and introduced a simple, energy-efficient product at a price that was affordable to China's vast middle and lower-middle classes, and small enough to fit in their kitchens. As sales steadily climbed, Liang stimulated demand by using the company's ever-declining cost per unit to reduce the product's price. Galanz's domestic market share rose from 2 percent in 1993 to 76 percent of a much larger market by 2000. Armed with a business model that could earn attractive profits at low price points, Galanz moved up-market to manufacture larger machines that had more features. It began to disrupt the microwave oven markets in developed countries by marketing its machines on a private-label basis to large MNC producers of home appliances. By 2002, it had become the largest producer of microwave ovens in the world, with a global market share of 35 percent.

Connecting the World

Galanz's success demonstrates the possibility for disruptive change to affect people in the middle of the pyramid. But the feasibility of disruptive business models has also been demonstrated in numerous experiments at the very bottom, where more than four billion people earn less than $1,500 in purchasing power parity annually. Perhaps the best-known such experiment occurred in the Grameen family of enterprises in Bangladesh, described in Chapter 3, "The Sustainable Value Portfolio." The original Grameen Bank, one of the originators of micro-credit in the developing world more than 20 years ago, has since spawned several other ventures, including Grameen Telecom, launched in the late 1990s, which focused on bringing information and communication technology to rural Bangladesh in the form of "village phones."

Iqbal Quadir originally conceived of the idea in 1993, after his New York firm's computer network went down. It reminded him of his childhood days in rural Bangladesh when he used to waste entire days walking long distances because there was virtually no phone service outside of the city.[19] Today more than half of humanity (3 billion people) is still without reliable telecommunications service. Telephone service in rural areas has been slowed by the size of the capital investment required to extend the wireline infrastructure profitably from urban areas. Grameen Telecom's mission has therefore been to bring telecommunications service to the rural poor in Bangladesh (average per capita income of $286 per year). At this income level, the existing business model for telephone service would not be feasible—only disruption could do the job.

Accordingly, at the initiation of Professor Yunus, two independent companies were formed in 1997, one for profit (GrameenPhone), and another not for profit (Grameen Telecom). GrameenPhone is a consortium made up of four partners: Telenor of Norway (51%), Grameen Telecom (35%), Marubeni of Japan (9.5%), and Gonophone Development Company (4.5%). GrameenPhone was the recipient of the telecommunications license. It focused on serving all urban areas in Bangladesh by building a nationwide cellular network. Grameen Telecom buys bulk airtime from GrameenPhone and retails it through Grameen borrowers in the rural villages. Initially, few gave the venture much hope because only the richest city-dwellers in Bangladesh could afford their own mobile phones. But by changing its business model, Grameen Telecom was able to pilot-test and launch a venture that has proved to be highly profitable. The bank loaned the money to women in rural villages to establish them as independent entrepreneurs to sell mobile phone services. They received loans of up to $175 to purchase a mobile phone and a small solar recharger unit. The loan also included the necessary training needed to use and service the equipment. The pilot project started in 1997 with 950 villages, but in Bangladesh alone there was a potential market for tens of thousands of "village phones."

The results of the pilot test were impressive.[20] Village phone operators increased their income on average by about $300 per year, raising their status in their villages considerably. Most of these women spent their additional income on education and health care for their children, providing an additional development bonus. For users of the phone service, there was considerable consumer surplus. Rather than making the time-consuming and expensive trip to secure information about crop prices or to place orders with distributors through a slow, unreliable postal system, users could now simply place a call. Each call saved the average user $2.70 to $10—a whopping 2.5 to 10 percent of household monthly income. Significant reduction in travel, combined with the avoidance of a wireline infrastructure, provided significant environmental advantages as well.

The business model also proved to be potentially very profitable for the company. The rural phones in the pilot project booked three times the revenue per phone as their urban counterparts ($100 per month in revenue for a village phone versus about $30 per month in the city). If extended to all of rural Bangladesh, it was estimated that the business could generate revenues in excess of $100 million per year. If a similar model were applied to rural India and China, tens of billions of dollars of revenue would be possible.

In fact, the performance of GrameenPhone over the past half-dozen years has exceeded even the wildest dreams of those involved with the pilot project.[21] By August 2004, the company had a subscriber base of more than 2 million and provided telephone access to more than 50 million people—including half of Bangladesh's rural population. In 2003, the company had grown net profits to $74 million on revenues approaching $300 million. Annual revenues from each village phone had grown to nearly $4,000 per year. Phone ladies were earning, on average, more than $1,000 per year. While it may not sound like much in places like the United States or Western Europe, this level of income has moved the phone ladies' families squarely into the middle class.

In fact, demand for rural phone services was so strong that additional phone ladies were necessary in many villages. By 2004, there were nearly 75,000 phone ladies, and that number was expected to top 100,000 before the end of the calendar year. If you do the math, that means that GrameenPhone is approaching a half-billion dollars in revenue as a company in Bangladesh alone. This is all the more impressive when it is realized that, until 2004, the government denied access to the wireline infrastructure, meaning that all calls had to be made from one Grameen phone to another.

Recently, GrameenPhone began expanding its service to include rural Internet access, through the use of Internet kiosks. N-Logue, an emerging telecom player in India, has adopted a similar business model but has developed new technology to dramatically lower connection costs in rural areas using wireless local loop (WLL) technology that separates voice and data traffic. The revenue and profit potential for this business is enormous.[22]

Whereas fixed and mobile wireless technology is not performance- or cost-competitive with wireline access to the Internet in developed nations, it is vastly superior to the alternative in much of the developing world: nonconsumption. Telecommunications giants in developed countries have spent billions on 3G technology and spectrum licenses, hoping to provide enough bandwidth for current customers to do wire- lessly the things for which they now use the wireline Internet. These investments have crippled many of these companies, and they are unlikely ever to produce adequate returns. Far better is to compete against nonconsumption at the base of the pyramid—and migrate from that profitable base toward successively more sophisticated customers and applications in global markets.

The case of Grameen Telecom illustrates how disruptive business model innovation can incubate sophisticated technologies at the base of the pyramid in ways that offer tremendous growth potential for busi- nesses and positive social and environmental benefits for the rural poor. Great Leaps Downward hold the potential to generate enormous growth and to address the root causes of antiglobalization sentiments, facilitat- ing sustainable development. This is true even for the most sophisti- cated new technologies, such as solar energy, LED lighting, and bioengineered foods. The base of the pyramid can be the best place to start, as we explore next.

Power to the People

Consider the case for distributed generation of power. The electric power infrastructure in the developed world is based upon large, cen- tralized power facilities (fueled by coal, oil, gas, or nuclear technology) and an extensive grid system for the transmission and distribution of power. Incremental innovation has improved the efficiency of these power plants over the years, but significant inefficiencies still exist in generation and distribution. Extending the grid system to distant rural areas is capital intensive (costing, on average, $10,000–$20,000 per mile), and the pricing required to recoup those massive investments would limit consumption. As a consequence, there are still more than 2 billion people in the world with no access to dependable electric power. These people instead use dangerous and polluting fuels such as kerosene, diesel, candles, and dung.

In rich countries, there is growing investment in the distributed generation of power (DG), including such technologies as solar photovoltaics, wind, fuel cells, and microturbines. In fact, venture capital investment in DG surpassed $800 million in 2000, up from only about $100 million in 1996. These technologies generate small quantities of electricity (less than 1mW) near the actual point of use, thereby avoiding the need for expensive distribution. DG technologies also lend themselves to the use of renewable fuels (such as the sun or wind, as well as biomass, in the case of fuel cells and microturbines).

Engineers and marketers are struggling against a stringent standard, working to bring down the cost of these technologies to make them competitive with conventional sources of power in the developed world, where the existence of a well-developed, sunk-cost grid system and subsidies for fossil fuels wipe away any cost advantage associated with distributed generation. In these markets, cost-accounting systems and rate structures tailored to the centralized generation of power using fossil fuels make it difficult for such technologies to gain a foothold in the mainstream markets because they have yet to achieve cost parity in the eyes of the consumer. Photovoltaic electricity, for example, still costs about $1–$2 per kilowatt hour, compared to 7¢–15¢ per kilowatt hour for grid-connected electricity. Customers in the developed world are also understandably leery about taking on the additional risks and responsibilities of solar panels or fuel cells while the after-sale service infrastructure remains in its infancy.

But DG faces few of these obstacles among the rural poor in the developing world. It may be decades before the electrical grid system is extended to provide service to those who currently lack access to dependable electric power. As a consequence, the rural poor spend a significant portion of their income—as much as $10 per month—on candles, kerosene, and batteries to have access to lighting at night and periodic electrical service.[23] Furthermore, generating electricity using kerosene and batteries is expensive, costing $5–$10 or more per kilowatt hour. If offered a viable substitute, these people might abandon these dangerous, polluting, and expensive technologies in favor of clean, efficient, and renewable electric power. Yet few producers of DG have targeted the rural poor at the base of the pyramid as their early market for these technologies, despite the fact that the market is potentially huge and is populated by people who would be delighted with technologies that cannot compete along the metrics used in developed markets.

The crucial breakthrough for sustainable energy technologies, therefore, will not be in a laboratory. Instead, sustainable energy must be incubated and refined where the technology can be profitably deployed through disruptive strategies, in markets where it does not compete against established technologies. This means producers must tailor the technology for use in poor rural areas and develop production, sales, service, and microfinancing packages that enable nonconsumers to gain access.

Consider the innovative technology and business model created by the nonprofit Light Up the World (LUTW).[24] Dedicated to bringing a safe source of light at night to the billions of people without electric power around the world, LUTW recently teamed with Stanford University to develop an affordable rural (off-grid) lighting system that combines solar photovoltaics with light-emitting diode (LED) technology.

LED is an emerging lighting technology that is extremely energy-efficient (80–90 percent more efficient than incandescent light bulbs), long-lived (lasts 8–10 years), and durable (virtually unbreakable). Despite these advantages, however, to date, LEDs have been limited to niche applications such as traffic signals, brake lights, and electronic displays, where vibrant color and durability are important. In recent years, however, white LED technology has been developed that holds the potential to replace light bulbs in the mainstream lighting market. Yet even though all the large lighting companies (including GE, Philips, and Osram-Sylvania) have growing LED businesses, there have been few commercial inroads into this vast market, despite the potential for massive energy and financial savings. We can explain this in part by the large installed base of light fixtures (which will not accommodate LEDs). It is also a result of the propensity for top-of-the-pyramid consumers to benchmark any substitute lighting technology against conventional incandescent bulbs, which cost less than a dollar but last only a matter of months (LEDs cost 10 times as much but last for nearly a decade). Indeed, the slow rate of compact fluorescent bulb adoption has already demonstrated the difficulty of changing consumer preferences to a substitute with a higher first cost but a lower life-cycle cost.

Of course, none of these problems exists if we focus instead on the billions of rural poor without access to electricity. There is no installed base of light bulb fixtures, nor are there any preconceived notions about how an electric lighting system should operate. And by combining the highly energy-efficient LED lighting arrays with solar power, we can dramatically reduce total system cost, downsizing the solar panel needed to power the system. Indeed, LUTW and Stanford have been able to design a system that includes the LED lighting arrays, the solar panel, the battery, wiring, and controls in a "rural lighting system" package that can be sold for as little as $40 retail. For a poor family making less than $500 per year, this would be equivalent to the purchase of a car by a top of the pyramid family. Because the family is already spending as much as $5–10 each month on candles, kerosene, lanterns, and batteries, all that is required is a microfinancing package, along with a reliable local microentrepreneur to sell and service the equipment. This is precisely the approach that LUTW and Stanford have taken in launching a commercial venture to serve this market.

A business model like this could tap into a market of more than two billion people. With the volume and experience from the sale and service of solar and LED at the base of the pyramid, it would be only a matter of time before this technology became so efficient—and affordable—that it began to eat its way into the low-end markets in urban areas, perhaps starting with shantytowns, where grid-based electric power is expensive and unreliable. For example, the Solar Electric Light Company (SELCO), a for-profit enterprise that serves the middle-of-the-pyramid market with full-scale solar home electric lighting systems that sell for as much as $500 each, has a thriving business in India and Southeast Asia. Ultimately, such systems could become so attractive and affordable that even the wealthy at the top of the pyramid would find them difficult to resist. Given the enormous growth potential of this business model, it comes as no surprise that electronics giant Philips launched such a commercial venture in rural India during 2004.

In sum, sustainable energy pioneers who focus on the base of the pyramid could set the stage for one of the biggest business bonanzas in the history of commerce, because extensive adoption and experience there would almost certainly lead to dramatic improvements in cost and quality. If firms such as Philips create a business model that can be profitable in these markets, solar energy has a chance. But this is the *only* strategy by which this technology can succeed without massive and ongoing government subsidy.

Food, Health, and Hope?

A Great Leap Downward could also reverse the present course of the agricultural biotechnology and genetically modified (GM) plant and animal industries, which continue to struggle for economic viability and social acceptance. Most early efforts to bring this technology to market were aimed at rapid penetration of the mainstream market. For example, despite its mantra of "Food, Health, and Hope," Monsanto focused virtually its entire strategy during the 1990s on designing genetically engineered seeds to lower costs for farmers growing commodity crops (such as corn, soybean, and cotton) in the developed world, especially the United States.

Reducing chemical and input usage through genes that made the plants pest-resistant (such as Bt Cotton) or resistant to the application of herbicides (such as Roundup Ready) made such seeds hard for farmers in the United States to resist because they were under intense margin pressure from food processors and manufacturers. The large-scale and centralized nature of the American agribusiness system meant that producers rapidly planted and purchased GM crops. Indeed, the acreage dedicated to GM crops in the United States increased from virtually zero in 1995 to more than 60 million acres by the end of the 1990s.[25]

However, as we have seen, attempts to expand beyond the United States met with growing opposition. In Europe, environmentalists and consumers began to resist the import and planting of such seeds. A backlash movement set in motion and focused on several issues. First, consumers perceived no benefit to eating GM crops. Indeed, only farmers benefited from the first generation of seeds, and consumers were asked to take whatever risk there might be (such as allergic reaction), with no compensating health or nutrition benefit. Second, environmentalists grew more concerned that unforeseen ecological problems could be unleashed by the rapid rate of GM adoption by farmers, including the possibility of crossing with wild plants and the production of "super weeds." Third, critics from the developing world grew increasingly concerned that a few MNCs might come to control the world's seed supply, denying poor, small-shareholder farmers around the world the ability to save seed and engage in other age-old agricultural practices. Food manufacturers and retailers began to boycott GM crops, in some cases paying a premium for conventionally grown foods. By the late 1990s, the backlash had become so severe that Monsanto and other agricultural biotechnology producers were forced to scale back their business operations and reconsider the future of GM food.

The recent bioagricultural experience provides important lessons in technological innovation and commercialization. Disruptive innovation theory would predict that the attempt to pit GM foods against the established options in complex mainstream markets so soon would be fraught with difficulty. Reducing farmers' cost is not enough to guarantee acceptance of a radically new technology when customers already are well satisfied with the quality, quantity, and affordability of present food alternatives. Indeed, the greatest need for additional nutrition and agricultural productivity resides not with American agribusiness, but rather, at the base of the pyramid, where billions of small-shareholder farmers labor to produce crops, frequently for their own consumption, at very low levels of efficiency and productivity.

Properly designed and introduced, GM seeds might dramatically improve the lives of small farmers by lowering costs, enhancing pest resistance and productivity, conserving water and soil, and increasing nutritional value of foods made from such crops as rice, sweet potatoes, and cassava. Through microcredit and other forms of collaboration with small farmers, it might be possible to design a business model that results in a whole new approach to sustainable agriculture. Incubating such experiments from the ground up rather than introducing the technology on a massive scale from the top down also might encourage a more reasoned understanding of any significant environmental issues. Eventually, these approaches to agriculture might become so productive and successful that they could move up-market to out-compete the chemical- and energy-intensive agribusiness model prevalent in the United States. When we are building major new growth markets with new technology, the shortest distance between two points often is not a straight line.

A New Development Paradigm

The theory of disruptive innovation suggests that existing mainstream markets are the wrong place to look for major new waves of growth. Indeed, forcing a potentially disruptive innovation into a conventional business model, thereby moving it into head-on competition with incumbents, may only ensure its early demise. Instead, we argue that the vast, untapped market at the "base of the pyramid" is an ideal place for the incubation of new, sustainable technologies.

Our thinking about the potential rewards resulting from a great leap to the base of the pyramid extends this strategy as a framework not just for corporate growth, but also for more balanced and effective macro-economic development in poor countries. Such an approach is potentially significant because existing strategies for economic development now appear to be all but bankrupt.[26] Import substitution, for example, which emphasized the development of domestic capacity to serve established home markets, was discredited more than 20 years ago; its protectionist stance failed to produce competitive or efficient national producers.[27]

More recently, the export-led growth strategies advocated by the so-called Washington Consensus have come under increasing fire as well.[28] By asserting that more developing countries can generate growth by producing commodities and goods for export to the top of the pyramid, the doctrine of export-led growth has resulted in excess capacity and global deflation. Indeed, after a decade of international financial crises, mounting Third World debt, environmental devastation, and rising inequity, the Washington Consensus is crumbling. It now appears clear that the only way to spur sustainable growth for the long term is to design a development strategy that focuses on the unmet needs in the developing world itself, the base of the pyramid. Indeed, the Great Leap Downward holds the prospect of lifting the poor out of poverty, averting environmental meltdown, and opening the way to sustainable growth for the global economy.

Consider the case of Mexico. Since signing on to the North American Free Trade Agreement (NAFTA) a decade ago, the country has been caught in a no-win situation. By opening its borders to foreign investment, Mexico became a haven for Maquiladora plants near the U.S. border and new export-oriented MNC assembly facilities in search of low labor costs or lax environmental enforcement. There can be no doubt that these foreign direct investments created factory wage jobs in the short term. Unfortunately, few of these investments provide any long-term development payoff for Mexico.

There are two reasons for this conundrum. First, as even lower-cost locations (such as China) became more attractive, many of the plants and assembly facilities closed their doors and moved overseas, leaving Mexico's workers high and dry. Like unemployed factory workers in the U.S., they are victims of the global "race to the bottom" for the lowest wages and operating costs. Second, the export-oriented investments in Mexico have provided few of the skills or capabilities needed to compete more effectively in the game of global capitalism. Indeed, few Mexican companies are now better able to compete against the highly sophisticated U.S., European, and Japanese multinationals for the top of the pyramid markets as a result of these investments. In short, low factor costs alone do not translate into knowledge or skills that have value in the highly competitive marketplace of today's global capitalism.

The combination of NAFTA and the draconian structural adjustment policies imposed on Mexico by the International Monetary Fund have served only to hasten the country's slide into rising inequity, social rebellion, and financial meltdown. It should come as no surprise, then, that some enlightened business leaders and government officials in Mexico have become increasingly interested in the Great Leap Downward as a potential way out of this trap: By using the power of commerce as a vehicle for serving the needs of the country's massive underclass, Mexico can incubate entirely new enterprises with the unique capabilities needed to become the globally competitive companies of the future. Just like China and Galanz, Mexico could become a wellspring for the truly disruptive—and sustainable—enterprises of the twenty-first century.

Taking the Leap

If history is any guide, most of the growth opportunities in the vast, untapped market at the base of the pyramid will be seized by entrepreneurs (such as Grameen and Galanz) in developing countries, just as the opportunities in impoverished postwar Japan were captured by innovators such as Sony, Honda, and Toyota. In addition, countries such as Mexico, India, and China may well make the Great Leap Downward their primary strategy for national economic development. Indeed, we may be witnessing the birth of the next generation of multinational corporations, nurtured in the base of the pyramid and ready to take on the high-cost structures and rigid management models of the existing MNC incumbents.

Today's global corporations, however, should not assume that such an outcome is inevitable; they, too, can seize these growth opportunities before they become threats. As is always the case in pursuing disruptive innovation, however, such companies will need to manage these new opportunities independently from the processes and values of their mainstream incumbent businesses. Even more importantly, they will have to build new business models that include strategies, organizational structures, and management processes actually suited to conditions at the base of the pyramid.

Notes

1. C. K. Prahalad and Ken Lieberthal, "The End of Corporate Imperialism," *Harvard Business Review* July–August (1998), www.hbsp.harvard.edu/hbr/index.html.

2. C. K. Prahalad and Stuart Hart, "The Fortune at the Bottom of the Pyramid," *Strategy+Business* January (2002): 54–67.

3. Including C. K. Prahalad and Michael Gordon (University of Michigan), Clayton Christensen (Harvard Business School), Miguel Angel Rodríguez and Joan Enric Ricart (IESE Business School), Sanjay Sharma (Wilfrid Laurier University), Alan Hammond (World Resources Institute), Nicholas Guttierez (Tec Monterrey), and Jim Johnson, Ted London, Mark Milstein, Erik Simanis, and Lisa Jones (University of North Carolina).

4. At the suggestion of my UNC colleague Ted London, we changed the name from "Bottom" to "Base" of the Pyramid to remove any hint that those on the lower end of the income scale are in any way inferior to those at the high end of the income scale.

5. The BOP Learning Lab's contributing members include DuPont, HP, J&J, P&G, SC Johnson, Ford, Dow, Coke, and Tetrapak. Nonprofit organizations such as the Grameen Foundation, ApproTEC, Tata Energy and Resources Institute, and the World Resources Institute are also actively involved.

6. Parts of this chapter are excerpted from Stuart Hart and Clayton Christensen, "The Great Leap: Driving Innovation from the Base of the Pyramid," *Sloan Management Review* 44(1) (2002): 51–56.

7. Portions of this section are excerpted from Prahalad and Hart, "The Fortune at the Bottom."

8. For an extended discussion of this issue, see Ted London and Stuart Hart, "Reinventing Strategies for Emerging Markets: Beyond the Transnational Model," *Journal of International Business Studies*, forthcoming.

9. C. K. Prahalad and Allen Hammond, "Serving the World's Poor, Profitably," *Harvard Business Review* 80(9) (2002): 48–57.

10. Ted London and Stuart Hart, "Reinventing Strategies."

11. Hernando de Soto, *The Mystery of Capital: Why Capitalism Triumphs in the West and Fails Everywhere Else* (New York: Basic Books, 2000).

12. Ibid.

13. Ibid.

14. Parts of the following section are excerpted from Stuart Hart and Clayton Christensen, "The Great Leap."

15. See Clayton Christensen, *The Innovator's Dilemma: When New Technologies Cause Great Firms to Fail* (Boston: Harvard Business School Press, 1997).

16. Stuart Hart and Clayton Christensen, "The Great Leap."

17. Clayton Christensen, Thomas Craig, and Stuart Hart, "The Great Disruption," *Foreign Affairs* 80(2) (2001): 80–95.

18. My thanks to Clay Christensen for this example.

19. Iqbal Quadir, presentation at the Wharton Global Compact Conference, University of Pennsylvania, 17 September 2004.

20. For details, see Muhammad Yunus, *Banker to the Poor* (Dhaka: The University Press Limited, 1998); D. Richardson, R. Ramirez, and M. Haq, *Grameen Telecom's Village Phone Programme in Rural Bangladesh: A Multi-Media Study* (Guelph, Ontario: TeleCommons Development Group, 2000).

21. Personal communication with Muhammad Yunas, April 2004, and Iqbal Quadir, September 2004.

22. J. Howard, C. Simms, and E. Simanis, *Sustainable Deployment for Rural Connectivity: the N-Logue Model* (Washington, D.C.: World Resources Institute, 2001).

23. Light Up the World Foundation, LUTW_factsheetdec23.pdf, p. 5.

24. Light Up the World, www.lightuptheworld.org.

25. Erik Simanis and Stuart Hart. *The Monsanto Company (A): Quest for Sustainability* (Washington, D.C.: World Resources Institute, 2000).

26. Thomas Palley, "A New Development Paradigm: Domestic Demand Led Growth," *Foreign Policy Focus* (September 2002): 1–8.

27. See Jagdish Bhagwati, *In Defense of Globalization* (New York: Oxford University Press, 2004).

28. See, for example, Joseph Stiglitz, *Globalization and Its Discontents* (New York: W. W. Norton & Company, 2002).

6

REACHING THE BASE
OF THE PYRAMID

Now is the time for the leaders of multinational corporations (MNCs) to expand their conception of globalization and strategy.[1] For boards, senior executives, and business leaders with the audacity and desire to compete at the base of the world economic pyramid, the prospective rewards include growth, profits, and incalculable contributions to humankind. As we have seen, countries that are not encumbered by billions of dollars of sunk costs in centralized infrastructure are ideal incubators for environmentally sustainable technologies and products that might one day benefit the entire world. Furthermore, MNC investment at the base of the pyramid means lifting billions of people out of poverty and desperation—and averting the social decay, political chaos, terrorism, and environmental meltdown that is certain to result if the gap between rich and poor continues to widen.

As C. K. Prahalad and I have argued, doing business with the world's four billion poorest people—two-thirds of the total population—will require radical innovations in both technology and business models. It will require MNCs to re-evaluate price-performance relationships for products and services. It will demand a new level of capital efficiency and new ways of measuring financial success. Companies will be forced to transform their understanding of scale from "bigger is better" to highly distributed small-scale operations married to world-scale capabilities.

In short, the poorest populations present a prodigious new managerial challenge for the world's wealthiest companies. Indeed, over the past few years, it has become apparent that there is a large prospective market to be served in the BOP. It has also become clear that the prospect transcends mere market potential: The opportunity is to use commerce as a driving force for human betterment and environmental restoration—to literally raise the base of the pyramid. Attempts to adapt the top of the pyramid model for use at the base, however, appear destined to fail. Only through a concerted focus on the base of the pyramid will it be possible for large corporations to combine a humanitarian, even activist, orientation with the conventional motivations of growth and profitability.

BOP Pioneers

Hindustan Lever, Ltd. (HLL), a subsidiary of Great Britain's Unilever PLC, has been a pioneer among MNCs exploring markets at the base of the pyramid. For more than 50 years, HLL served the small elite in India with the income to buy the MNC's products. Then in the 1990s, HLL noted that an Indian firm, Nirma, Ltd., was offering detergent products for poor consumers; in fact, Nirma had created an entirely new business system designed to meet the needs of underserved consumers, mostly from poor, rural areas. This included a new product formulation, a low-cost manufacturing process, a wide distribution network, special packaging for daily purchasing, and pricing for consumers with limited means.

In typical MNC fashion, HLL initially dismissed Nirma's strategy—it appeared, on the surface, to have no implications for HLL's served market at the top of the pyramid. However, as Nirma rapidly grew, HLL could see that its local competitor was winning in a market it had foolishly disregarded. Furthermore, as Nirma grew, it began to migrate up-market from the strong base in the BOP; HLL finally saw its vulnerability—and its opportunity. In 1995, the company responded with its own offering for the BOP market, drastically altering its traditional business model.[2]

HLL's new detergent product, Wheel, was reformulated to substantially reduce the ratio of oil to water, responding to the fact that the poor often wash clothes in rivers and other public water systems. Most raw materials were sourced from local suppliers. Production, marketing, and distribution were all decentralized to leverage the large labor pool in rural India, quickly creating selling channels through the thousands of small outlets where people at the base of the pyramid shop. HLL also changed the cost structure of its detergent business so it could introduce Wheel at a low price point.

Today Nirma and HLL are close competitors in the detergent market, with about 40 percent market share each, according to India Infoline.com, a business intelligence and market research service covering the Indian market. And the BOP accounts for more than half of HLL's total revenues—and profits. Unilever's own analysis of competition in the detergent business, however, reveals even more about the profit potential in the BOP marketplace (see Exhibit 6.1). Contrary to popular assumptions, the BOP can be a very profitable market, especially if MNCs change their business models.

Exhibit 6.1
Nirma Versus HLL in India's Detergent Market (1999)

	Nirma	HLL (Wheel)	HLL (High-End)
Total sales ($ million)	150	100	180
Gross margin (%)	18	18	25
Return on capital (%)	121	93	22

Source: Presentation by John Ripley, Senior Vice President, Unilever, at the
Academy of Management Meeting, 10 August 1999.

It's the Business Model, Stupid

As Exhibit 6.1 makes clear, in the consumer goods industry, the BOP is
not a market that allows for the traditional pursuit of high margins;
instead, volume and capital efficiency are the name of this game.
Margins are likely to be low (by current norms), but unit sales
extremely high. Managers who focus on gross margins will miss the
opportunity; managers who innovate and focus on economic profit will
be rewarded.

Thus, getting the metrics right is critically important to success in
the BOP: Imposing the established performance criteria from the top of
the pyramid will almost certainly kill the opportunity. The decentralized
nature of Unilever's corporate structure enabled HLL to "fly under the
radar" long enough to establish a successful new business model for the
BOP. More centralized MNCs might not allow such latitude to experiment; yet without it, the BOP will almost certainly remain elusive.

Yet despite its early success in the market, Wheel's introduction
was far from perfect. Although it represented a considerable improvement over the low-cost but harsh formulation offered by Nirma, HLL's
detergent was phosphate-based, which meant that it still polluted public
waterways. Wheel also introduced a new solid waste problem in the
form of millions of spent sachet (single-use) packets. Only after HLL's

experiment in serving the poor was validated and supported by the parent company was it possible to connect Unilever's corporate capability in environmental management and sustainability to HLL's innovative approach to reaching the BOP market. Solving these environmental challenges in the BOP will clearly require the combination of corporate know-how and local knowledge.

As a direct result of business model innovation, first-mover Nirma is today one of the largest branded detergent makers in the world. Meanwhile, HLL, stimulated by its emergent rival and its changed business model, registered a 20 percent growth in revenues per year and a 25 percent growth in profits per year for 1995–2000. Over the same period, HLL's market capitalization grew to $12 billion, a growth rate of 40 percent per year. HLL's parent company, Unilever, has also benefited from its subsidiary's experience in India. Unilever transported HLL's business principles (not the product or the brand) to create a new detergent market among the poor in Brazil. The brand Ala has been a runaway success. Even more important, Unilever has adopted the base of the pyramid as a corporate strategic priority. Indeed, by 2004, the BOP accounted for nearly 20 percent of Unilever's sales on a global basis.[3]

Recently, HLL launched another round of business model innovation. India has more than half a million villages, home to tens of millions of people who are inaccessible by traditional product distribution models. Through "Project Shakti," the company has taken a page out of GrameenPhone's book by seeking to develop a cadre of women microentrepreneurs at the village level.[4] HLL has already trained more than 10,000 Shakti Entrepreneurs (SEs), with a goal of having more than 25,000 by the end of 2005. Ultimately, the company might build a network of a million or more SEs located throughout the rural villages of India. SEs are imparted basic selling and accounting skills to enable them to operate as micro-entrepreneurs earning a steady income from the sales of HLL's products. In addition, the women are trained to be health and hygiene communicators in a bid to improve the standard of living of the community they operate in. SEs also serve as listening posts for future needs. If successful, Project Shakti's unique win-win direct-distribution model may supplant the current complex and unwieldy approach to BOP distribution through thousands of small-scale distributors and small "mom and pop" shops.

Clearly, the base of the pyramid presents unique challenges for MNCs: It violates nearly every assumption associated with successfully serving the top of the pyramid. In point of fact, the biggest challenge for MNCs may have less to do with technology, intellectual property, or rule of law, even though these issues have dominated most of the work to date relating to emerging markets.[5] Instead, the fundamental challenge may be one of business model innovation—breaking free of the established mindsets, systems, and metrics that constrain the imagination of incumbent firms.

As the Unilever case demonstrates, to identify needs and opportunities in the BOP, MNC managers must learn to look beyond their current served market. This can be done in several ways. First, MNCs can seek to identify and remove constraints that prevent the poor from taking control of their own futures. Second, through their business models, MNCs can seek to increase the earning power of the poor. Finally, MNCs can consciously look to create new economic and social potential at the base of the pyramid. We explore each of these in greater detail in the following sections.

Removing Constraints

Business exists to solve problems. Most material needs have already been provided for people at the top of the pyramid, which is why it is so difficult to identify successful new business strategies—customers are already quite well served. The reverse logic applies at the base of the pyramid—major needs remain unmet for massive numbers of people.

Barriers, constraints, gaps, and snafus abound for the poor. What we need to realize as businesspeople is that learning to see these constraints from the point of view of the poor is the best way to identify new break-through business strategies that offer both profit and growth potential for the firm—and a significantly better life for those in the BOP.

As C. K. Prahalad and Al Hammond point out in their recent article in the *Harvard Business Review*, the poor—especially those in urban slums and shantytowns—live in high-cost economies.[6] Their needs are typically not well met by local vendors. In fact, quite frequently, the poor are victims of active exploitation by local moneylenders, corrupt officials, and low-quality service providers. Prahalad and Hammond present data showing that the poor often pay anywhere from twice to 20 times as much as consumers at the top of the pyramid for basic goods and services such as water, food, medicine, phone service, and, as we have seen, access to credit. If we adjust for income level, these differentials become downright obscene. Thus, there is an enormous opportunity to create consumer surplus in the BOP, if we could only open our eyes to the reality on the ground.

We must learn to identify and remove the constraints—"unfreedoms," according to Nobel Prize–winning economist, Amartya Sen[7]—that prevent those in the BOP from realizing their full potential. Unfreedoms mean that the poor often suffer from a systematic lack of opportunity, poor health, and even premature death. These constraints can come in many shapes and sizes: usurious interest rates for credit, poor-quality products, exorbitant prices, exploitive business models, or a total lack of problem recognition.

Cemex, Mexico's largest cement company, provides a glimpse into how to go about constraint identification as a vehicle for reaching the BOP.[8] The 1994 financial crisis in Mexico was a major blow to the company's domestic business, which constituted nearly half of Cemex's cement sales at the time. The construction sector, in particular, was one of the hardest hit in Mexico. However, Cemex executives noted that whereas revenues from upper- and middle-class customers dropped by half, cement sales to the poorest tier of the population were hardly affected. In fact, sales to the poor seemed to follow a completely different logic than those in the affluent market (it would later be recognized that the formal and informal economies do, indeed, follow completely different logics). Given that cement sales to the poor constituted 40 percent of Cemex's Mexican business and that the company knew little about this customer segment, corporate leadership decided that it was worthy of further investigation.

In 1998, a team of Cemex employees began to explore this issue in greater depth. They began by issuing a "Declaration of Ignorance," an open admission that the company knew virtually nothing about 40 percent of its Mexican market. They then resolved to learn all they could about the needs and problems of the people in the urban slums and shantytowns where demand for the company's cement was the strongest. To accomplish this, the team lived in the shantytowns for six months. Their mission was to better understand the context in the BOP, not to sell more cement.

Initially the team, led by Hector Ureta, had a difficult time appreciating the situation.[9] At first glance, the shantytowns appeared to be chaotic assemblages of half-built squatter homes stretching as far as the eye can see. Building materials lay around exposed to the elements—and theft. Partially constructed rooms with steel rebar rods reaching skyward formed the streetscape. It was easy to assume that the people must be ignorant or stupid to engage in such poorly planned and executed construction activity. But after spending several months living in this context, the team came to realize that the people were doing the best possible job that could be done, given the constraints and the circumstances.

Poor, do-it-yourself homebuilders in the shantytowns, they learned, often take 4 years to complete just one room and 13 years to finish a small four-room house. The reason is that banks and other businesses will not engage with poor residents of informal settlements where the legal status of their property ownership is murky. Haphazard design, combined with material theft and spoilage, conspire to make home construction a costly and risky proposition. Vendors prey upon the poor, selling them off-quality goods in quantities that are inappropriate because they have little bargaining power or ability to complain. The Cemex team came to realize that if these constraints could be removed, it might be possible for the poor to build much better-quality homes in less time, while also saving money on materials in the process. And, yes, they might also grow the cement business as well.

To accomplish this end, the team created a new business model. Through its program called Patrimonio Hoy, which, roughly translated, means "Equity Today," Cemex formed savings clubs that allowed aspiring homebuilders to make weekly savings payments. These savings clubs built upon the already prevalent Tandas, community savings plans that had been common in the marginalized sectors in Mexico for decades. In exchange, Cemex provided material storage and architectural support so that homes could be well designed and built in sensible stages. Given its clout as a major buyer, Cemex could negotiate with material suppliers for the best possible prices and quality, something that the shantytown dwellers themselves were unable to do. Participants in the program built their houses three times faster, with higher-quality materials and designs, and at two-thirds the cost. Patrimonio Hoy has been growing 250 percent per year and has enrolled more than 20,000 poor families since its inception. The goal is to reach one million families in Mexico in five years.

The Patrimonio Hoy experience demonstrates how important it is to view the BOP through a new set of lenses to see the opportunity. Rather than assuming that poor people are irrational, stupid, or lazy, it behooves MNCs to instead assume that people in the BOP are doing the best they can under the circumstances. The key is to ask the question, why are they doing things this way? If we can gain a better understanding of the constraints that cause this behavior, we can construct new business models designed to remove these constraints—and profit in the process.

Increasing Earning Power

According to the International Labor Organization's *World Employment Report 2001*, nearly a billion people—roughly one-third of the world's work force—either are underemployed or have such menial jobs that it is not possible to support themselves or their families. The harsh realities of structural adjustment in many of the world's poorest countries have made it all but impossible for those in the BOP to survive exclusively through self-provisioning, barter, and community exchange. Helping the world's poor to elevate themselves above this desperation line by increasing earning power is thus a business opportunity to do well and do good simultaneously. *Creating consumer surplus* and *generating income* are crucial here. A few farsighted organizations have already begun to blaze this trail, with startlingly positive results.

As we saw in the case of Cemex's Patrimonio Hoy program, it is possible, through business model innovation, to create significant consumer surplus for BOP customers while simultaneously making a healthy profit. Indeed, do-it-yourself homebuilders in Mexico's shantytowns saved considerable time and money through the program, while Cemex realized significant incremental cement sales and profits. The creation of consumer surplus in the BOP is possible because, more often than not, the poor are badly served by local vendors. In some instances, particularly in rural areas, however, there are actual service vacuums.

This was the situation faced by Grameen Telecom, as discussed in detail in the last chapter. Because phone service was nonexistent in rural Bangladesh before the introduction of Grameen's service, the relevant point of comparison was how much time and money villagers were spending to gain access to information such as crop prices and currency exchange rates. Although the phone service offered by Grameen was considered expensive by developed world standards, users still saved between 2.5 and 10 percent of household monthly income ($2.70–$10) with each call because the alternative to making the call was spending days traveling to secure the necessary information—an expensive and risky proposition.

Providing consumer surplus through innovative new products and services is important to increased earning power; saving the poor time and/or money frees up resources to be used more productively for other purposes. Procter & Gamble's new clothes rinse product for the rural poor, for example, reduces by two-thirds the amount of water needed to rinse clothes after washing with detergent. It saves an enormous amount of time as well because, instead of finding and hauling as much water as before, people can engage in more productive activities.

Even more important than the provision of consumer surplus, however, is the actual generation of income in the BOP. Businesses that lead to income generation are therefore of special importance. Perhaps the quintessential example of such a business is the microcredit model introduced by Muhammad Yunus and the Grameen Bank. The loans made to the poor through the bank lead directly to income generation through microentrepreneurship and other forms of local enterprise development. In addition to providing credit, companies can develop new technologies to raise BOP incomes and start businesses.

One example of such a venture is Appropriate Technologies for Enterprise Creation (ApproTEC), founded by Dr. Martin Fisher in 1991.[10] Begun as a non-profit, ApproTEC has helped to create thousands of jobs in Kenya and other parts of East Africa, where more than half the population lives on less than $1 per day, by developing enabling technologies and working with local entrepreneurs to launch businesses using those technologies. Profits from the new small-scale businesses enable thousands of poor families to escape poverty, educate their children, afford health care, and plan their futures.

ApproTEC's best-selling technology is the leg-operated Money-maker Micro-irrigation Pump. These simple but effective water pumps, which retail for less than $100, enable poor farmers to grow high-value fruits and vegetables year-round by supplying their crops with much-needed water. On average, these farmers earn an additional $1,200 profit per year, recovering their investment in three months, and increase overall farm income by a factor of 10. Since its inception in the early 1990s, ApproTEC has helped to create 35,000 new microenter-prises in East Africa, with a total of $36 million per year in new profits. Revenues generated by these enterprises equal more than 0.5 percent of Kenya's GDP. Today, more than 800 new businesses are being started every month using ApproTEC technology.

ApproTEC has recently teamed up with SC Johnson Company in Kenya to create more sustainable livelihoods for thousands of poor farmers dependent on growing pyrethrum for a living.[11] When SC Johnson launched its best-selling brand Raid® in 1956 as the world's first commercial aerosol insecticide, the company chose to use environ-mentally benign pyrethrum as the active ingredient. Pyrethrum is the fourth-largest export crop in Kenya, after tea, coffee, and horticultural plants. The Pyrethrum Board of Kenya (PBK) is a parastatal agency reporting to the Ministry of Agriculture that operates as a monopoly, controlling all aspects of Kenya's pyrethrum production, processing, marketing, and export. PBK produces nearly 70 percent of the world's supply of pyrethrum through a network of 200,000 subsistence farmers and their families (nearly 1 million people) organized into cooperatives and self-help groups throughout Kenya's central highlands. SC Johnson has been its biggest customer by far since 1956.

Unfortunately, droughts in Kenya during the 1990s threatened the quality and stability of the natural pyrethrum supply. When Japanese giant Sumitomo developed a lower-cost synthetic alternative, SC Johnson was presented with a difficult choice: Either switch totally to the synthetic or work with the Kenyan producers to lower the cost, improve the quality, and ensure the long-term availability of the natural product. The company chose the latter strategy.

In a new partnership with SC Johnson and ApproTEC, PBK now monitors pyrethrum quality and quantity, and provides ongoing assistance to farmers in the form of access to higher-quality seed. A pilot project involving 600 farmers seeks to increase net household incomes on average from $100 to $750–$1,000 per year. Such a boost in income would enable poor farmers to dramatically improve food security, health, and nutrition. In addition, it is expected that pyrethrum production per acre will increase substantially, and quality will also improve, enabling the company to continue to source the natural botanical at a competitive price rather than switching to the synthetic chemical.

ApproTEC's ability to generate income for the users of its technologies is beyond question. However, ApproTEC now faces the challenge of sustaining its own growth and development. It is clear that it cannot continue to rely exclusively on donor capital to fund the technology development work. Indeed, fundraising has now become the primary activity for the organization's leaders. Accordingly, ApproTEC has embarked on a strategy to move a part of its operation toward a for-profit model, through direct distribution of its technology to end users. Indeed, the partnership with SC Johnson represents one way for it to achieve this end. Only by generating a surplus itself can ApproTEC continue to generate income for others.

Increasing earning power is of vital importance in the BOP, especially in a post-structural adjustment world where poor countries are increasingly dependent upon the cash economy and the generation of foreign currency to survive. MNCs can therefore identify opportunities to both create consumer surplus and generate income through innovative technologies and business models. As with removing constraints, opportunities to increase earning power provide a useful lens for identifying the best opportunities to reach the base of the pyramid.

Creating New Potential

Because BOP communities are often physically or economically isolated, better distribution systems and communication links are essential to sustainable development. Few poor countries have distribution systems that reach more than half the population—hence the continued dependence of the poorest consumers on often low-quality local products and services and exploitative moneylenders. MNCs can therefore create new potential in the BOP by enabling *outreach* (providing distribution channels for local products) and *in-reach* (providing access to affordable products, services, and information).

With regard to outreach, MNCs can play a key role in sourcing or distributing the products of BOP enterprises for use in top of the pyramid markets, giving BOP enterprises their first links to international markets. Indeed, it is possible through partnerships to leverage traditional knowledge bases to produce more sustainable—and, in some cases—superior products for consumption by affluent customers. Anita Roddick, CEO of the Body Shop International PLC, demonstrated the power of this strategy in the early 1990s through her company's "trade, not aid" program of sourcing local raw material and products from indigenous people.

More recently, the Starbucks Corporation, in cooperation with Conservation International, has pioneered a program to source coffee directly from farmers in the Chiapas region of Mexico. These farms grow coffee organically using shade-grown practices, which preserve songbird habitat and prevent soil loss. Starbucks markets the product to U.S. consumers as a high-quality, premium coffee; the Mexican farmers benefit economically from the sourcing arrangement, which eliminates middlemen from the business model. This direct relationship also improves the local farmers' understanding and knowledge of the market at the top of the pyramid and its customer expectations, making a steady transition from the informal to the formal economy possible.

Daimler-Chrysler has also been instrumental in the launch of an outreach-oriented alliance in Brazil called POEMA (Poverty and Environment in Amazonia Research and Development).[12] This alliance is focused on the development of natural fibers for use in the production of interior car parts. With financial and technical assistance from the company, POEMA pioneered the use of coconut fibers and latex sourced from the Amazon in the production of headrests, sun visors, and seat cushions in the Class A Mercedes-Benz model. After a successful pilot project, a for-profit enterprise, POEMAtec Amazon Natural Fibers, was created near the city of Belem in northeastern Brazil. Daimler-Chrysler has since signed a 10-year supply contract with the new company.

Before POEMAtec, coconut fibers were considered waste. Now they are a source of income. POEMAtec worked with the small landholders in the region to help them switch from slash-and-burn agriculture of single crops to a multicrop system that includes coconut palms, rubber, cacao, bananas, and Brazilian chestnut trees. Sourcing communities were set up with processing centers to extract the coconut fibers and produce the latex. These raw materials were then sold to POEMAtec for the manufacture of the final product. The parts produced by the alliance meet all Daimler-Chrysler's stringent quality requirements and are also about 5 percent cheaper to produce than conventional plastic components. Approximately 4,000 new jobs have been created, including agricultural producers, processing plant workers, and POEMAtec employees. Average family income in the community has increased from about $36 per month to nearly $300 per month since the beginning of the alliance. The results of this BOP marketing outreach alliance in Brazil have also been transferred to South Africa and the Philippines.

With regard to in-reach, information technologies such as phones and Internet connections hold the potential to literally transform the way BOP communities view the world. Indeed, information poverty may be the single biggest roadblock to sustainable development.

Through in-reach, it is possible to imagine, for the first time in history, a single, interconnected market uniting the world in the quest for a truly sustainable form of economic development. This process could transform the "digital divide" into a "digital dividend" for the companies willing to take the initiative.

New ventures such as N-Logue in India are developing information technology and business models suited to the particular requirements of the rural poor at the base of the pyramid. Through shared-access models (for example, Internet kiosks) and focused technology development, companies are dramatically reducing the cost of being connected. For example, IT connectivity typically costs $850–$2,800 per line in the developed world; the CorDECT (wireless local loop) technology employed by N-Logue has reduced this cost to less than $400 per line, with a goal of $100 per line, which would bring telecommunications within reach of virtually everyone in India.[13]

Recognizing the opportunity to create new economic potential, the Indian tobacco giant ITC has spawned a network of electronic meeting places in more than 4,000 rural villages in India dubbed *e-choupals*.[14] To address the obvious shortages—phone lines, electricity, and literate farmers—the company has provided satellite links, solar batteries, and carefully chosen microentrepreneurs to run the meeting places. As part of a diversification strategy into a broader range of agribusinesses, ITC (formerly the Imperial Tobacco Company) has made the e-choupal initiative an integral part of its rural development business strategy.

The traditional agricultural system was centered on *mandis,* the markets where farmers brought their produce to be auctioned. Given the obvious power asymmetries (that is, the auctioneers had better information about commodity prices than the farmers), small farmers were often paid far less than they deserved for their produce. To facilitate better information access, ITC created websites for the various crops covered: soya, wheat, coffee, and shrimp. This enabled farmers to level the playing field by gaining better access to market conditions, prices, and even other potential buyers. By eliminating the stranglehold of the man-dis, ITC has been able to source agricultural commodities at more favorable prices, while at the same time increasing the bargaining power—and incomes—of the small farmers.[15] Thus, two of the big roadblocks faced by rural economies are mitigated by e-choupals: Virtual aggregation provides bargaining power for even the smallest producers, and better information helps overcome uncertainty and isolation.

Once a virtual meeting place is established in a village, there is no shortage of other potential users: governments putting their services online, consumer goods firms that are otherwise unable to reach rural villages, microcredit providers, and so on. The possibilities are virtually limitless. Thus, rather than selling a defined end-product such as a con-sumer good, e-choupals create the *potential* for many new, perhaps unanticipated, economic activities to blossom, driven by local needs and capabilities.

ITC intends to reach 100,000 villages with its network in the next decade. The rural connectivity brought by initiatives such as e-choupal and N-Logue could literally transform the countryside in India. Ventures like this, which provide both in-reach and outreach, constitute the ultimate in creation of potential. For MNCs, therefore, identifying opportunities to create new potential constitutes another important vehicle for reaching the base of the pyramid.

Assessing Sustainability Impact

Identifying the opportunity is only the first step in successfully reaching the base of the pyramid. While serving a real need through the firm's product or service is necessary for a successful strategy, it is not suffi-cient. It is equally important to evaluate the effect of the *entire* business system on the communities and environments where it is to be intro-duced. That means monitoring and assessing the triple bottom line (social, environmental, and economic) impact of the business system. This step is necessary because often the biggest impacts—positive and negative—are felt through the upstream (supply chain) or downstream (end use) effects of the company's activities rather than directly through its immediate products or services. Provision of credit, for instance, may not appear to have much impact in itself; the activities enabled by credit, however, may have wide-scale impacts. Furthermore, an MNC's entry into the BOP may have implications for existing organizations and institutions that play an important role in the community. Understanding these total system impacts is thus crucial to assessing whether a company's activities enhance or inhibit sustainable development.

In assessing sustainability impact, managers need to recognize that *any* new business intervention has both positive and negative effects. The problems that a sustainable global enterprise solves should, of course, be more significant than the new ones it creates. Unfortunately, from a societal perspective, many new technologies and businesses do not pass this test; the problems they create are more significant than the problems they solve. Take, for example, the nuclear power industry. In its beginning stages, the industry was seen as the source of pollution-free electricity that was too cheap to meter. It was heralded as the salvation of the world: It would rescue us from dependence upon nonrenewable and polluting fuels such as coal, oil, and gas. However, as it turned out, the nuclear power industry created massive new problems: We had not fully thought through how to deal with the expensive process of decommissioning old nuclear facilities, nor had the disposal of high-level radioactive waste been adequately addressed.

The operation of the facilities themselves also proved to be problematic, with accidents raising public fears—and operating costs—to astronomical levels. In the end, new nuclear facilities became so expensive to build and engendered so much public resistance that it no longer made sense to construct them, at least in the United States. Today nuclear power is viable only where massive government subsidies make it so: France and Japan. Therefore, in evaluating the sustainability impact of a BOP business initiative, a comprehensive and continuous assessment of both the upside and the downside of the total business system is critical.

Village Phones: The Triple Bottom Line

Let us return to the case of Grameen Telecom, described in detail in Chapter 5, "The Great Leap Downward," for an in-depth assessment of sustainability impacts. As you may recall, the venture was established as a nonprofit experiment in a few hundred villages before it was introduced on a widespread basis. This was done intentionally to allow time to test the model, identify problems, and make midcourse corrections prior to scale-up. Grameen enlisted the aid of local universities and NGOs in conducting the impact assessment, both to facilitate the work and to ensure the independence and legitimacy of the results.[16]

The results of the sustainability assessment for the village phones are summarized in Exhibit 6.2.[17] The diagram displays the triple bottom line (economic, social, and environmental) impacts associated with the introduction of mobile phone service in the 950 villages that constituted the pilot test in rural Bangladesh. Economically, the introduction of phone service was clearly a net positive. As we have seen, not only did the "phone ladies" themselves realize a significant increase in their income, but, more important, users of the service realized significant consumer surplus (each call saved 2.5–10 percent of household monthly income, equivalent to a savings of $2.70–$10 per call). In some cases, the phone service produced dramatic increases in income for users. For example, with better access to competitive agricultural prices, local farmers were able to get substantially better prices for their crops. Indeed, the efficiency of the village economies was significantly enhanced through more rapid and accurate information flow. In the words of Iqbal Quadir, "Connectivity is productivity." Phone ladies and other local businesspeople also became more aware of and capable in the ways of the formal economy, increasing the prospects for further growth and development in the future.

Exhibit 6.2
Sustainability Assessment: Grameen Telecom

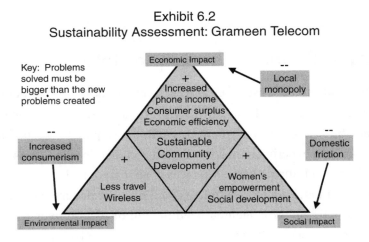

Socially, the introduction of the village phone gave the phone ladies status and visibility within their villages (if you wanted to make a phone call, you had to seek them out or come to their home). The incremental income these women contributed to their households also gave them a bigger voice in family decision-making. They spent most of the new income from the village phone on their children, in the form of tuition for schooling, clothes, and health care. This raised their standard of living and opened up opportunities for their children that would not have otherwise existed.

Environmentally, the availability of phone service meant that fewer trips to the city in inefficient and polluting buses and cars were necessary. Furthermore, by moving directly to wireless telecommunications, Grameen Telecom enabled poor villages to avoid the expensive, material-intensive, and environmentally destructive step of installing cables and phone lines. The village phone, in other words, enabled the poorest communities in rural Bangladesh to leap directly to the most modern and least-polluting technology available.

Although Grameen Telecom's sustainability impact has been overwhelmingly positive, it has, predictably, created some new problems on each of the three dimensions. From the social perspective, in some cases, phone ladies' newfound earning power introduced friction and even conflict within households that were previously dominated by the husbands. Some have even experienced increased physical abuse and violence. Not surprisingly, there are those who view this as being disruptive to local communities and cultural traditions. Others, however, including most of the phone ladies themselves, view it as a necessary step toward the emancipation of women throughout the world. It may also hold the key to stabilizing population growth because raising the status of poor women is now recognized as being one of the most effective ways of lowering fertility rates.

Other observers are concerned that the introduction of phone service into rural areas, with its attendant rise in income and economic activity, will lead to increased consumerism and environmental degradation. Although this is a legitimate concern, it would appear that the alternative—keeping the majority of people in the world isolated and without access to information—has even larger negative consequences. Indeed, through the Great Leap Downward, discussed in the previous chapter, we may be able to successfully incubate and launch the renewable and inherently clean technologies of tomorrow in the BOP.

Perhaps the most significant problem that has arisen has been the emergence of monopolistic practices by some of the phone ladies.[18] As demand for rural phone services grew in the past half-dozen years, the initial business model of having a single phone operator in each village has proven problematic: With demand exceeding supply in many villages, prices rose and phone ladies' incomes soared. Some phone ladies were becoming "rich" by village standards, with incomes grossly out of proportion to what they once were. To address this problem, the company removed its limit of one phone lady per village, creating a "free market" for phone service in the villages of Bangladesh. In short order, the number of phone ladies virtually doubled. With competition, prices came down and the new incomes returned to a more reasonable level. As noted in the last chapter, the company expects that, by the end of 2004, there will be 100,000 phone ladies in Bangladesh, each averaging $1,500–$2,000 in revenues (and roughly $500–$700 in profits) each year. The new problem has been translated into yet another opportunity.

The case of Grameen Telecom underscores the importance of tracking the sustainability impact of the entire business system. By starting with a nonprofit pilot experiment, Grameen was able to understand and document the economic, social, and environmental impacts of its business system from the beginning. It was also able to create a mechanism for continuously monitoring the triple bottom line performance of its business. By recognizing that any intervention will not only solve problems but also create new ones, Grameen Telecom has been able to identify and address new problems as they emerge through the continuous and creative adjustment of the business model.

The MNC Advantage

Multinationals have much to learn from the approach Grameen took in introducing its rural mobile phone service. In fact, even readers who are sympathetic to the argument so far may be wondering why MNCs should concern themselves with the BOP: Even if multinational managers are emotionally persuaded, it is not obvious that large corporations have real advantages over locally oriented firms and nonprofits such as Grameen Telecom. In addition, MNCs must overcome significant negative reputational equity, given the extractive nature of much of their past behavior in the traditional economy. However, there are several compelling reasons for MNCs to embark on this journey:

- **Resources.** Building a commercial infrastructure for the base of the pyramid is a resource- and management-intensive task. Developing environmentally sustainable products and services requires significant research. Distribution channels and communication networks require extensive effort to develop and sustain. *Few local entrepreneurs have the managerial or technological resources to create this infrastructure.*

- **Convening of power.** MNCs can be nodes for building the commercial infrastructure, providing access to knowledge, managerial imagination, and financial resources. Without MNCs as partners, well-intentioned NGOs, communities, local governments, entrepreneurs, and even multilateral development agencies will continue to flounder in their attempts to bring development to the base. *MNCs are well positioned to unite the range of actors required to reach the BOP.*

- **Knowledge transfer.** MNCs are able to transfer knowledge from one BOP market to another, such as from China to Brazil or India, as Unilever and others have demonstrated. Although practices and products have to be customized to serve local needs, *MNCs, with their unique global knowledge base, have an advantage that is not easily accessible by local entrepreneurs.*

- **Upmarket migration.** Not only can MNCs leverage learning across the base of the pyramid, but they also have the capacity to move innovations up-market all the way to the top of the pyramid. As we have seen, the BOP is a testing ground for disruptive innovations that enable a more sustainable way of living. *Many of the innovations for the base can be adapted for use in the resource- and energy-intensive markets of the developed world.*

A Common Cause

Recognizing the four billion people who comprise the base of the pyramid is a great opportunity for MNCs. It also represents a chance for business, government, and civil society to join together in a common cause. Indeed, pursuing strategies for the base of the pyramid may hold the potential to dissolve the conflict between proponents of free trade and global capitalism on the one hand, and adherents of environmental and social sustainability on the other.

However, the products and services currently offered at the top of the pyramid are not appropriate for the BOP, and reaching out to the base will require fundamentally different approaches than those even in the emerging markets of the developing world. Changes in technology, credit, cost, and distribution are critical prerequisites. Only large firms with global reach have the technological, managerial, and financial resources needed to realize this opportunity.

New commerce in the BOP will not be restricted to businesses serving such basic needs as food, textiles, and housing. The base of the pyramid is waiting for high-tech businesses such as financial services, cellular telecommunications, and affordable computers. In fact, as we have seen, for many emerging disruptive technologies (such as fuel cells, photovoltaics, satellite-based telecommunications, biotechnology, and nanotechnology), the base of the pyramid may prove to be the most attractive early market.

To date, however, NGOs and local businesses with far fewer resources than the MNCs have been more innovative and made more progress in developing these markets. It is tragic that as Western capitalists we have implicitly assumed that the rich will be served by the corporate sector (MNCs), while governments and NGOs will protect the poor and the environment. This division of labor is stronger than most realize. Managers in MNCs, public policymakers, and NGO activists all suffer from this historical divide. A huge opportunity lies in breaking this code, linking the entire human community in a seamless market organized around the concept of sustainable growth and development.

Collectively, MNCs have only begun to scratch the surface of this massive opportunity. Those in the private sector who commit their companies to strategies for the base of the pyramid can lead the movement toward a more inclusive capitalism. It is imperative, however, that managers recognize the nature of business leadership required in the BOP arena. Imagination, tolerance for ambiguity, stamina, passion, empathy, self-reflection, and courage may be as important as intelligence, analytical skill, and knowledge. And as the final section of the book shows, leaders need to develop a deeper understanding of the complexities and subtleties of sustainable development in the context of the BOP if they are to become truly indigenous.

Notes

1. This introduction and other parts of this chapter are adapted from C. K. Prahalad and Stuart Hart, "The Fortune at the Bottom of the Pyramid," *Strategy+Business* 26 (2002): 2–14,

2. Brian Ellison, Dasha Moller, and Miguel Angel Rodriguez, *Hindustan Lever: Reinventing the Wheel* (Barcelona, Spain: IESE Business School, 2003).

3. Ibid.

4. My thanks to Sharat Dhall, head of Project Shakti at HLL, for this information, which he presented at the Zurich Sustainability Forum in August 2004.

5. See, for example, R. Hoskisson, L. Eden, C. Lau, and M. Wright, "Strategy in Emerging Economies," *Academy of Management Journal* 43(3) (2000): 249–267; and D. Arnold and J. Quelch, "New Strategies in Emerging Economies," *Sloan Management Review* 40(1) (1998): 7–20.

6. C. K. Prahalad and Alan Hammond, "Serving the World's Poor, Profitably," *Harvard Business Review* 80(9) (2002): 48–57.

7. Amartya Sen, *Development as Freedom* (New York: Anchor Books, 1999).

8. Ruth Romo and Francisco Ballester, *Cemex: Patrimonio Hoy and Contrumex* (Mexico City: IPADE [English translation], 2004).

9. My thanks to Hector Ureta for his visit to Chapel Hill in April 2004 to tell the story of Patrimonio Hoy to the students in a class jointly taught by Ted London and me, called "Business Strategy for the Base of the Pyramid."

10. Martin Fisher, *ApproTEC: Kick Starting Economic Growth in Africa* (San Francisco: ApproTEC report, 2004).

11. My thanks to Scott Johnson at SC Johnson for this example.

12. The description of this alliance is excerpted from Yerina Mugica and Ted London, *Partnering for Mutual Success: Daimler-Chrysler-POEMAtec Alliance* (Chapel Hill, NC: Kenan-Flagler Business School, 2004).

13. Joy Howard, Charis Simms, and Erik Simanis, *Sustainable Deployment for Rural Conductivity: The N-Logue Model* (Washington, D.C.: World Resources Institute, 2001).

14. For a full description of e-choupals, see *The Economist*, "Yogeth Deveshwar, The Boss of India's Biggest Tobacco Firm, Is Putting Rural India Online," 5 June (2004).

15. For more information on the e-choupals, see C. K. Prahalad, *The Fortune at the Bottom of the Pyramid* (University of Pennsylvania: Wharton School Publishing, 2005).

16. See D. Richardson, R. Ramirez, and M. Haq, *Grameen Telecom's Village Phone Programme in Rural Bangladesh* (Geulph, Ontario: International Telecommunications Union, 2000).

17. This is my interpretation of the results, placed in the framework of the triple bottom line. My thanks to John Elkington for letting me borrow this concept. For details on this framework, see John Elkington, *Cannibals with Forks: The Triple Bottom Line of 21st Century Business* (Oxford: Capstone Publishing Ltd, 1997). For full text of the pilot study, see D. Richardson, R. Ramirez, and M. Haq, *Grameen Telecom's Village Phone Programme*.

18. Personal communication with Muhammad Yunus, April 2004.

Part Three

BECOMING INDIGENOUS

7

BROADENING THE CORPORATE BANDWIDTH

When we set our sights on the world's "poor," we tend not to see complex societies with unique histories that also have economies. Instead, we see societies that *are* economies—albeit "underdeveloped" ones, from our point of view.[1] Indeed, my colleague Erik Simanis at the University of North Carolina has made it very clear to me that our conceptual categories, which seem as though they were decreed by God, are only one way of looking at the world.[2] Whether we speak of industry boundaries—automobiles, computers, energy, telecommunications—or societal categories—economy, government, education, church, family, community—all serve to blind us to the actual conditions and constraints that exist for those beyond our realm, particularly at the base of the pyramid.

Because we tend to impose our preexisting categories on the BOP, we often fail to see business opportunities of potentially vast proportion. Existing core competencies and strategies within companies further constrain our thinking. The BOP thus presents MNCs with a unique opportunity, a "license to imagine," to reconceptualize the corporation in a manner that can recognize and serve the diversity of needs and values of all people in the world.[3] This does not mean selling extractive products and services to the poor; it means learning how to *codevelop* a commercial model aimed at improving the lives of those who have been bypassed or actively exploited by globalization. Cultural sensitivity, environmental sustainability, and mutual learning hold the keys to this process.

Unfortunately, most managers in MNCs have little knowledge or understanding of those in the BOP, let alone their views about social equity, environmental quality, or what represents a "good life." Indeed, it has been strongly argued that the dominant conceptualizations of "development" and "modernization" reflect a Western cultural bias and a preoccupation with simply raising GDP per capita.[4] Together, these shortcomings significantly hinder efforts to imagine and build healthy BOP communities and markets.[5] Successfully serving the needs of the entire human community therefore requires that corporations broaden their bandwidth and hear the true voices of those on the periphery of the global economy.

Learning from Ladakh

In her book *Ancient Futures: Learning from Ladakh,* Helena Norberg-Hodge provides a bird's-eye view of both the problem—and the opportunity—confronting global capitalism.[6] Trained as a linguist, Norberg-Hodge in the mid-1970s set about the task of documenting the language of the Ladakhi people, an ancient tribal society of the Himalayan region who had lived a self-contained existence, largely undisturbed for centuries, due to their remote location. Having mastered the language in the first year, she became increasingly fascinated by the way of life of the people of Ladakh.

Despite the rigorous climate, short growing season, and arid environment, the people had learned how to grow crops and utilize water for irrigation on a sustainable basis. They had evolved a society in which nothing was wasted or thrown away—a use was found for everything. The concept of crime was virtually nonexistent. The Ladakhis had developed a natural sense of responsibility toward each other and their environment, and were, by and large, happy, healthy, and fulfilled. They led a rich artistic, symbolic, and ceremonial life, "working" no more than about four months out of the year, during the short growing season. Norberg-Hodge was utterly struck by what she described as their *joie de vivre*, true joy and contentment. She set about documenting their way of life and committed to spending roughly six months in Ladakh annually, a practice she continues to this day.

However, things began to change rather abruptly in the late 1970s and '80s. Given the growing conflict with Pakistan over the contested region of Kashmir, of which Ladakh was a part, the Indian government threw the area open to tourism, and concerted efforts were initiated to "develop" the region. This process, as usual, consisted primarily of building up the infrastructure, especially roads and utilities. Western-style health centers and schools were also established in even the most remote villages. Other fundamental changes included a growing police force, courts, banks, and radio and television. Spurred on by the development efforts, the formal sector grew rapidly. Traffic increased exponentially, with hundreds of trucks a day making the long journey to the Himalayan plateau. Jeeps and buses, crammed with thousands of tourists, added to the congestion and air pollution in the provincial capital of Leh.

The sudden influx of Western influence caused growing numbers of Ladakhis—the young men, in particular—to develop feelings of inferiority. Tourists would spend more money in one day than a typical Ladakhi family would earn in a year. Ladakhis did not realize that money played a completely different role for the foreigners; that back home they needed it to survive, whereas in their traditional culture, villagers provided for their own basic needs without money. Western media provided overwhelming images of wealth, luxury, ease, and glamour (the side effects of pollution, stress, drug addiction, and homelessness were never shown). By contrast, the Ladakhis' own lives seemed primitive and trivial. As local people became more focused on earning money, the age-old practices of communal farming and local self-reliance began to erode. Cash cropping became the norm. More young people left for the city to find paid work, leading to a building boom in and around Leh, where urban sprawl began to resemble the slums that characterize cities throughout the Third World.

With the breakdown of the Ladakhi traditional extended family and the practice of polyandry,[7] the population, which had been virtually stable for centuries, began to grow at a rate higher than the Indian average. For the first time, a noticeable gap between rich and poor developed. With unemployment on the rise, crime became a growing problem. Children no longer greeted strangers with wonder and laughter, but rather as beggars or worse. Modern education ignored the old ways and made the children think of themselves as inferior. As mutual aid gave way to dependence on faraway forces, people began to feel powerless to make decisions concerning their own lives. Striving for the modern ideal required that Ladahkis, in effect, reject their own culture. The resulting alienation gave rise to a growing resentment and anger, which lay behind much of the violence and religious fundamentalism that has come to plague the region.

In effect, the "development" of the region led to the systematic dismantling of Ladakhi culture and a growing economic dependence, cultural rejection, and environmental degradation. Although per-capita incomes definitely rose, it is quite clear that happiness, security, and contentment did not. That is not to say that there have been no benefits from development. Many aspects of the traditional culture were far from ideal: Communication with the outside world was limited, illiteracy rates were high (although this had little impact on the functioning of the traditional culture), and infant mortality was higher and life expectancy shorter than in the developed world. The introduction of money and technology, and the advent of modern medicine did bring with them certain benefits. However, on balance, the traditional nature-based society, with all its flaws and limitations, was probably more sustainable, both socially and environmentally, for the Ladakhis.

The Post-Development Challenge

The Ladakh situation is a microcosm of what has played out across the Third World over the past 50 years under the banner of development. As one of the last subsistence societies to survive virtually intact into the 1970s, it provided a unique vantage point from which to observe the process of development unfold. Throughout most of the Third World, the process began much earlier, in the 1950s, following the creation of the post-war Bretton Woods Institutions of the World Bank, International Monetary Fund (IMF), and the GATT.

As many have pointed out, the modern concepts of poverty and development were constructed only following World War II.[8] For the United States, the dominant concern at that time was the reconstruction of Europe. Reconstitution of the colonial system was a key component of reconstruction because continued access to raw materials was seen as crucial not only for European recovery, but also for U.S. growth. By the late 1940s, however, many of the former colonies had achieved independence. The consolidation of the communist block had created three worlds: the free industrialized nations (First World), the communist industrialized nations (Second World), and the poor, nonindustrialized nations (Third World). There was a need, therefore, to define a new world order based not on subjugation, but rather on development.

In 1949, U.S. President Harry Truman announced in his inaugural address the concept of a "fair deal" for the entire world. An essential component of this was his appeal to the U.S. and the world to solve the problems of the "underdeveloped areas" of the globe. The intent was quite ambitious: to replicate the features that characterized the "advanced" societies of the time—industrialization, urbanization, and rapid growth of production and living standards, along with the adoption of modern education and cultural values—throughout the world. Greater production was seen as the key to prosperity and peace.

This was an audacious and visionary goal, to be sure. Within a few years, it was universally embraced by the First World and many Third World countries as well. Unfortunately, this framing ignored the immense cultural diversity, unique historical circumstances, and varied skills and capabilities of the Third World by focusing attention primarily on increasing production and standard of living. In short, poverty came to be defined across the world through a single metric—*income poverty*—and the solution to poverty was economic growth. The reality, we now realize, is that "standard of living" can actually be quite high in places where GDP per capita is quite low. Bhutan, for example, where people still provide for many of their own needs and produce beautiful art and music, is considered to be one of the poorest countries of the world because its gross domestic product is virtually zero.[9] With GDP as the metric, no distinction is made between homeless beggars who live on the street and the Bhutanese or Ladakhi farmers. In both cases, there may be no income, but the life behind the statistics is entirely different.

In this way, poverty has been used to define whole peoples not according to what they are or what they want to be, but according to what they lack (income). This, it turns out, is development's fatal flaw. It has systematically failed to recognize the wealth of *indigenous* resources and alternatives. We have projected on the rest of the world our own Western post-war fixation with industrial production as the only path to prosperity. As a consequence, we have committed the better part of 50 years to using one-size-fits-all solutions to what are really complex, diverse, and unique problems.

Paradoxically, the development era, quite unintentionally, has *created* the base of the pyramid as we know it today. Traditional societies such as the Ladakh have been systematically disrupted by the development process. As peasants, nomads, and tribal peoples have been either lured away or driven from their land to urban slums in search of wage labor, poverty is often the result, not the cause. Populations that were once stable ballooned out of control as the old social norms and extended family structures that once kept them in check steadily eroded (why do we think that the human population has exploded from 2 billion to 6.5 billion since the end of World War II?). Increasing dependence on the money economy means that income eventually *does* become the most critical factor; unfortunately, job opportunities in the money economy have not been adequate to match the tens of millions of poor people flooding into the job market. Thus, massive poverty in the modern sense appeared only when development broke down community ties and cut off millions of people from access to land, water, and other resources.

The postwar development paradigm has come under increasing criticism in recent years not only from post-colonialists and antiglobalizers such as Wolfgang Sachs, David Korten, and Arturo Escobar, but also from development insiders such as Joe Stiglitz, Jeff Sachs, and George Soros.[1] At this point in history, it is probably safe to say that the development era as articulated after World War II is officially dead. Of the major multilateral development institutions, the World Bank and the IFC may be the farthest along in recognizing that this is the case. The question, then, is, what will the post-development paradigm look like?

Clearly, this need not be a dichotomous choice between full-scale modernization and returning to the old ways: Neither Old Ladakh nor New Ladakh is viable any longer. As we have seen, a sustainable enterprise-led strategy has the potential to avoid the pitfalls of one-size-fits-all policies (such as structural adjustment), with development experts dictating the way people should live. Through decentralized business models and disruptive innovation, it is possible to foment a bottom-up revolution of wealth creation and life enhancement. As Norberg-Hodge observed, the real lesson of Ladakh is the realization that plateau-dwelling farmers in the Himalayas have as much to teach us about how to live as we have to teach them. They need not sacrifice the sort of social and ecological balance that they have enjoyed for centuries. To do so, however, they will need to build on their own ancient foundations rather than tear them down, as is the way of conventional development. It is time that we get on with this enterprise in a spirit of mutual respect and learning, rather than implied or explicit superiority.

As businesspeople, therefore, we cannot know in advance what is required to serve the real needs of those who have been bypassed or damaged by the globalization process. A new capability is needed, focused on hearing these voices for the first time. Rather than engaging only known or powerful stakeholders of existing businesses, we need to systematically identify, explore, and integrate the views of those on the periphery or at the "fringe"—the poor, the weak, the isolated, the disinterested, and even the voices of other species with which we share the planet (through a human interpreter, of course). Accordingly, my colleague Sanjay Sharma and I have proposed the idea of *radical transactiveness* (RT), the ability to access and combine knowledge with fringe stakeholders possessing radically differing views, to build the competitive imagination necessary for future business success and the pursuit of a truly sustainable form of global development.[11]

Radical Transactiveness

RT is "radical" because it focuses on gaining access to stakeholders previously considered extreme or fringe, for the express purpose of facilitating disruptive change and creating competitive imagination. RT is "transactive" because it seeks to engage the firm in a two-way dialogue with stakeholders so that each influences and is influenced by the other.[12] Interactions among diverse stakeholders extend the boundaries of the firm, offering the possibility for learning and growth not envisioned at the beginning of the process. RT thus allows a firm to understand the complex and evolving issues that may affect its future competitive position.

Exhibit 7.1 depicts the difference between core stakeholders—those visible and readily identifiable parties with a stake in the firm's existing operations—and fringe, or peripheral, stakeholders. Whereas core stakeholders gain a seat at the table by virtue of the power, legitimacy, or urgency of their claims, fringe stakeholders are typically disconnected from or invisible to the firm. They may be affected by the firm but have little, if any, direct connection to the firm's current activities. However, fringe stakeholders may hold knowledge and perspectives that are key both to anticipating potential problems and to identifying innovative opportunities and business models for the future. Hewlett-Packard's "i-Community," in the village of Kuppam in India, for example, was established to learn the possibilities for information technology and Internet use by the rural poor in developing countries. This is intended to help HP imagine and design the products and services that would respond to the real problems and needs of rural India.[13]

Exhibit 7.1
Engaging Fringe Stakeholders

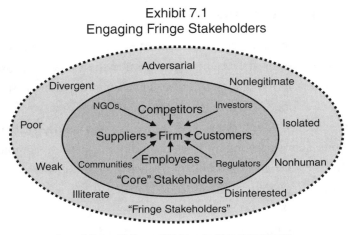

Source: S. Hart and S. Sharma, 2004. "Engaging Fringe Stakeholders for
Competitive Imagination." *Academy of Management Executive,* 18(1) (2004): 7-18.

By opening communication channels to previously untapped
sources of intelligence, RT helps the firm maintain a dynamic alignment
of its strategy with the changing environment. Knowledge and learning
from fringe stakeholders signal to the firm the investments it should
make in appropriate resources and capabilities, allowing it to generate
new value-creating strategies.[14] For example, Hindustan Lever Limited
(HLL, Unilever's Indian subsidiary) requires its managers to spend six
weeks living in rural areas, to generate knowledge about the hygiene
needs and practices of the rural poor. This knowledge has resulted in
new product ideas (such as a combined soap and shampoo bar) and pro-
motional programs (such as street theater) for rural markets. These
innovations have also been adopted by Unilever subsidiaries in Brazil
and other developing countries.

As Sanjay Sharma and I have suggested, RT consists of two sub-
capabilities: 1. The ability to extend the scope of the firm (fan out); and
2. The ability to integrate diverse and disconfirming knowledge (fan-in).
These two phases are similar to the concepts of idea generation (diver-
gence) and idea evaluation (convergence) described in the traditional
problem-solving literature.[15]

Fanning Out: Extending the Scope of the Firm

Competitive imagination requires divergent thinking by managers to identify the unmet needs of new, yet-to-be served markets. Divergent thinking is also necessary to envision new, disruptive technologies and business models that enable the firm to deliver functionality to customers faster, better, or cheaper than competitors. The knowledge needed to drive such innovation is usually widely dispersed outside the firm, within stakeholder groups that may be neither important nor salient, nor part of a firm's current network.

As the previous HP and HLL examples show, these stakeholders are often at the unseen periphery of the firm's stakeholder network, such as the urban homeless or the rural poor in developing countries, or are even nonhuman (for example, endangered species and nature).[16] In fact, Janine Benyus, author of the path-breaking book *Biomimicry*, argues that by including *biologists* in the technology development process, it might be possible for companies to emulate (rather than dominate) nature in its designs. Spiders, for example, can manufacture a material (spider webs) at ambient temperature using no toxics that is stronger (pound for pound) than Kevlar. By treating nature as a mentor in product design, it may be possible to create a whole new generation of inherently clean and sustainable products. Distant voices from the fringe thus provide a panoramic view of a firm's changing circumstances and opportunities.

To be truly effective, fanning out requires the reversal of traditional stakeholder-management models, by "putting the last first."[17] This means making a conscious effort to completely reverse the rules of stakeholder saliency by identifying actors who have been completely invisible to the firm in the past. It is extremely difficult for managers in existing businesses to identify fringe stakeholders such as the rural poor, urban shantytown dwellers, or advocates for nature's rights.

However, placing managers in situations that are the opposite of their current contexts opens them to hearing stakeholder voices from the periphery.

Recently, for example, in an effort to expand the scope of the firm, Grameen Bank founder Muhammad Yunus challenged his employees to embrace the poorest of the poor by focusing the bank's attention on beggars.[18] Beggars, he noted, had generally been excluded from the bank's portfolio because most current clients did not want to include them as part of their peer lending group, for fear that they would not pay back their loans. As a consequence, Yunus requested that every employee take the personal responsibility to recruit one beggar to become a client of the bank. This required each employee to directly confront the reality of the poorest of the poor. As of October 2004, over 23,000 beggars were recruited to the bank and have been saved from the humiliation of taking handouts. In the process, bank employees have greatly expanded their conception of what is possible by working directly with the beggars to get them on the path to microentrepreneurship. In one case, for example, a limbless beggar who previously simply sat all day with a cup in hand, transformed his "strategic location" near the village center into a miniconvenience mart. With a $50 loan guarantee from the bank, the beggar now sells bananas, cookies, and beverages sourced from a local shop with a less desirable location.

Another example, this time in the context of an MNC, is the Biotechnology Advisory Panel set up by DuPont to consciously seek divergent views from the periphery to help it formulate a more robust strategy for biotechnology development. The company has purposefully sought to include a diversity of stakeholders from India, Africa, and Latin America in its deliberations. It has also invited environmental advocates, such as the former head of Greenpeace International, to provide divergent views on the issue. Exposing senior managers and business leaders to radically different perspectives has resulted in significant modifications and improvements to the company's approach to and strategy for biotechnology commercialization. New ideas have been generated for future business models in accordance with the company's push to move away from products based upon petrochemical feedstocks and into knowledge-intensive businesses with a biological base.

Exhibit 7.2 identifies the actions that firms can undertake to extend the scope of the firm. The costs in terms of managerial time and effort are likely to be a fraction of what a large firm would normally spend on research and development to generate new ideas and innovations.

Exhibit 7.2
Extending the Scope of the Firm

Objective: Identify and engage managers in business contexts that are the reverse of those which the business currently faces to generate imagination and ideas about potential new products and services.
Process:
1. Conduct research around issues such as climate change, biomimicry, social equity, poverty, human rights, etc., to identify stakeholders that are as different as possible from the current constituencies of the firm. The focus is on those regions and communities that have been heavily disrupted by globalization—communities with exploding population, environmental degradation, and associated migration to urban areas, lack of education, mobility, communications, basic hygiene and nutrition.
2. Create an inventory of potential sites and contexts where learning can take place for generating ideas for new business models that are sustainable in terms of economic potential, zero pollution, biodiversity and ecosystem disruption, and enable capacity building in local communities.
3. Send managers to these jurisdictions to immerse themselves in the cultures, to understand the needs and functionalities required, and to explore the feasibility of new approaches for meeting customer needs in a radically different, innovative and sustainable manner.
Costs: Training, managerial time, travel and other forms of operating slack
Benefits: Generating radical new ideas for products and services and business models

Source: Adapted from S. Hart and S. Sharma 2004. "Engaging Fringe Stakeholders for Competitive Imagination." *Academy of Management Executive*, 18(1): 7-18.

Managers should begin intense interactions with fringe stakeholders only after suitable cultural and ecosystem sensitivity training. They then can immerse themselves in radically different contexts to learn firsthand about the needs of those that they do not cater to with existing products. As a result, they come to understand the potential for and feasibility of applying innovative technologies to develop new business models and products. For example, Procter and Gamble has launched a pilot venture in rural Nicaragua to help its managers generate creative ideas by immersing themselves in a context where the company currently has no presence, infrastructure, or partners. By doing so, they avoid having the voices from the fringe contaminated by the dominant logic of the marketing model used to serve their existing markets.

Extending the scope of the firm by reaching out and seeking knowledge from fringe stakeholders enables managers to suspend disbelief, thereby broadening the corporate bandwidth. New knowledge is generated only when managers escape from the old ideas and mindsets that underpin the current business system. Effective fan-out thus focuses on engaging with unconventional and nontraditional stakeholders to understand dynamic and complex problems that might result in new, breakthrough products, technologies, or strategies.

Fanning In: Integrating Diverse and Disconfirming Information

Once the company's boundaries have been expanded and divergent thinking has opened up the firm to both new concerns and emerging opportunities for the future, the challenge is to integrate this new information into practical, useable strategies. Having initiated contact with these stakeholders, managers need to build bridges so that extended, informal conversations can take place. The transfer of tacit or unwritten knowledge residing in people and their traditions requires intense interaction; it cannot be transferred in large group meetings or during formal negotiations. Practical strategies emerge only after the apparent contradictions between knowledge from fringe stakeholders and the current business model have been reconciled.

Just as living in a different country allows managers to better identify appropriate product/service modifications in developed markets, spending time in homeless shelters, rural areas in developing countries, or areas where nature has been depleted or devastated provides a radically different physical and mental context to spark the imagination. To be able to absorb knowledge from fringe stakeholders, however, especially those that are adversarial or peripheral to the firm's current operations, managers need to empathize with differences in perspectives. Empathy depends upon deep listening and speaking in depth with those who have different views.

As we have seen, HLL generates empathy by requiring all company employees to spend six weeks living in rural villages and actively seeking local consumer insights and preferences as they develop new products.[19] The company has also created an R&D center in rural India that focuses specifically on technology and product development to serve the needs of the poor and that sources raw materials almost exclusively from local producers. HLL uses a wide variety of local partners to distribute their products and also invests in developing the capabilities of those partners. By developing local understanding and empathy, and experimenting with codevelopment through new partnerships, HLL has been able to generate substantial revenues and profits from operating in low-income markets.

By reconciling disconfirming information, Arvind Mills was able to create an entirely new value-delivery system for affordable blue jeans in India.[20] As the world's fifth-largest denim manufacturer, Arvind found Indian domestic denim sales limited because a $20–$40 pair of jeans is neither affordable to the masses nor widely distributed. In direct response, Arvind introduced Ruf and Tuf jeans, a ready-to-make kit of components (denim, zipper, rivets, patch) priced at about $6. A network of 4,000 tailors, many in small rural towns and villages, assemble the pants for customers, providing employment and building a motivated and decentralized distribution system for the kits. Ruf and Tuf jeans are now the largest-selling jeans in India, easily surpassing Levi's and other brand names from the United States and Europe.

In contrast, the failure of Nike's attempt in the late 1990s to produce an athletic footwear product for the booming low-income populations in China can be traced, at least in part, to a lack of empathy and
inability to reconcile disconfirming information.[21] Based upon a relatively low price point ($10–$15 per pair), the "World Shoe" was
designed (without extensive contact with potential customers) as a
product that could appeal to the masses who could not afford Nike's
top-of-the-line products. In China, Nike relied exclusively on its existing contract factory network to produce the product, utilized the firm's
established in-country channels to distribute the World Shoe, and did
not develop a context-specific marketing plan for the product. In fact,
the World Shoe was displayed side by side with the $150 Air Maxx in
upscale retail outlets in Beijing and Shanghai. Relying on familiar partners and the existing business model for high-end athletic footwear
products left the World Shoe struggling to meet its sales goals. The initiative was terminated in 2002.

Designing and producing a lower-cost shoe using the existing business system meant, paradoxically, that Nike failed to reach its target
customer. The company failed to develop an empathetic understanding
of the context before designing the product. Nike was also singularly
unsuccessful in resolving the contradictions that existed between its
current business model and the one that would be required to appropriately serve the need for affordable athletic footwear. Thus, competitive
imagination is sparked only when the company commits to integrating
the disconfirming information introduced by fringe stakeholders.

As we saw in the last chapter, Mexico's largest cement company,
Cemex, provides a more instructive example.[22] Cemex has achieved
extraordinary profitability through a shrewd strategy of targeting developing countries such as Bangladesh, Egypt, Indonesia, Thailand, and
others in Latin America. The poorest residents of these developing
countries represent a special opportunity because they are currently
served inadequately, if at all. Cemex learned how to tap the enormous

market of low-income customers in developing countries by first study-ing how to do business with the poor in Mexico. By gaining an in-depth understanding of the constraints and conditions that existed in the shantytowns of Mexico, Cemex was able to forge a business model that reconciled the company's need for growth with the idiosyncratic needs of poor, do-it-yourself homebuilders.

Other examples reinforce the point. To help reconcile contradic-tions and leverage learning, DuPont has designated a senior executive to serve as point person for all new initiatives in the company aimed at the base of the pyramid. In this way, efforts of individual project teams can be better coordinated and learning more effectively communicated from one part of the company to another. Similarly, Unilever has created an international committee to transfer BOP-based innovations, such as HLL's products and promotion programs, to other countries and markets.

As Exhibit 7.3 shows, integrating diverse and disconfirming infor-mation means engaging, on an ongoing basis, with fringe stakeholders. This is how the radical new ideas and business models identified in the previous step are operationalized, tested, and leveraged. Such imple-mentation takes into account the real needs of remote stakeholders and builds in the capacity to adjust and learn based upon actual experience. This step focuses on the implementation of practical solutions to the problems and opportunities identified in the fan-out stage. The final challenge is then to link both stages of the RT process into a coherent approach for new strategy formulation and implementation.

Together, the capabilities of stakeholder fan-out and fan-in rein-force each other. By integrating knowledge from fringe stakeholders, radical transactiveness has the potential to challenge fundamental busi-ness models and frames of reference, leading to new bases of growth and competitive advantage. This capability also helps the firm engage stakeholders in an ongoing two-way dialogue that enables it to antici-pate and respond to their concerns instead of facing unanticipated con-flicts such as those faced by Monsanto.

Exhibit 7.3
Integrating Diverse and Disconfirming Information

Objective: Incubate, implement, and leverage radical innovations and new business
models.
Process:
1.   Organize and facilitate stakeholder dialogues involving line managers, product
       developers, and technologists in collaboration with fringe stakeholder.
       representatives to develop specific new product concepts and markets.
2.   Incubate innovations and new business models by setting up task forces
       consisting of operating managers, R&D engineers and staff managers, some of
       whom have experienced the radically different stakeholder contexts.
3.   Open continuing conversations with stakeholders in extreme contexts to test
       and refine ideas for products, services and business models, ensuring that
       stakeholder needs are met and their concerns regarding negative social and
       environmental impacts are addressed.
4.   Coordinate and exchange information in organizational committees that are
       horizontally diverse (SBUs, functional areas, geographic locations) and vertically
       diverse (across corporate hierarchies).
Costs: Coordination of taskforces and ongoing transactiveness with stakeholders.
Benefits: Generating disruptive innovations in products, services, and business models
       while addressing the economic, social and environmental concerns of
       stakeholders at the fringe and preventing the creation of adversarial swarms.

Source: Adapted from S. Hart and S. Sharma 2004. "Engaging Fringe Stakeholders for
Competitive Imagination." *Academy of Management Executive*, 18(1): 7-18.

From Transparency to Transactiveness

Radical transactiveness helps firms cast a wider, more inclusive net to
generate competitive imagination about possible future products, services, markets, and business models. It complements other approaches to
business creativity, such as increased employee diversity, lateral thinking, and conventional R&D and technology management. To leverage
the disruptive innovations that have emerged from HLL and other grass-
roots initiatives, for example, Unilever has begun adding managers
from these developing country subsidiaries to its board of directors and
top management committees at the head office. Such diversity is now
paying dividends in the form of increased innovation in conventional
R&D and product development.

The RT framework proposes that firms go beyond the traditional
logic of stakeholder engagement by consciously seeking out remote
stakeholders that have previously had no connection with the company.
Putting the last first reverses the logic of the established business and

seeks to generate imagination and ideas about unmet needs, potential new products, and business innovations. Fanning–in, then, requires training managers to empathize with diverse and disconfirming stakeholder perspectives, and understand the culture, thought processes, and language of distant stakeholders. To convert the insights thus gained into practical business strategies, however, it is crucial to reconcile the contradictions between current reality and the needs and requirements of those on the fringe.

RT thus means going far beyond the notion of radical *transparency*, which entails full and open disclosure of the firm's current activities, strategies, and impacts. Radical transparency, which has become increasingly common over the past decade, is targeted primarily at managing core stakeholders—those who can directly affect the current business by virtue of their power, urgency, or salience.[23] It seeks "permission" to operate from those interests and groups that might otherwise withhold resources, approval, or legitimacy.

Unfortunately, in an interconnected world populated by tens of thousands of NGOs and activist groups, it is increasingly perilous to depend upon radical transparency alone. The experiences of organizations such as Monsanto, Nike, Shell, and the World Trade Organization demonstrate that fringe stakeholders with no direct connection to the organization's activity can have a significant impact on the company's ability to execute. RT thus helps the firm anticipate and even preempt such difficulties by identifying new strategies for a smarter, more inclusive form of globalization—strategies that seek, from the outset, to address social, cultural, and environmental issues.

From Alien to Native

Radical transactiveness provides the basis for widening the corporate bandwidth that is crucial to the development of a more indigenous form of enterprise. The conventional development paradigm of the past half-century has been based on a deductive approach to problem solving. It has imposed a problem definition (income poverty) and a solution (economic growth and development) without any real knowledge or understanding of the history, complexity, or indigenous resources that existed in the Third World. Top-down policy prescriptions and large-scale infrastructure development have made inroads into some problems, such as infant mortality, curable disease, and illiteracy, but they have created bigger problems in the process—a burgeoning mass of truly impoverished people with little hope or opportunity for the future.

As corporations have globalized their strategies over the past few decades, they have succeeded in developing worldwide supply chains capable of serving a customer base around the globe. However, these strategies—even ones focused on being locally responsive—still rely heavily on world-scale production and one-size-fits all solutions. These solutions may be appropriate for the wealthy at the top of the pyramid, but they hold little hope of being either appropriate to the real needs of the poor or within their means. To serve the poor effectively, companies need to hear the voices of those who historically have been excluded from capitalism's reach. Developing this skill will enable companies to make the transition from being alien forces in the world, with strategies that extract natural resources, plunder rural villages, and accelerate the rush to the city, to becoming native to the places in which they operate.

Unfortunately, most MNC strategies to date—even those developed with sustainability in mind—have remained alien. Monsanto's aborted attempt to commercialize genetically modified seeds, and Nike's failed effort to develop an athletic shoe for low-income markets in China, provide two instructive examples. Even the few MNC success stories described in this chapter and elsewhere—Hindustan Lever's BOP business development in rural India, Hewlett-Packard's i-Community in Kuppam, and Cemex's Patrimonio Hoy program—represent important first steps, but still have a ways to go before we can think of them as indigenous business models. Broadening the bandwidth is the first step in the development of native capability. The next chapter delves more deeply into what it means to become truly indigenous.

Notes

1. This insight is drawn from Wolfgang Sachs, *Planet Dialectics* (New York: Zed Books, 1999).
2. Some of Erik's most powerful ideas can be found in Erik Simanis, *Entrepreneurship and Global Development: An Antiessentialist Critique and Extension* (Chapel Hill: University of North Carolina, working paper, 2002).
3. My thanks again to Erik Simanis for this wonderful concept.
4. See, for example, Arturo Escobar, *Encountering Development* (Princeton, NJ: Princeton University Press, 1995).
5. My thanks to Erik Simanis and Gordon Enk for some of the language here; it is excerpted from our joint *Project Proposal for a Protocol for Strategic Initiatives at the Base of the Pyramid* (Ithaca, NY: Cornell University, 2004).
6. Helena Norberg-Hodge, *Ancient Futures: Learning from Ladakh* (Berkeley, CA: Sierra Club Books, 1991).
7. Polyandry refers to the practice of a woman having more than one husband. Such a practice limited the number of women having children and contributed to keeping the population in check.
8. See, for example, Wolfgang Sachs, *Planet Dialectics*; Gilbert Rist, *The History of Development* (New York: Zed Books, 1997).
9. Helena Norberg-Hodge, *Ancient Futures*.
10. See Wolfgang Sachs, *Planet Dialectics*; Arturo Escobar, *Encountering Development*; David Korten, *When Corporations Rule the World* (San Francisco, CA: Berrett-Kohler, 1995); Joseph Stiglitz, *Globalization and Its Discontents* (New York: W.W. Norton, 2002); Jeffrey Sachs, "Helping the World's Poorest," *The Economist* (14 August 1998): 17–20; and George Soros, *On Globalization* (New York: Public Affairs, 2002).
11. Portions of the following section are excerpted from Stuart Hart and Sanjay Sharma, "Engaging Fringe Stakeholders for Competitive Imagination," *Academy of Management Executive* 18(1) (2004): 7–18.
12. The idea of a "transactive" approach to planning in the public domain was first articulated in John Friedmann, *Retracking America: A Theory of Transactive Planning* (New York: Anchor Press, 1973).
13. For a detailed description, see Deborah Dunn and Keith Yamashita, "Microcapitalism and the Megacorporation," *Harvard Business Review* (August 2003): 46–54.

14. Kathy Eisenhardt and Jeffrey Martin, "Dynamic Capabilities: What Are They?" *Strategic Management Journal* 21 (special issue) (2000): 1105–1121; and David Teece, Gary Pisano, and Art Shuen, "Dynamic Capabilities and Strategic Management," *Strategic Management Journal* 18 (1997): 509–533.

15. For an excellent summary of this literature, see Gordon Enk and Stuart Hart, Stuart, "An Eight Step Approach to Strategic Problem Solving," *Human Systems Management* 5 (1985): 245–258 .

16. For examples of each of these, see David Collins, "Serving the Homeless and Low-Income Communities Through Business and Society/Business Ethics Class Projects: The University of Wisconsin-Madison Plan," *Journal of Business Ethics* 15(1) (1996): 67–85; C. K. Prahalad and Stuart Hart, "The Fortune at the Bottom of the Pyramid," *Strategy+Business* 26 (2002): 1–14; and Mark Starik, "Should Trees Have Managerial Standing? Toward Stakeholder Status for Non-human Nature," *Journal of Business Ethics* 14(3) (1995): 207–217.

17. For an in-depth discussion of this concept, see Robert Chambers, *Rural Development: Putting the Last First* (London: Longman, 1984).

18. Personal communication with Muhammad Yunus, April 2004.

19. See Miguel Angel Rodriegez, *Reinventing the Wheel: Hindustan Lever in India* (Barcelona, Spain: IESE, 2002).

20. M. Baghai, S. Coley, D. White, and C. Conn, "Staircases to Growth," *McKinsey Quarterly* 4 (1996): 39–61.

21. See Heather McDonald, Ted London, and Stuart Hart, *Expanding the Playing Field: Nike's World Shoe Project* (Washington, D.C.: World Resources Institute, 2002).

22. See K. Herbst, "Enabling the Poor to Build Housing: Pursuing Profit and Social Development Together," *Changemakers.net Journal* September (2002).

23. Witness the explosion of standards and reporting initiatives over the past decade (The Global Reporting Initiative, The Global Compact, ISO 14000, SA 8000, and so on).

8

DEVELOPING NATIVE
CAPABILITY

If MNCs are to thrive in the twenty-first century, they must broaden their base and share their gains more widely, they must play a central role in narrowing the gap between rich and poor, and they must incubate and commercialize the disruptive technologies of tomorrow that leapfrog us toward a more sustainable world. These objectives cannot be achieved if companies produce only so-called "global products" for consumption primarily by rich consumers. They must come to understand and nurture local markets and cultures, leverage local solutions, and generate wealth at the lowest points on the pyramid. Producing in rather than extracting wealth from these communities will be the guiding principle. The objective is indigenous enterprise, co-creating technologies, products, and services to meet local needs and building local businesses from the bottom up.

To do this, MNCs must combine their advanced technology and global reach with deep local understanding. Although technology is important, strategies for the base of the pyramid cannot be realized without engaging local people. Indeed, efforts led by MNCs or development agencies trying to "solve" the problems of the poor or impose technological solutions have generally failed. For MNCs, the best approach is to marry their global best practices with newfound local knowledge and understanding gleaned from widening the corporate bandwidth.

But whether an MNC enters the BOP directly or collaborates with an NGO or entrepreneur from the base, the development principles remain the same: New business models must not be disruptive to the cultures and lifestyles of local people. An effective combination of local and global knowledge is needed, not a replication of the Western system. This combination requires the development of a new, native capability to complement competencies in global efficiency, national responsiveness, and learning transfer that most MNCs possess. As organic agriculture pioneer Wes Jackson says, we must figure out how, once again, to become native to this place.[1]

Expanding Our Concept of the Global Economy

To date, our tendency has been to take a very narrow view of what constitutes "the economy." We have framed the global economy, especially in the rich countries of the First World, as consisting exclusively of wage labor within firms that produce goods and services. We have focused almost exclusively on a narrow range of macroeconomic indicators, such as GDP per capita, thereby failing to take into account myriad other forms of economic activity that are critically important to people around the world. Not surprisingly, then, when we attempt to impose this model of global capitalism on the rest of the world, we encounter significant resistance precisely because we have failed to appreciate how the majority of people in the world currently live.

Scholars such as J. K. Gibson-Graham have pointed out, for example, that the formal money economy represents only the tip of the iceberg of economic activity in the world (see Exhibit 8.1). Beneath the formal, private sector–based economy lies not only the public sector (schools, governments, agencies) and the informal economy (barter, self-provisioning, moonlighting, household production), as we have seen, but also myriad other arrangements and activities, such as producer cooperatives, communal enterprises, not-for-profit organizations, volunteering, gift giving, and what Hazel Henderson calls the love economy: work performed without pay by hundreds of millions of mothers, fathers, aunts, uncles, and grandparents in raising their families.[2]

Exhibit 8.1
The Global Economy Expanded

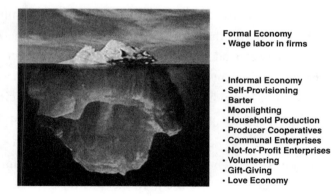

Formal Economy
• Wage labor in firms

• **Informal Economy**
• **Self-Provisioning**
• **Barter**
• **Moonlighting**
• **Household Production**
• **Producer Cooperatives**
• **Communal Enterprises**
• **Not-for-Profit Enterprises**
• **Volunteering**
• **Gift-Giving**
• **Love Economy**

Source: Adapted from a slide first created by Ted London.

When we add all of these activities together, they total many times what we record in our official GNP numbers in measuring the health of the economy. Our narrow measure is one reason, of course, why so-called developing countries look so anemic when it comes to economic growth and success: The majority of actual economic activity is taking place beneath the surface, in the public-sector, informal, and love economies. That is not to say that these economic activities are always efficiently accomplished, equitably distributed, or environmentally sustainable. Indeed, as we have seen, there are literally billions of people at the base of the economic pyramid whose needs are still being poorly met or who are actively exploited by extractive local producers, warlords, or despots.

The opportunity, therefore, is to expand our concept of both the economy and capitalism. Neither is a monolithic idea. Markets are ubiquitous throughout the world, from street vendors in the Third World to the New York Stock Exchange. A more inclusive form of capitalism can catalyze and spawn a range of economic activities and practices, even in those sectors that are currently considered noncapitalist (the informal sector, cooperatives, and family-based enterprise).

Capitalism, in other words, need not be hegemonic: Through the strategies they create, companies can expand the scope of the global economy beyond its current focus on the production of commodity goods for the wealthy in the formal economy. Similarly, the global financial system can expand its horizons beyond its current preoccupation with the free movement of capital, which has served primarily the interests of the wealthy while destabilizing foreign currencies and further impoverishing the poor, to become a truly effective tool in spreading opportunity and fighting poverty.

As businesspeople, we must now awaken to these possibilities. By creating a more inclusive form of enterprise, one that is based in the local context and built from the bottom up, we can combine the best of both worlds—the resources and technological capacity of the formal economy, and the indigenous knowledge, human face, and cultural understanding of the informal sector and love economy. This is fundamentally different from the idea of corporate social responsibility, which relies on mere philanthropy to compensate for the damage done by conventional (alien) business strategies; instead, I am proposing that companies develop a new sense of intimacy with and embeddedness in the world so that they might better understand the real problems that need to be solved for the majority of humanity.[3] The profit motive, seen through this lens, then serves to *accelerate* the pace of positive change by solving problems and creating new wealth, not by extracting resources from the many only to give them to the few.

As we saw in the last chapter, widening the corporate bandwidth through radical transactiveness is an important first step in the development of native capability, the skills and competencies needed for firms to become thoroughly embedded in the local context. Not surprisingly, becoming indigenous requires firms to bridge the formal and informal economies because development at the base of the economic pyramid does not follow traditional patterns found in the developed world. As my colleague Ted London at the University of North Carolina suggests, this means focusing on what is *positive* in the BOP, not just what is negative (corruption) or missing (Western-style institutions). The successful distributed energy and microloan ventures discussed in previous chapters, for example, show that small-scale, decentralized initiatives are well matched to the conditions in low-income markets. Indeed, they meet those markets' conditions better than the developed-world mantra of centralization of control and economies of scale, which require rule of law and well-functioning central institutions from the outset.

There is much to be learned from analyzing the strategies and practices of actual ventures—for-profit as well as not-for-profit—focused on the BOP. As Ted London and I found in our study of BOP-based ventures, successfully serving the base of the pyramid appears to require a completely different strategic approach.[4] In the sections that follow, I describe some of the critical skills and practices underpinning native capability that have emerged from our ongoing study of BOP ventures during the past four years.

Engage First, Design Second

As we saw in Chapter 5, "The Great Leap Downward," when Cemex issued its "Declaration of Ignorance" regarding the use of its cement products by low-income customers in Mexico, it gave a group of managers the challenge of living in the shantytowns for six months, to develop a better understanding of the constraints and problems faced by do-it-yourself homebuilders. There was one additional requirement: that they not think about cement at all during their time in the shantytowns. This prohibition, as it turned out, was a critically important one. Freed of the burden of the short-term commercial agenda, the Cemex managers were able to win the trust of the local people, which ultimately led to new and unanticipated insights into how the company might better serve their needs. It also yielded a key insight about how to become indigenous: Local engagement should always precede product or service development. The Patrimonio Hoy program, with its wonderful embeddedness in the local shantytown environment, would never have happened if the project teams' primary objective had been to simply sell more cement.

When it comes to entering the BOP, then, large corporations must resist the temptation to behave like the proverbial child with a hammer, to whom everything begins to look like a nail. Pushing the company's existing products and solutions onto shantytown dwellers and rural villagers may indeed produce incremental sales in the near term, but will almost certainly fail in the long run because the solutions remain alien; witness Nike's failed attempt to introduce an athletic footwear product in the BOP. Hewlett-Packard, on the other hand, clearly acknowledged the importance of engagement before design by establishing its Living Laboratory in Kuppam, India, set up as a listening post to better understand and identify how information technology might be used to benefit those at the base of the pyramid. Indeed, through extended engagement, HP has identified several potential new services and business models that it would have otherwise never seen.

After living in Kuppum for an extended period, for example, it became evident to HP staff that there was an unmet need for secure storage of important documents. This led to the launch of a new business (Surakshita Dakhalalu), a service which provides for the digital scanning and storage of important documents for a charge of about 40 cents per entry.

A precommercial period of engagement is thus essential to do the deep listening required to develop empathetic understanding. Building trust also enables managers to engage in two-way learning with local people. The poor may, in fact, help them to see the shortcomings in their own company—and perhaps even their way of life. As journalist Tom Friedman noted in his book *The Lexus and the Olive Tree*, people everywhere need the material wealth and sustenance supplied through work, trade, and the market as symbolized by the Lexus. However, people also need the olive tree—the sense of belonging, community, connection to nature, and larger purpose that comes from family, tribe, tradition, religion, and other nonmaterial sources.[5]

Today the top of the pyramid, particularly in the U.S., has more than succeeded in supplying the Lexus for its people; in fact, obesity and overconsumption have become increasingly common, suggesting that, as a culture, we have overshot the mark on this dimension. However, the olive tree has, for some time, been in retreat at the top of the pyramid: Career mobility, urbanization, and the automobile culture have served to undermine family, erode communities, and dampen a sense of belonging to place. Religious fundamentalism may be seen, at least in part, as a compensatory response to the progressive loss of the olive tree in modern society.

The situation is exactly the opposite at the base of the pyramid: While lacking in the Lexus dimension, Third World communities still earn their livelihoods in ways consistent with the preservation of their cultures and of their natural environments. The olive tree continues to thrive, despite threats from resource extraction, environmental degradation, and cultural disruption. It is here that those of us at the top of the pyramid can rediscover community and the wisdom of indigenous systems of agriculture, industry, shelter, water, and medicine if we allow ourselves to look.

In northern Nigeria, for example, a local teacher, Mohammed Bah Abba, was motivated by his interest in indigenous African technology to seek a practical, local solution to the problems of food spoilage, which causes disease and loss of income for thousands in the area.[6] Northern Nigeria is an impoverished region where people in rural communities eke out a living from subsistence farming. With no electricity and, therefore, no refrigeration, perishable foods spoil within days. Bah Abba's extremely simple and inexpensive earthenware pot-in-pot cooling device is starting to revolutionize lives in this semidesert area. This technology, which draws upon the ancient art of pottery and employs local pot makers, requires no external energy supply to preserve fruit, vegetables, and other perishables in hot, arid climates. The innovative cooling system consists of two earthenware pots of different diameters, one placed inside the other. The space between the two pots is filled with wet sand. The water contained in the sand between the two pots evaporates toward the outer surface of the larger pot, where drier outside air is circulating. The evaporation process causes a drop in temperature of several degrees, cooling the inner container, destroying harmful microorganisms, and preserving perishable foods. Bah Abba launched an enterprise using more than 500 local potters as producers to make them available to the rural poor. By 2004, he was producing tens of thousands of pots annually with a retail price of about $1, and the enterprise had grown to encompass three additional countries in Africa, including Chad, Cameroon, and Niger.

Through engagement, then, we can awaken to new possibilities. In the process, we may discover the potential for new products and services—not to mention new ways of living—that could never have been envisioned before. For decades, Peace Corps volunteers have learned this lesson firsthand. When they first join, most young volunteers expect that they will be applying "advanced" knowledge from the rich countries to "help" the poor. Upon completion of their assignment, however, most freely admit that they learned more from the poor whom they were supposed to be helping, than the poor did from them.

For corporations, it may be difficult to truly engage because of the baggage associated with the existing commercial agenda—the tyranny of the current core competencies. For example, although focused on engagement, and an *ecosystem approach* to identifying needs and leverage points, HP still built its Kuppam i-community primarily around *IT*; similarly, Cemex sent its managers into Mexico's shantytowns to learn about poor *homebuilders*, even if they were also instructed to forget about cement sales, at least for a while. The mindset associated with the current business still blinds managers to new possibilities.

One way to overcome such biases is to put together consortia to do the engagement work. Including representatives from different industries might make it possible to cross-fertilize ideas and for each industry to stimulate the others. A consortium that included a wider diversity of industries might have been able to see that, despite their best intentions, Cemex's preoccupation with cement blinded it to the potential for leveraging more sustainable building methods as part of its offering. Furthermore, the presence of a microfinance expert might have been able to see that, in addition to creating a mechanism for paying for building materials, the Patrimonio Hoy program might incorporate a service to help shantytown dwellers gain legal title to the houses they build. Engagement thus opens up the possibility of identifying real needs from the point of view of the local people themselves. It also helps to focus and direct the technology and product development required to become truly native to a place.

Coinvent Custom Solutions

Companies interested in developing responsive technologies and products at the base of the pyramid can learn much from fields such as rural sociology, applied anthropology, and empathy-based design. Indeed, techniques such as participatory rural appraisal, rapid assessment processes, and quick ethnography open up valuable ways to hear the true voices of marginalized populations and begin the processes of understanding, mutual learning, and the creation of responsive strategies.[7] All these techniques stress the importance of codeveloping custom solutions to problems through two-way information flow. Rather than imposing pre-existing solutions from above, the emphasis is on working with local partners to codesign every aspect of the product or service, including its delivery.

In our study of BOP ventures, Ted London and I discovered that successful initiatives—those that became embedded in the local community—maximized the *functionality* of the product or service in terms that were important to local users. This often meant allowing the product and business model to coevolve. As one of our respondents indicated, successful initiatives require "everybody who touches it to make money."[8] Poorly performing ventures, on the other hand, tended to view the value proposition in terms of the product itself and often completed the development process at a geographically distant location, such as the corporate R&D center, before the business model was designed.

WorldSpace Corporation, for example, was created to provide direct satellite delivery of digital audio communications and multimedia services to the underserved emerging markets of the world, including Africa, the Middle East, Asia, and Latin America. The WorldSpace satellite network, which was launched in the late 1990s, consisted of three geostationary satellites capable of delivering more than 40 channels of crystal clear audio and multimedia programming directly to portable receivers, enabled with a proprietary chip. To recoup the cost of the satellite infrastructure, WorldSpace priced receivers in the $250–$500 range. Ultimately, it expected this unique global service to transmit quality information, education, and entertainment programming to a service area that included five billion people.[9]

Founder Noah Samara's original vision was to use direct audio broadcast via satellite to stop the spread of AIDS in Africa, but that horizon quickly expanded. In addition to spreading knowledge to make people healthier, better educated, and more aware of the precious environment in which they live, WorldSpace was also seen as a vehicle for bringing the poor the best music and literature of their native cultures, along with those from the great cultures of faraway lands.

Although the technology development associated with the WorldSpace venture was impressive, the company ultimately failed to secure a critical mass of users. Receiver price was clearly a roadblock to widespread adoption. However, even more significant was the company's inability to provide programming that users found useful or compelling. Because it relied on the central generation of content to be broadcast to large areas in the developing world, the company was unable to accommodate the varying tastes and priorities of local users. The centralized nature of the business model virtually prevented the kind of codevelopment and coevolution that is crucial to success. Despite its best intentions, WorldSpace was an alien technology, unable by its nature to develop a local face.

Contrast this with the approach taken by rural IT provider N-Logue.[10] Employing a specially designed wireless local loop (WLL) technology developed by the Indian Institute of Technology in Madras, N-Logue was able to offer village-based communication services through a coinvention strategy. The business model consists of three levels of interdependent networks. At the corporate level, N-Logue facilitates the relationships among the wide range of organizations (equipment vendors, NGOs, content providers, and government) that enable and support the entire system. At the next level, N-Logue maintains a regional network of franchised Local Service Partners (LSPs) who work in tandem with the corporation to set up Access Center nodes to which individual kiosk operators are connected. At the lowest level, local microentrepreneurs are recruited by the LSPs to establish village-level kiosk franchises that provide Internet and Voice over IP telephone access to the local population.

The kiosks essentially function as combination rural Internet cafes and pay phone booths. While N-Logue provides kiosk owners with training, support, and technical assistance, and LSPs provide some general content platforms that they might adopt, the local microfranchisees themselves are responsible for deciding upon the actual product and service offerings and marketing strategies they will use. These have included not only access to specific content, based on the local needs of villagers, but also computer training classes, CD-ROM movie viewing, and other specially tailored services. Allowing kiosk operators to develop their own business strategies has resulted in locally appropriate solutions and new offerings that are difficult to develop within a centralized business structure.

As the N-Logue example makes clear, the context-specific nature of the base of the pyramid dictates that companies adopt a participatory approach to product and service development, in concert with local users. Coinventing custom solutions thus extends far beyond the idea of being locally responsive (adapting pre-existing solutions to local conditions), which pervades most of the thinking about global strategy in MNCs. To develop native capability, then, companies must learn how to coinvent and coevolve products and services so that they are appropriately embedded in the local ecosystem and culture from the start.

Experiment with Low-Cost Probes

To facilitate the development of native capability, multiple low-cost experiments appear vastly superior to a single, large-scale market probe. Small-scale experimentation offers the potential for rapid and continuous learning, as well as for modular scale-up if the experiment proves successful. Low-cost probes also make it easy to shut down failed projects before they become expensive burdens on the company. Such initiatives must be evaluated for funding using a separate set of criteria and metrics, however, because they will almost never meet the short-term revenue and profitability targets associated with projects designed to expand existing businesses.

In this regard, it is beneficial to use a real-options approach rather than rely exclusively on the more conventional discounted cash flow logic to evaluate these projects.[11] Real-options analysis brings the logic of the private equity market into the firm, with an expected payoff in the time frame of five to seven years rather than the excessively short-term logic associated with conventional capital budgeting or excessively long-term logic associated with traditional R&D.[12] It effectively segments the project into several affordable chunks so that the decision to move forward can be made iteratively, after the completion of each stage, rather then through an "all-or-nothing" decision at the start of the project.

Without the flexibility afforded by real-options analysis, there will be the inevitable tendency to convert BOP experiments into philanthropy. This pitfall should be avoided at all cost because experience shows that giving away technology rarely succeeds in solving the problem.[13] The fact that it is often easier to convert BOP initiatives into corporate donations than it is to make the case for running them as viable business experiments shows how inflexible most MNCs are when it comes to project evaluation and capital budgeting. The solution is to broaden the analytical lens for investment rather than taking the easy way out through the corporate foundation.

P&G, for example, has struggled to make the business case for its nutritional beverage drink, Nutristar, and its point-of-use water purification technology, PuR—both new products targeted at the BOP. Both have gone through multiple rounds of small-scale market experimentation. Each stage has produced important information about how best to adapt the business model for successful commercialization. Unfortunately, multiple rounds of market probes do not stack up very well using discounted cash flow analysis as the measuring stick. The champions for each of these projects are now under intense pressure to turn them over, at least in part, to the philanthropic arm of the company. As George Carpenter, vice president for Sustainability at P&G, noted, however, philanthropy is a trap: Giving away such new technologies can never be financially sustainable because the scale of the problem far exceeds the corporate foundation's ability to address it.[14]

Creating a separate pool of investment capital to fund such low-cost probes, along with a separate organizational entity to house them, is one way to address this challenge. Without this early protection, the logic of short-term performance in today's business will almost certainly guarantee failure.[15] Nike's failed attempt to commercialize the World Shoe through its current production and marketing infrastructure makes this point only too clearly. Indeed, as Clay Christensen and Michael Raynor point out in their new book *The Innovator's Solution*, with disruptive new ventures, it is important to be *impatient* for profit, but *patient* for growth because it takes time for such ventures to reach the point of being scaleable.[16]

When it comes to the base of the pyramid, Christensen and Raynor's observation may be even more important because evidence suggests that when the point of scale-up is reached, growth can proceed at an explosive rate. For example, C. K. Prahalad shows that the time frame for new technology and product diffusion, which may take 10–15 years to play out in the developed market, is being collapsed into a short period of perhaps 3–5 years in the BOP.[17] The implication for MNCs is clear: Don't give up on BOP ventures if they appear to be stalled after a few years; they may be just reaching the point that they are ready to take off—and when they do, be prepared for a rapid ascent!

Fly Under the Radar

World Water Corporation was founded in 1984 in response to a perceived vacuum in private business activity supplying water and power in developing countries.[18] With help from a team of Princeton University engineers, the company developed its first patented product in 1992, a solar thermal power system. Since then, it has added proprietary photovoltaic technology, most notably the AquaSafe solar powered water pump. This technology can pump 10 times the volume of any other solar water pump in the world—more than 2,000 gallons of water per minute from rivers and other surface water. The technology can also be used to pump ground water up to 1,000 feet deep, to bring up clean water from wells. Given that water shortages are expected to be a major problem in the twenty-first century, the company was confident that its powerful solar water systems would find a big market worldwide. Based upon this optimistic projection, the company went public in 1997.

By 2000, World Water Corporation had established operations in 17 developing countries. Typically, the company worked through the central government to sign long-term agreements to serve as consultant and contractor for water and energy programs, with a focus on rural areas. For example, World Water signed an agreement to become master consultant and contractor for all water and energy programs for the newly elected government in Somalia in 2000. The company had signed similar agreements in Pakistan and the Philippines, working with the leadership of both countries. The pilot phase of the Somalia project was worth $2.5 million and was planned to cover 25 communities.

To ensure that these very poor countries actually pay for their equipment and services, the company deals only in hard currency; it also seeks to collect down payments of 10–15 percent at the start of each project. World Water also teams up with American banks and international financial institutions where possible to help the countries pay for the projects.

Unfortunately, despite World Water's best efforts, the unstable and corrupt nature of its clients' governments has put the viability of the company at serious risk. The highly visible nature of the agreements makes the scale and scope of the agreement—and the potential profit for World Water—readily apparent to a broad range of bureaucrats, government officials, and others who might benefit from either derailing the project or currying favor before it is allowed to move forward.

As a result of these problems, the company's international business prospects have soured considerably. Over the past few years, in fact, it has sought to increase its presence in the U.S. market, particularly California, where a combination of water scarcity and electric power interruptions make World Water's product attractive. World Water's stock price did not budge, despite the heady projections for growth in 2000: It was still trading at about 30 cents per share in August 2004.

Contrast this experience with the one described in Chapter 6, "Reaching the Base of the Pyramid," for ApproTEC, the Kenya-based venture focused on technology and microenterprise development for the rural poor in East Africa. ApproTEC also focused on water pumping in the Third World but took a very different approach, both technologically and in terms of business model. As we have seen, ApproTEC's Moneymaker Microirrigation Pump is manually operated by small farmers and was codesigned with them to ensure product acceptance. At less than $100, the pump was directly affordable by the end consumer, meaning that ApproTEC could launch its business on a small-scale basis and allow it to grow organically over time. It bypassed the need to deal with the central governments of Kenya and Tanzania, thereby avoiding the complexity and corruption that World Water exposed itself to.

In short, ApproTEC, like most other successful ventures in the BOP that we have been able to identify, flew under the radar of corruption, thereby avoiding all the problems that go along with having to deal with difficult—and changeable—central regimes. By constructing a business model that went directly to the user and building it up from a local base of support, ApproTEC was able to engender trust and gain experience with the user community. This helps to avoid the corruption trap of bribes and "speed money" associated with weak central governments or failed states. Avoiding dependence on central institutions—national governments, corrupt regimes, and central infrastructure planning—thus appears to be a critical aspect of native capability. In the final analysis, while both ApproTEC and World Water sought to help the rural poor gain better access to clean water, the former was able to become indigenous while the latter remained alien.

It is ironic that large corporations are willing to invest in massive—and often risky—projects while eschewing the smaller-scale, bottom-up approach described earlier. The belief that it is necessary to start big to get big is pervasive and may prove to be one of the most vexing challenges when it comes to serving the poor. Enron, for example, invested more than $2 billion in its Dabhol energy project in India, only to see the investment go up in smoke when corruption, changing political winds, and unacceptably high electricity prices turned stakeholders against the project. This aborted project also cost the American taxpayers more than $700 million in foregone loan guarantees by the Overseas Private Investment Corporation. What might have happened if even a fraction of this money had been invested in small-scale experiments in distributed energy generation?

Work with Nontraditional Partners

Ventures that face challenging new environments usually need to turn to partner organizations for missing resources and expertise. Indeed, governments often require MNCs to have a local corporate partner to ensure market access in emerging economies. Tarun Khanna and his associates, for example, have shown that partnering with the large business conglomerates in the developing world—the chaebols, grupos, and business houses—helps MNCs fill the institutional void by ensuring property rights, capital availability, and political support.[19]

When entering the base of the pyramid, however, firms may need to dramatically expand the potential field of alliance partners because the large national players familiar with the ways of global capitalism seldom serve the rural poor or shantytown dwellers in their own countries. Indeed, in our analysis of BOP ventures, Ted London and I found that successful strategies (such as ApproTEC's) rely heavily on nontraditional partners, including nonprofit organizations, community groups, and local (even village-level) governments. Unsuccessful strategies (such as World Water's), on the other hand, tend to rely on traditional partners, such as national governments and large local companies. Not surprisingly, these traditional partners are as far removed from low-income markets in terms of knowledge and experience as the firms trying to launch the venture.

One BOP venture in Kenya, Honey Care Africa, created a particularly interesting three-way partnership with the private sector, the development sector, and the local community. Honey Care was established to make beekeeping accessible to poor farmers and to create a domestic source of high-quality honey for Kenya. The company has achieved success by doubling the income of many poor farmers, providing high-quality honey for the Kenyan market, and creating economic, social, and environmental value for local communities. Today Honey Care is the largest producer of high-quality honey in East Africa.[20]

Traditionally, Kenyan communities used log hives, baskets, or clay pots for beekeeping. Unfortunately, although they were cheap to set up, these crude techniques produced small volumes of poor-quality honey. Honey Care thus based its business model on making advanced (yet context-appropriate) beekeeping equipment available to these small farmers. They procure this equipment from a third-party producer and sell it to a development-sector partner, which, in turn, works with local microcredit institutions to provide financing for small farmers to purchase the equipment. The company guarantees a steady income for the farmers by committing to purchase all their honey production, ensuring a loyal source of supply. Honey Care then sells the honey to distributors and retailers for sale to end consumers. The company has established a virtuous circle by creating a collaborative model that enables it to better understand and leverage the local social context. By working with nontraditional partners who were embedded in the local scene, it has been able to become indigenous while leveraging its core competencies in equipment procurement and marketing.

As another example, Bata, a leading retailer of shoes with operations throughout the developing world, has entered into an innovative partnership with the NGO Care in Bangladesh to gain access to rural areas in the country where their products have yet to penetrate.[21] Bata's products are well-suited to the BOP; indeed, they have developed a line of low-cost ($2-$5) yet high-quality shoes and sandals. Care, which has been in Bangladesh for more than 50 years, has invested extensively in entrepreneurial training for rural women. Indeed, Care has trained in excess of 80,000 poor rural women throughout the country to run micro-enterprises, which include small grocery stores, handicraft production and retailing, commercial dairy operations, and bicycle rental businesses. By partnering with Care, Bata gains access to this network of rural microentrepreneurs interested in expanding their businesses to include shoe sales. In exchange, the rural women gain visibility and credibility as business people because few in the rural areas have any direct affiliation with a multinational brand. If the Bangladesh experiment is successful, the model could be spread to many other countries throughout the developing world.

Working with nontraditional partners thus means going far beyond the typical focus on customers and suppliers. By including civil society, community groups, and local players, firms are better able to understand and leverage existing strengths in the environment rather than trying to change that environment to resemble the Western way. Nontraditional partners provide intelligence on the local context, local legitimacy, and access to needed resources, none of which is available to MNCs attempting to go it alone.[22]

Build Social, Not Legal, Contracts

Despite the advantages of working with nontraditional partners, MNCs have tended to ally themselves with the small number of entities in the developing world that understand the current global capitalist system, value their existing products, and respect intellectual property. Not surprisingly, local partners have most often been large domestic firms, central governments, or state-owned enterprises, whose primary business experience is centered on the urban elite in the developing world. As my colleague Ted London likes to point out, however, reaching the base of the pyramid requires entry strategies that move past preoccupation with Western-style rule of law and intellectual property protection because these do not exist in the base of the pyramid.[23]

As anyone who has traveled extensively in the developing world knows, counterfeit products and knock-offs abound, whether we are talking about Rolex watches, Nike running shoes, CDs and videos, computer software, or prescription drugs. Given the high cost structure and fat margins associated with most products for the top of the pyramid, companies depend on intellectual property protection—patents, trademarks, and copyrights—to guarantee their franchise. Viewed from this perspective, the Third World appears hostile to MNCs, a place where value will be hijacked rather than added. However, when we look from the perspective of those at the base of the pyramid, we begin to see other commercial models.

In the informal sectors, relationships are primarily grounded in social, not legal, contracts, and the organizations with the most expertise in serving these populations—local government and civil society—

have a strong social orientation. As the experience of the Grameen Bank clearly demonstrates, successfully operating in this space requires a capability to understand and appreciate the benefits of the existing social infrastructure, not complain about its lack of Western-style institutions. Grameen's lending model, for example, entails no legally enforceable instruments whatsoever. Because there is no collateral, legal papers would be useless. If a borrower defaults, the bank staff works with her to restructure the debt or plan an alternative repayment schedule. The entire business model is based upon social capital and trust.

Although Nike's World Shoe venture was a commercial failure, it did, at the very least, demonstrate that the best way to deal with the counterfeit problem is not by using legal remedies against Third World countries, but rather by attempting to create products that poor people can actually afford. This requires a very different strategy, cost structure, and business model. Rather than cajoling its existing contract manufacturers in Asia to produce the low-end World Shoes (there was little incentive do so because they were rewarded based on contribution margin), what if Nike had chosen to partner with the counterfeiters instead? Indeed, counterfeit producers possessed exactly what Nike lacked—production capacity—as well as distribution capabilities to reach precisely the low-income markets that Nike was trying to capture. Nike could have provided a dramatically improved shoe design (with the real Nike Swoosh) and also transferred its social and environmental practices to the counterfeit producers, a potential win-win for both parties, not to mention the workers, customers, and the environment. The result might have been a business model that competes based on social capital, quality, and value for money rather than trademark and legal protection.

Perhaps the pharmaceutical industry could also benefit by focusing on social rather than purely legal contracts. At present, the search for new drugs is focused almost entirely on the (often cosmetic) afflictions of the rich while overlooking the fatal illnesses of the poor. Indeed, medicines against tropical diseases like malaria, sleeping sickness, and tuberculosis make up a miniscule 1 percent of new drug patents. Lack of patent protection (and inability to pay) are usually cited as the reasons for this disproportionate figure. The reality, however, is that ignorance is to blame: Few people in pharmaceutical companies really know anything about either the challenges or the opportunities in the Third World.

Drug companies defend their current, lucrative markets in places such as the United States by agreeing—sometimes under duress—to run either tiered pricing programs (as with AIDS drugs) or drug-donation programs (as with Merck and river blindness treatment). Neither approach is financially sustainable: Any effort to seriously address the public health crisis that rages in the Third World through drug give-aways would bankrupt the industry. But what if the drug companies began with some real engagement, perhaps through low-cost probes, to develop commercial businesses in poor communities selling drugs that have already gone off patent (for example, pain relievers are sorely needed but are often unavailable). Such an initiative would work wonders for the industry's tarnished image around the world and would also build a direct relationship with the people most in need. Through this experience, the firms might also be able to identify some new and creative ways to address the public health problems of the world's poor—and make money doing it. Indeed, Western drug companies ignore this space at their peril: The Indian pharmaceutical industry, for example, has already learned, out of necessity, how to deliver drugs coming off patent in the U.S. at a fraction of the cost charged by the established drug companies.[24]

Neville Williams, founder of SELCO, the largest supplier of solar electric home systems in India, argues that the key to success in the BOP is trust, not technology.[25] SELCO has built a reputation among the poor by making solar electricity affordable (through a network of participating banks) and reliable (through the creation of solar service centers). Because the poor are frequently exploited by predatory lenders and unscrupulous vendors, SELCO's reputation for fair dealing, dependability, and continuing care has become the key to its growth (about 30 percent per year). Indeed, Williams believes that trust and social capital form the real basis for sustainable competitive advantage at the base of the pyramid: Once poor customers come to trust you, they are disinclined to leave because most have experienced only poor service, unscrupulous vendors, or blatant exploitation. As Shell and other MNCs begin to enter the solar electric home system business, they are realizing that the business model is more important than the technology. There is a reason why many in India now refer to solar home electric systems generically as "SELCOs." The reason is trust—and trust cannot be copied.

Moving Beyond the Transnational Model

The current transnational model emphasizes global efficiency (world-scale production and global supply chains), national responsiveness (modifying products and operations to suit country differences), and worldwide learning (sharing experience across units within the firm) as the crucial capabilities for a successful multinational corporation.[26] As Ted London's work and our joint analysis of BOP ventures has shown, however, these conventional capabilities are clearly inadequate. In fact, at times, reliance on these in the context of the BOP can actually be damaging.[27]

For MNCs to flourish in the twenty-first century, it appears that they must acquire a new capability—a native capability—to complement their existing skills. Native capability requires that MNCs expand their conception of the global economy to include the varied economic activities that occur outside of the formal, wage-based economy. They must embrace the informal, barter, household, and love economies, and tailor their business models to enhance the way people currently live. Creating sustainable livelihoods means strengthening local communities and restoring the environment, not extracting resources and forcing people to move in the pursuit of factory jobs. Spanning these worlds provides the basis for developing the climate needed for business to thrive by building respect for agreements, transaction transparency, and mutual trust. Indeed, MNCs, in partnership with local entrepreneurs, NGOs, and local governments, can help build a system of governance *from the ground up* rather than waiting for corrupt central governments to reform.

Native capability means learning to engage extensively with the local people on their terms in a true spirit of mutuality. It means working on bottom-up coinvention of more sustainable ways of living. It means experimenting with small-scale, low-cost probes and flying under the radar to work directly with local communities, rather than seeking to cut deals with corrupt central regimes or national champion firms. It means working with nontraditional partners—civil society, communities, and town and village governments—where the real knowledge about local conditions resides. And it means building the business model around social rather than legal contracts because trust and social capital are the *lingua franca* in the BOP.

Native capability enables the corporation to become truly *embedded*—part of the local landscape rather than an alien force that imposes its will from the outside. Embeddedness takes time to develop and cannot be quickly duplicated by competitors. Competitive advantage is then based upon deep understanding of and integration with the local environment. Companies earn it by creating a web of trusted connections with a diversity of organizations and building on the available social infrastructure. Rather than looking to overcome limitations in the environment—such as a lack of central institutions and rule of law—native capability emphasizes the crafting of strategies that build on *existing* conditions and resources.

Unlike the conventional transnational model, which focuses on transferring proprietary resources from within the firm, native capability assumes that the critical knowledge for success lies beyond the firm's boundaries. MNCs, not their local partners, are the ones that must do the unlearning. Given that, competitive advantage is premised less on protecting existing proprietary technology or intellectual property, and more on developing trust and social capital. Generic principles and learnings from specific settings, however, can and must be transferred and applied in other BOP contexts; that is how the capability is fostered and spread. The time has come for MNCs to move beyond the traditional conception of transnational success. And developing native capability is one of the keys to creating a truly sustainable global enterprise.

Notes

1. Wes Jackson, *Becoming Native to This Place* (New York: Counterpoint, 1994).

2. J. K. Gibson-Graham, *The End of Capitalism (As We Knew It)* (Oxford: Blackwell Publishers, 1996); J. K. Gibson-Graham, "A Diverse Economy: Rethinking Economy and Economic Representation," working paper; and Hazel Henderson, *Beyond Globalization* (West Hartford, CT: Kumarian Press, 1999).

3. My thanks to Ted London for letting me borrow the wonderful concept of "social embeddedness" from our joint work together. I should also acknowledge the work of Mark Granovetter who first articulated the phrase: "Economic action and social structure: The problem of embeddedness." *American Journal of Sociology*, 91(3) (1985): 481–510.

4. This exploratory study, which has been conducted through the Base of the Pyramid Learning Laboratory over the past four years, involved on-going interviews with dozens of MNC managers, 24 original BOP venture case studies, and analysis of archival materials. For details, see Ted London and Stuart Hart, "Reinventing Strategies for Emerging Markets: Beyond the Transnational Model," *Journal of International Business Studies*, 35 (2004): 350–370.

5. Thomas Friedman, *The Lexus and the Olive Tree* (New York: Anchor Books, 2000).

6. See "Nigerian Wins Prize for Developing Clay Pot Cooler," www.mclglobal.com/History/Sep2000/29i2000/29i0t.html. I thank Erik Simanis at UNC for drawing it to my attention.

7. Robert Chambers, *Whose Reality Counts: Putting the First Last* (London: ITDG Publishing, 1997); James Beebe, *Rapid Assessment Process: An Introduction* (New York: Altamira Press, 2001); and W. Penn Handwerker, *Quick Ethnography* (New York: Altamira Press, 2001).

8. Ted London and Stuart Hart, "Reinventing Strategies."

9. See World Space Corporation Frequently Asked Questions, www.worldspace.com.

10. For a more complete description of N-Logue, see Joy Howard, Charis Simms, and Erik Simanis, *Sustainable Deployment for Rural Connectivity: The N-Logue Model* (Washington, D.C.: World Resources Institute, 2001).

11. See M. Amran and N. Kulatilaka, *Real Options* (Boston: Harvard Business School Press, 1999); and M. Milstein and T. Alessandri, "New Tools for New Times: Using Real Options to Identify Value in Strategies for Sustainable Development" (paper presented at the Academy of Management Annual Meeting, Toronto, Ontario, 2000).

12. Richard Foster and Sarah Kaplan, *Creative Destruction* (New York: Doubleday, 2001).

13. The experience with the appropriate technology movement and foreign aid programs over the past 40 years leaves little doubt that giving technologies to the poor fosters neither the pride of ownership nor the personal stake needed to ensure continued utilization.

14. George Carpenter, presentation at the Sustainable Enterprise Academy, York University, Toronto, Canada, April 2004.

15. See Clayton Christensen, *The Innovator's Dilemma* (Boston: Harvard Business School Press, 1998).

16. Clayton Christenson and Michael Raynor, *The Innovator's Solution* (Cambridge, MA: Harvard Business School Press, 2003).

17. C. K. Prahalad, *The Fortune at the Bottom of the Pyramid* (University of Pennsylvania: Wharton School Publishing, 2005).

18. See www.worldwater.com/company_history.htlm.

19. See, for example, Tarun Khanna and Krisna Palepu, "Why Focused Strategies May Be Wrong for Emerging Markets," *Harvard Business Review* July–August (1997): 41–51.

20. See "IFC-Backed Kenyan SME Project Wins Sustainable Development Prize," 7 January (2003), http://web.worldbank.org.

21. My thanks to Jesse Moore of Care Canada for this example, which he presented at the Base of the Pyramid Learning Laboratory in September 2004.

22. Dennis Rondinelli and Ted London, "How Corporations and Environmental Groups Cooperate: Assessing Cross-Sector Alliances and Collaborations," *Academy of Management Executive* 17(1) (2003): 61–76.

23. See Ted London and Stuart Hart, "Reinventing Strategies."

24. C. K. Prahalad, *The Fortune at the Bottom of the Pyramid.*

25. Neville Williams, personal communication, April 2004.

26. See, for example, Chris Bartlett and Sumatra Ghoshal, *Managing Across Borders* (Boston: Harvard Business School Press, 1989); and C. K. Prahalad and Yves Doz, *The Multinational Mission* (New York: Free Press, 1987).

27. Ted London makes this case most persuasively in his Ph.D. dissertation: *How Capabilities Are Created: A Process Study of New Market Entry* (draft) (Chapel Hill, NC: University of North Carolina, 2004).

9

TOWARD A SUSTAINABLE
GLOBAL ENTERPRISE

When the hijacked planes flew into the World Trade Center towers and the Pentagon on September 11, 2001, many believed that the world had changed fundamentally. They were wrong. The world was exactly the same as it had been the day before. The horrific events of 9/11 simply focused our attention in a new way: It was now clear that the world was inextricably interconnected and that unrest in one part of the globe would not remain geographically isolated.

Many in the wealthy nations of the West—particularly the United States—became aware, perhaps for the first time, of what others in developing countries had known for a long time: When people are desperate, disenfranchised, or humiliated, they will resort to just about anything to relieve that condition. Most will seek resolution through modest means, such as working harder, migrating to find new opportunities, or perhaps even resorting to petty crime. Others will turn to organized protest or seek political solutions. A few will resort to the ultimate expression of alienation and repudiation: terrorism.

There is little doubt that the *leaders* of terrorist organizations are, more often than not, driven by extremist ideologies. Militant Islam, for example, weaves together fundamentalist religious beliefs, moral values, and a radical political agenda to create a particularly virulent form of such extremism. As the leaders of such groups know, however, special circumstances are required to attract the large numbers of people needed to effectively advance the cause. Most people are not born to be suicide bombers or militia members. It takes a lifetime of neglect, despair, dashed hopes, thwarted opportunities, or worse—intimidation, exploitation and humiliation—to drive most people to such extremes. Only by reversing the conditions that breed such behavior—poverty, inequity, hopelessness, loss of dignity—will we deal with the root causes of the problem. Yet while thousands of lives were lost or altered forever by the events of 9/11, and hundreds of known terrorist leaders have since been killed or captured, these underlying conditions remain largely unchanged—or have perhaps even worsened. Terrorism, in short, is a symptom; the underlying problem is unsustainable development.

Draining the Swamp

The Middle East in the early twenty-first century provides perhaps the starkest example of unsustainable development in modern history.[1] Oil has made a few elites enormously wealthy and powerful, while the masses have seen little of the benefit. Western dependence on oil has allowed dictators and despots to reign supreme, as long as they ensure that the oil keeps flowing. Indeed, Washington and the West have supported the very Muslim tyrannies that al Qaeda and other extremist groups seek to destroy.[2] Tragically, then, the developed world's growing dependence on oil from the Middle East virtually ensures that this vicious cycle will continue. And to make matters worse, the massive consumption of fossil fuels with its attendant carbon emissions endangers the very climate system upon which we all depend.

A proud culture boasting scientific and artistic achievement second to none, the Arab world today is a shadow of its former self, rife with hopelessness, despair, and a profound sense of humiliation. Journalist Tom Friedman describes the problem in the Middle East as not so much a poverty of *money*, but rather a poverty of *dignity*.[3] Western popular culture, often a direct affront to Islamic values, has permeated every corner of the region. Indeed, Islam's traditional emphasis on charity, social security for all, and the integration of the sacred into everyday life seems, to many Arabs, to be at odds with the Western conception of development and modernization.[4]

Tens of millions of young Muslim boys in the Middle East are coming of age at a time of record unemployment and lack of opportunity. Doctors, lawyers, and other professionals are churned out of universities only to work as day laborers and waiters. Religious extremism and nihilism provide potentially attractive escapes from the grinding sense of frustration and humiliation. Should we be surprised that growing numbers of young Muslims are attracted to a cause that takes away their pain by providing a sense of purpose, however misguided, as well as affiliation and economic security?

What is needed, therefore, is a compelling and persuasive *alternative* to extremist ideologies and terrorism—a vision of hope, mutual respect, and opportunity—that can offer the prospect of a better life to the masses in the Middle East. What if we spent a small fraction of the money committed to military effort to empower and support small-scale enterprise development throughout the region? What if we flooded the region with teachers, health care providers, social workers, small business developers, and microfinanciers rather than merely soldiers and Western contractors?

What if we saw the Middle East as the ultimate challenge in the creation of a more sustainable world? Couldn't all the strategies discussed in this book—clean technology, the Great Leap Downward, creative destruction, radical transactiveness, native capability—serve as potential antidotes to the current vicious cycle of violence? Imagine, for example, incubating the renewable, distributed energy system of the future in the very belly of the petroleum beast itself. Could there not be a more delicious irony? But more important, could there not be a more pressing need?

The Next Tsunami

On the day after Christmas in 2004, a great tidal wave washed over most of the coastal communities of South Asia, leaving death and destruction on an unprecedented scale in its wake. With over 150,000 dead and tens of billions of dollars in damage, the world rallied to the aid of the millions of victims: Governments rose to the challenge by contributing hundreds of millions of dollars in disaster relief; charitable contributions from private citizens from across the world reached record levels in an outpouring of support and sympathy. Companies ramped up production to supply the needed goods and services from water purification equipment to emergency shelter to medical supplies. NGOs, disaster relief agencies, and even the military mobilized on a massive scale to airlift and distribute emergency aid to the hundreds of remote communities that had been devastated by the disaster.

In Indonesia, Thailand, and Sri Lanka, extremist movements, terrorist groups, and warring factions set aside their differences, at least for short term, to address the human suffering and devastation that lay in the great Tsunami's wake. Indeed, the possibility for unity—between rich and poor; Christian, Buddhist, Hindu, and Muslim; corporate, government and civil society; developed and developing—was palpable. The flood had created the pretext for collaboration and common cause, at least for a while. But what happens after the immediate tragedy passes and world attention is drawn away to other issues, as it inevitably will be? With the passage of time, will the aid dry up leaving these communities destitute and impoverished? Will the region then become an even greater hotbed for extremist movements and terrorist activity? Or can we envision another wave after the Great Tsunami—one based upon the principles developed in this book?

Indeed, with the South Asia coastline in ruins, there is an opportunity to drive the reconstruction process through an *enterprise-based* model organized around a vision of sustainable development. For visionary companies, this offers the chance to leapfrog directly to clean technology, wireless telecommunications, distributed generation of renewable energy, point of use water purification, sustainable agriculture, and environmentally-sound building techniques. For the financial sector, the opportunity exists to help local people pull themselves back up by the bootstraps through micro-finance and micro-entrepreneurship, rather than perpetuating a deepening cycle of aid-based dependence.

In short, the next wave could be an orchestrated effort to bring inclusive capitalism to the region, with the potential to diffuse forever the insurgency movements that result from inequity, poverty, isolation, and hopelessness. Imagine the possibility of creating common cause with Indonesia—the largest Muslim nation in the World—to create a sustainable future for the country's devastated west coast. It might be possible to transform an entire generation's view of the United States and western capitalism. The time is now for the major corporations of the world to step up to this challenge—to forge the partnerships with the multilaterals, governments, NGOs, and local players necessary to make it happen.

In the wake of September 11, 2001 and December 26, 2004, then, we find ourselves at a crossroads. Political solutions to the world's social and environmental problems have not been forthcoming, the framework conditions needed for global governance have remained elusive, aid and philanthropy have not been adequate to the challenge, and the use of force appears to create more problems than it solves. Economic globalization has shown promise, but thus far, it has not managed to reach the majority of humanity. Increasingly, people around the world are asking the question, must capitalism's thirst for growth and profits serve only to exacerbate poverty and environmental deterioration? If the answer to this question is yes, as a growing chorus of antiglobalization activists believe, then there is little hope.

As I propose in this book, however, the answer to this question must be an emphatic "no." The major challenge—and opportunity—of our time is to create a form of commerce that uplifts the entire human community of 6.5 billion and does so in a way that respects both natural and cultural diversity. Indeed, that is the only realistic and viable pathway to a sustainable world. And business can—and must—lead the way.

Becoming Indigenous

The chapters that came before charted the course to a more inclusive and sustainable form of commerce. Exhibit 9.1 summarizes the journey that we have taken in this book. As we have seen, *greening* has been an important first step because it eliminated the myth that a trade-off exists between a firm's financial and societal performance. Driven by the realization that pollution is waste and dialogue with stakeholders is superior to court battles, greening opened the door for companies to take a proactive stance toward social and environmental issues. Indeed, pollution prevention and product stewardship have succeeded in reducing waste, emissions, and impact, while simultaneously reducing cost, risk, and stakeholder resistance. The incremental gains associated with greening, however, have been clearly inadequate: They only slow the rate of destruction rather than fundamentally changing course.

Moving *beyond greening*, therefore, is critical both to a sustainable world and to a sustainable enterprise. Driven by an accelerating rate of technological change and the growing realization that something fundamental must change if we are to accommodate a population of 8 billion to 10 billion human beings on the planet, beyond greening provides the motivation for companies to think in terms of reorientation rather than just adjustment. Leapfrogging to inherently clean technologies through disruptive business models at the base of the pyramid enables companies to confront directly the two biggest problems facing humanity: poverty and global-scale environmental degradation. These also provide the basis for the repositioning and growth that will be needed for companies to thrive in the future.

Exhibit 9.1
The Path to Inclusive Commerce

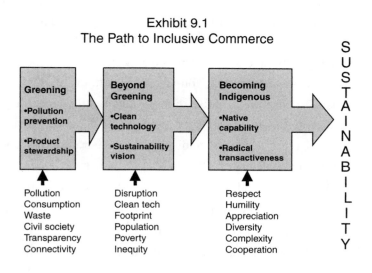

As we have seen, however, strategies for the base of the pyramid and clean technology, if narrowly construed, still position companies as outsiders, alien to both the cultures and the ecosystems within which they do business. The next sustainability challenge, therefore, is to become *indigenous*. By hearing the true voices of those who have previously been bypassed by globalization, and by learning to codevelop technologies, products, and services with nature and local people, MNCs can become native to the places where they operate. This requires a healthy dose of humility and respect, as well as a greater appreciation for the many and varied ways that people choose to live. Through bottom-up innovation on a human scale, MNCs effectively become part of the local landscape. In so doing, the corporate sector becomes a primary driving force for global sustainability. And in the process, visionary companies realize opportunities of untold proportion.

Enabling existing companies to first recognize and then pursue these opportunities is no small challenge. As we have seen, shattering the trade-off myth associated with pollution and prosperity was a crucial first step in realizing the full potential of greening. Moving beyond greening and becoming indigenous will require that we break free from the tyranny of another set of implicit trade-offs and assumptions. Indeed, the air is filled today with rejoinders such as "We can't serve the poor profitably," "Business should not be expected to solve the world's problems," and, most recently, "You are either with us, or you are with the terrorists." These are all false dichotomies that oversimplify and therefore obscure the possibilities for more nuanced and inclusive solutions. Focusing creative energy on dissolving these trade-offs—and the orthodox thinking that supports them—can provide an avenue for companies to identify the breakthrough business strategies of the future.

In this book, I have tried to suggest *what* companies might do to pursue the path of sustainable global enterprise—the strategies, practices, and capabilities that are required. What is less clear is *how* to pursue this path, particularly within the context of large, incumbent, multinational corporations. Indeed, as Raghuram Rajan and Luigi Zingales point out in their book *Saving Capitalism from the Capitalists*, it is precisely the large incumbent corporations that most often stand in the way of fundamental change.[5] I close the book, therefore, with some thoughts on what it will take to make sustainability happen in the real world of budgets, quarterly earnings reports, discounted cash-flow analysis, and the discipline of the investor community.[6] Leaders in companies will need to avoid the top-down bias, think as a disrupter, reinvent cost structures, transform the meaning of scale, and align the organization. Most important, to enable employees to build the sustainability cathedral, senior managers will have to step up to the challenge with visible and tangible commitments that far surpass what they have been willing to do to date.

Avoid the Top-Down Bias

Large corporations have great difficulty fomenting innovation from the bottom up. When firms are left to their own devices, new programs and strategies are decreed by senior managers and then sent down the reporting chain for implementation. Unfortunately, when it comes to sustainability, a top-down approach to implementation can seriously limit and even damage the company's hopes of realizing the opportunity. In fact, a strong market presence at the top of the pyramid can actually blind managers to the possibilities elsewhere.

P&G, for example, has had great difficulty shaking off the influence of its renowned brand-management system when entering low-income markets or looking to commercialize leapfrog technology. When the firm was test-marketing its new nutritional beverage product, Nutristar, for example, initial efforts were negatively affected by the company's traditional approach to product launch at the top of the pyramid. The local subsidiary in the Philippines was not familiar with the low-income segment of the population, and the company's standard approach failed to hear the true voice of the new customer. Ultimately, the team had to abandon this test market. They later decided to launch a pilot project in a country where the company did not currently have a local subsidiary. This enabled them to construct a true "learning" market by working with local communities and NGOs to do the pilot testing. Ironically, then, the corporation's strong presence around the world became a *liability* when it came to incubating new businesses at the base of the pyramid.[7]

DuPont has also struggled to devise ways to make the Great Leap Downward. Senior management has made reaching the base of the pyramid a strategic priority for the company; business leaders have been charged with initiating efforts in this regard. Indeed, a process has been put in place to identify, evaluate, and invest in new business opportunities in emerging markets. Yet despite this commitment, the process, which works through the company's existing business units, seeks primarily to extend existing technologies and products into underserved markets. In this sense, it is fundamentally an incremental initiative. Although there is nothing wrong with such a process (looking for product line extension opportunities is a good way to generate near-term growth), it underscores the difficulty that MNCs have when it comes to breaking the hold of the current business system.[8]

Even the vaunted Hindustan Lever's initial attempts to reach the base of the pyramid were incremental in character: minor formulation changes for soaps and shampoos, and single-use sachet packaging so that poor people could afford to buy it. Getting to bottom-up innovation through true engagement requires a fundamentally new and different approach. To enable this, senior managers need to create the structural conditions that enable internal entrepreneurs to break free of the current system. At a minimum, this calls for a separate investment fund and special incubation organization where these ventures can germinate without the same hurdle rates, corporate overhead burdens, and growth expectations carried by the existing business divisions.[9] It does not require a massive investment of resources. As we have seen, even a few million dollars committed in this manner has the potential to buy important options for the future—and create a growth engine that can help the company avoid saturation and stagnation in the current businesses. As noted economist E.F. Schumacher would say "Man is small, and therefore, beautiful. To go for giantism is to go for self-destruction."[10]

Think as a Disrupter

As the experience of the Grameen Bank shows, it is critical to think in terms of creative destruction rather than continuous improvement when it comes to the pursuit of sustainability. Often this means turning the existing technology and business model on their heads. That, in turn, means getting outside the current corporate straightjacket of central research and development. Such a system is particularly well suited to the current top of the pyramid model, with its emphasis on world scale, global supply chains, and one-size-fits-all products. It is singularly inappropriate, however, when it comes to bringing forward the sustainable technologies and business models of tomorrow.

To think as a disruptor, it is necessary to conduct R&D and market research focused on the *unique* situations and requirements of the poor, by region and by country. As a first step, such research can seek to adapt current technology to local needs. In fact, disruptive thinking can sometimes help to turn current shelf technology (technology that has yet to find a commercial application) into gold. Think about it: Many technologies are on the shelf because they are disruptive to the current business system. Empowering a team to look at these technologies through a new lens—the base of the pyramid, for example—can open up new horizons of possibility.

Many companies have resorted to donating patents to universities as a form of philanthropy and good will. Perhaps it would be wise instead to take a fresh look at these technologies, with the perspective of a disrupter. Over the past few months, for example, we have started a project at Cornell to re-evaluate the shelf technology in the university's intellectual property office.[11] Literally hundreds of patents are sitting dormant, mostly because no large corporation could be found with an interest in licensing them. In the space of a couple of weeks, a few MBA volunteers versed in sustainability and the Great Leap logic were able to identify more than a dozen patents that could provide the basis for start-up ventures focused on disruption and the base of the pyramid.

Perhaps even more important, however, research should seek to identify useful principles and potential applications from local practices. In the BOP, significant knowledge is transmitted orally from one generation to the next. Being respectful of traditions but willing to analyze them scientifically can lead us to new knowledge. Acupuncture was laughed at 30 years ago. Meditation was dismissed as a fad. Body Shop's creative CEO, Anita Roddick, built a business based on understanding the basis for local rituals and practices. For example, she observed that some African women use slices of pineapple to cleanse their skin. On the surface, this practice appears to be a meaningless ritual. However, research shows that the active ingredients in pineapple clear away dead skin cells better than chemical formulations.

To think disruptively, MNCs must develop major research facilities in developing regions such as China, India, Latin America, and Africa. The focus of these facilities, however, should not be conventional R&D. Instead, they can and must serve as jumping-off points for radical transactiveness and the development of native capability. Few MNCs have made much of an effort in this direction. Unilever is an exception: It has highly regarded research centers in India, employing more than 400 researchers dedicated to the problems of India's urban slums and rural villages.

Reinvent Cost Structures

Managers must dramatically reduce cost levels relative to those at the top of the pyramid. To create products and services the poor can afford, MNCs must reduce their costs by orders of magnitude to say, 10 percent of what they are today. This cannot be achieved by fine-tuning the current approaches to product development, production, and logistics. The entire business process must be rethought with a focus on functionality, not on the product itself.

As suggested earlier, focused R&D and technology development will be critical to reducing costs. Companies such as N-Logue in India, as we have seen, are focusing their R&D energies on affordability by creating Wireless Local Loop technology that dramatically lowers connectivity costs in rural area. Galanz has also used the unique expectations of low-income Chinese as a driver in developing highly affordable and energy-efficient microwave ovens. Thus, viewing the constraints imposed by the BOP as innovation drivers provides one important avenue for driving down costs.

The distributed and localized nature of most clean technology and BOP opportunities also offers opportunities for lowering costs through business model innovation. MNCs typically think in terms of capital intensity and labor productivity, based upon their experience at the top of the pyramid. Exactly the opposite logic applies in the BOP. Given the vast number of underemployed people at the base of the pyramid and the fragmented nature of the distribution system, the business model must provide jobs for many, as did Ruf and Tuf jeans from Arvind Mills: The company employed an army of local tailors as stockers, promoters, distributors, and service providers all rolled in one, even though the cost of the jeans was 80 percent below that of Levis. Thus, designing people-intensive rather than capital-intensive businesses provides another important vehicle for reinventing cost structures.

Lowering cost structures also forces a debate on ways to reduce investment intensity. This will inevitably lead to greater use of information technology to develop production and distribution systems. As noted, village-based phones are already transforming the pattern of communications throughout the developing world. Add to this the Internet, and we have a whole new way of communicating and creating economic development in poor, rural areas. Creative use of IT will emerge in these markets as a means to dramatically lower the costs associated with access to product and services, distribution, and credit management.

Transform the Meaning of Scale

The dominant logic for most MNCs today is that scale literally means "big"—world-scale factories, global supply chains, and international markets. Achieving scale means making big investments and spreading the costs over even bigger markets. Today's large corporations do not think twice about investing more than a billion dollars in one new project, whether it's a new car platform, a chip fab, a pulp mill, or an energy infrastructure project. Placing such big bets often produces spectacular success—but sometimes means horrific failure. Executives' careers are made and broken based upon how well they manage these investments. New businesses must start big to cover the corporate overhead, clear the hurdle rate, and generate the growth needed to feed the corporate monkey in the near term. Indeed, project-evaluation and capital-budgeting tools are carefully tuned to identify the best of the big ones. Projects that do not fit this description, either because they are initially too small or because they have a delayed payback, are shunted to the side, regardless of their potential. Only square pegs can fit in square holes.

The quest for sustainable global enterprise, however, demands that MNCs transform (or, at least, broaden) the meaning of *scale*. As we have seen, most clean technologies are disruptive; disruptive technologies are typically smaller in scale and more distributed in character. Indeed, many of the most exciting emerging technologies, such as nanotechnology, completely reverse the logic of "bigger is better": Production takes place at the molecular scale. Furthermore, effectively reaching the base of the pyramid requires a revolution in business models. Local engagement, codevelopment, and low-cost probes are the *modus operandi*. Achieving scale in this new arena means marrying distributed capability and learning with world-class technology and global reach. Growth is modular, not monolithic; it occurs from the bottom up through an organic process of coevolution rather than top down, through massive investment in world-scale facilities. It requires native capability, not global scale or local responsiveness.

Managers should therefore centralize only where there are clear and demonstrable advantages. Begin with the assumption that decentralization is the right choice until someone can prove to you otherwise. Question more intently the logic behind economies of scale implicit in world-scale proposals. Are they really a good use of scarce capital resources? Do they foreclose other pathways prematurely? Should some of the company's investment capital be spread over a wider range of smaller, more distributed experiments? Do some projects that appear too small initially have the potential to scale rapidly through modular, organic growth and become very large businesses? Questions like these can help managers to broaden and ultimately transform the meaning of scale.

Align the Organization

Pursuit of a sustainable global enterprise is often thwarted by inconsistent or even conflicting elements in organizational infrastructure. Strategies cannot be realized unless the organizational structure and formal systems enable them. Goals cannot be reached without the right people with the right skills using the right processes. Visions can never become real without a serious intent to actually reduce them to practice.[12]

Exhibit 9.2 lists the elements of organizational infrastructure that are critical to align. There is no question that setting a compelling and challenging vision and mission for corporate sustainability is a key to success. This enables senior leadership to challenge its people to do something great, to establish a "big, hairy, audacious" goal (BHAG), in the words of Jim Collins and Jerry Porras, a goal that is worthy of their highest aspirations, hopes, and dreams.[13] Ray Anderson, CEO of the Atlanta-based carpet manufacturer, Interface, has established a very hairy goal indeed for the company: to never take another drop of oil from the Earth. This is clearly audacious because the company's current core product—commercial carpet made from PVC and nylon—is based entirely on petrochemicals.

Although sustainability-based BHAGs are important, they cannot stand on their own because they define a future state that is well beyond the current grasp of most people in the company. It is necessary to articulate some tangible steps that allow people to make progress toward the vision. That is the purpose of clearly stated and measurable goals. DuPont, for example, has committed to a set of sustainability goals that move the company toward its vision of creating sustainable solutions essential to a better, safer, healthier life for people everywhere. One corporate goal, for example, is to reduce greenhouse gas emissions by two-thirds by 2010. This is an aggressive goal, to be sure, but it directs the attention of employees to the next steps they must take and clarifies appropriate strategies to pursue.

Too often, companies set lofty visions and goals for sustainability, only to have them fall apart at the level of strategy. When this happens, external stakeholders—particularly NGOs and civil society groups—conclude that the company is engaged in little more than public relations and "greenwashing." It is important, therefore, for companies to be clear on what their actual portfolio of strategies will be. The sustainable value portfolio developed in Chapter 3, "The Sustainable Value Portfolio" (and elaborated further in Exhibit 9.1), is a useful tool for planning the right mix of greening, beyond greening, and even indigenous programs and initiatives. DuPont, for example, has used this tool to help ensure that it has the mix of strategic activities needed to drive the company forward toward its goals, particularly in moving beyond greening.

Even where there is clarity with regard to strategy, however, companies can and often do run aground when it comes to implementation. Compelling vision, lofty goals, and aggressive strategies never make it out of the starting gate if the organizational structure and formal systems conspire to kill the projects and punish the people responsible for them. In fact, this misalignment may be one of the most significant problems facing large corporations today.

Exhibit 9.2
Aligning the Organization for Sustainability

- **Vision/Mission:** Setting the sustainability "BHAG"
- **Goals:** Establishing measurable targets
- **Strategy:** Identifying the sustainable value portfolio
- **Structure:** Creating separate experiments,ventures, and funding
- **Systems:** Designing new measurement, rewards, and project-evaluation tools
- **Processes:** Enabling new technology, product, market-development approaches
- **People:** Integrating sustainability into recruiting, leadership development, and performance evaluation

Nike's failed World Shoe initiative can be attributed, at least in part, to misalignment of strategy, structure, and measurement systems. The first mistake was to locate the venture within the athletic footwear business group; this forced the World Shoe group to make use of the manufacturing and distribution systems used for Nike's high-end products. Indeed, because existing contract manufacturers were rewarded based upon contribution margin, there was a built-in disincentive for them to even produce the low-priced World Shoes in the first place. Similarly, the company's pricing formula forced the fledgling venture to price the product beyond what its managers knew was acceptable to their target market, dooming it from the start. Finally, by forcing the venture to market its products through the company's existing distribution channels—primarily high-end retailers in China's large cities—Nike virtually guaranteed that it would never be able to reach its target customer base.

Establishing a *separate* venture for the World Shoe, one that had the freedom to design its own production, marketing, and distribution strategy apart from the established Nike pricing formula, might have given the venture a fair chance to realize its full potential, a market of potentially vast proportion. Instead, it was shut down after failing to make even the modest sales targets that had been set, defeated by the inflexibility of the corporate structure and formal systems.

It is thus of critical importance that large corporations make the organizational space necessary for innovative new ventures based on disruptive clean technologies and BOP markets to flourish. As we saw in Chapter 8, "Developing Native Capability," creating a separate organization and funding mechanism is an important starting point. That is not to say that such ventures should be allowed to lose money for an extended period of time. On the contrary, there is no reason such ventures cannot be profitable from the very start. As Clay Christensen and Michael Raynor suggest, when it comes to disruptive new ventures, senior management should be patient for growth and impatient for profit; expecting such ventures to become very big very fast fails to appreciate the organic and modular nature of their growth.[14]

Furthermore, the people who have the courage to undertake these experiments and ventures should not be punished if they fail. New and innovative measurement and reward systems are therefore crucial in moving us toward a sustainable global enterprise. The critical need for alignment of formal systems, particularly measurement systems, can be seen through Monsanto's experience in establishing a separate Sustainable Development Sector within the company in the mid-1990s.[15] CEO Bob Shapiro's instinct was exactly on target in establishing this sector. The company needed a place where innovative new ideas could be identified and pilot-tested if the businesses of the future were to come forward. During the mid- to late-1990s, the sector was working with a range of new technologies, as well as new partnerships in developing countries focused on the needs of poor, small shareholder farmers. Unfortunately, the pressures of the company's measurement system rendered most of these projects stillborn. By imposing the same growth and profitability targets on the fledgling new sustainability ventures as were used on investment proposals within the established business units (such as agricultural chemicals), the company effectively foreclosed its option on the future.

In addition to organizational structure and formal systems, it is important to align the informal (cultural) processes that exist within companies: the technology, product, and market-development processes, in particular. In fact, these processes may hold the key. It is relatively easy to change boxes on the organizational chart and alter the discount rate used to evaluate investment decisions; it is a bit more difficult—but perhaps more powerful—to change the way people behave in the company through the processes they follow. We have learned this lesson over the past two decades with such process-oriented programs as quality management, Six Sigma, and business process re-engineering, to name a few.

Designing processes that focus on the creation of sustainable technologies and businesses is a surprisingly underutilized tool in large corporations. It is a potentially very important way to guarantee some real action, unlike the rhetoric often associated with vision, goals, or even strategic plans. Philips, for example, has developed a very simple but elegant process for new sustainable business and market development. Philips businesses (and employees, in general) are invited to submit their ideas for projects that focus more effectively on the unmet needs of people worldwide. Project proposals need to outline the economic, environmental, social, and personal aspects of the solution that they intend to deliver. A separate pool of money has been created to fund the best of these new business experiments. In addition, the senior management of the company now requires each of Philips's businesses to move forward with at least one venture focused on the base of the pyramid each year.[16]

This brings us to the final element in organizational alignment: people. This element has been virtually ignored by most MNCs, but it could turn out to be the most significant of all. Much could be accomplished if the message contained in the corporate sustainability vision statement were actually integrated into corporate recruiting, leadership development, and performance evaluation. I can speak from firsthand experience when I say that, despite the best of intentions, few companies ensure that the recruiters they send to business schools are knowledgeable about sustainability issues. Even fewer firms include some understanding of or experience in sustainable enterprise as part of their hiring criteria for MBAs.

Research by my Cornell colleague Bob Frank suggests that ignoring students' commitment to social responsibility, ethics, and sustainability in the recruiting process may be a missed opportunity for firms committed to such aims.[17] Frank and his colleagues have found that there are significant salary differentials for "morally satisfying" jobs compared to those jobs seen as less socially motivated. In fact, research evidence clearly shows that students require large premiums before they are willing to work for less socially responsible employers. Thus, for companies, commitment to sustainability can serve as a magnet for recruiting the best people at a salary level below that of competitors lacking similar commitment.

When it comes to training and development, few MNCs have yet reached the point that they consider global sustainability a significant enough issue to make it an integral part of the leadership development process. Fewer still have made sustainability performance an integral part of the performance evaluation and promotion process. The time is now for corporations to close the loop on their own rhetoric by recruiting, developing, and rewarding people who display capability and imagination in moving the company and the world toward sustainability.

The importance of aligning these elements of organizational infrastructure should not be underestimated. Employees will quickly become cynical and even alienated if they run too frequently into roadblocks or have to take undue career risks to move the sustainability agenda forward. By pointing all the organizational arrows in the same direction,

MNC leaders can send a strong signal that encourages employees to step forward and invest their creative energies in the enterprise. Ultimately, that is the only way to ensure success.

Building the Cathedral

In his book *Reinventing the Bazaar*, John McMillan argues persuasively that large firms can never mimic the creative and innovative behavior of small firms, for one simple reason: ownership.[18] The owner of an asset has the right to any residual returns that it generates. If returns are unexpectedly high, the owner gets the windfall. Large firms can divide themselves into smaller units responsible for their own costs and revenues, thereby heightening incentives. Divisional managers can be paid according to their division's performance. But large firms can never precisely duplicate ownership. A divisional manager does not have residual control, so decisions can be overridden from above. If the division turns out to be wildly more successful than anyone foresaw when the manager's contract was written, the parent firm will probably find a way to harvest the profits. In short, not being an owner—lacking the rights to residual returns—puts a damper on the motivation to invest creatively and to take risks.

So how can MNCs possibly unleash the creative power of their people, a virtual prerequisite to realizing the full potential of sustainability? The answer is ownership! Not ownership of residual returns, but rather ownership of *ideas* and the ability to champion their development. MNCs must bestow on their people what my colleague Erik Simanis has described as the "license to imagine." Companies must enable their employees to pitch and run with new ideas—ideas that help to move us toward a sustainable world—in ways that would never be possible on their own or in small start-up enterprises. MNCs must, in short, make *meaning* for their employees and allow them the chance to align their personal values with what they do on the job everyday.

I am reminded of the story of three people at work on a construction site. All were doing the same job, but when each was asked what his job was, the answers varied. "Breaking rocks," replied the first. "Earning a living," answered the second. "Helping build a cathedral," said the third. Too many people in large corporations still view their work as either breaking rocks or, at best, earning a living. Sustainability is the cathedral building of the twenty-first century. There can be no more important goal, no nobler aspiration, and no greater business opportunity. What we lack in our companies is not resources or capabilities, but rather *imagination*. We must turn people lose to build the cathedral of sustainability.

Senior executives must develop the courage to speak out publicly regarding the importance of sustainable development and the role that they can play in its realization. Corporate governmental affairs must come to mean more than lobbying to maintain the status quo or bending the political process to serve the company's short-term interests. Instead, business must champion the needed global framework conditions—international protocols and agreements—that governments, civil society, and multilateral agencies have been unable to deliver on their own.

Building the cathedral of sustainability also requires senior executives to create the structural space for disruptive new technologies and business experiments to flourish. This includes allocating the necessary investment capital to fund their development, protecting the ventures—and their entrepreneurs—from the tyranny of the current incumbent business, and recognizing and rewarding those who succeed in nurturing the businesses of the future.

While senior executive leadership is crucial, it is also important for each individual and employee to take the bull by the horns. The best place to start is by charting your own personal vision and action plan for sustainability. What can you do, within the realm of your current role, to move the company—and the world—toward sustainability? Write it down. Commit to it. When you have created a practical vision of what you want to achieve, take note of the current reality. As Bryan Smith, my colleague in the Sustainable Enterprise Academy, points out, current reality is not the problem—it simply defines the set of resources, people, and opportunities that you have to work with. Note your current reality and then assess the gap between it and your vision.[19]

The wider the gap is between vision and the current reality, the more "creative tension" there is. Your challenge is to put together a coalition of people and resources, and then build the momentum within the organization to close the gap. That is how you realize the vision. When the first one is realized, move on to the second. Enroll others within the organization to make a similar commitment. Creating a sustainable global enterprise is not about waiting for the magic bullet to be handed down from senior management. Instead, it is about hundreds or even thousands of people in the organization deciding to commit to the pursuit of their personal visions and action plans, with global sustainability as the driving force.

Postscript

As we embark upon the new century, business has emerged as the most powerful institution on the planet. Seven-hundred years ago, it was religion; the world's cathedrals, mosques, and temples stand as testimony to the primacy of organized religion in the world at that time. Two hundred years ago, it was the state; no tour would be complete without visits to the impressive palaces, capitol buildings, and governmental complexes of the world that remind us of how centrally important government was in the age of enlightenment. Today the most powerful institution in the world is business: Witness the office towers, banks, and commercial centers that dominate today's largest cities. Although no one denies the continuing and crucial importance of government, religion, and civil society, there can be little doubt that commerce has become the dominant institution.

But, as we have seen, there are storm clouds on the horizon: Unless global capitalism can extend its bounty to the entire human community in a way that respects cultural diversity and husbands the natural capital upon which it depends, we may well witness the marginalization of this great institution in our lifetime. Unfortunately, there is no candidate institution waiting to step into the breach to assume leadership: Global governance is in its infancy, religious fundamentalism has become a divisive rather than constructive force, and civil society lacks the resources and technology to make a large enough impact on its own.

It now seems clear that environmental deterioration, global terrorism, and geopolitical meltdown all wait in the wings if business fails to step up to the challenge. The United States, the lone superpower in the world today, is mired in a parochial and counterproductive struggle between two outmoded ideologies: liberal versus conservative. Tragically, neither is appropriate for the challenges that lie ahead. We desperately need a third way, one premised on a combination of global interdependence, sustainability, and local self-reliance. Commerce may be the only institution with the resources, capabilities, and global reach to make it happen. Today capitalism truly does stand at a crossroads: My hope is that this book has shed some light on the appropriate path for business to take.

Notes

1. For in-depth treatments of the causes and consequences of the radical Islamic movement, see Benjamin Barber, *Jihad Versus McWorld* (New York: Ballantine Books, 1996); and *Fear's Empire* (New York: W.W. Norton, 2003).

2. An anonymous intelligence veteran makes a compelling argument that it is not opposition to the West's secular, democratic way of life that is behind the global Islamic insurgency, but rather the West's unsustainable policies toward and practices in the Middle East itself. See *Imperial Hubris* (anonymous) (Washington, D.C.: Brassey's Inc, 2004).

3. Tom Friedman (New York Times), presentation at Kenan-Flagler Business School, University of North Carolina, April 2003.

4. For an insightful discussion of the "hideous schizophrenia" implicit in Western conceptions of liberalism, see Paul Berman, *Terror and Liberalism* (New York: W.W. Norton, 2003).

5. Rajan Raghuram and Luigi Zingales, *Saving Capitalism from the Capitalists* (New York: Crown Business, 2003).

6. Portions of the following sections have drawn from C. K. Prahalad and Stuart Hart, "The Fortune at the Bottom of the Pyramid," *Strategy+Business* January (2002): 2–14.

7. George Carpenter (P&G), presentation at the Sustainable Enterprise Academy, April 2004.

8. Eduardo Wanick (DuPont), presentation at the Base of the Learning Laboratory meeting, Monterrey, Mexico, February 2004.

9. Clay Christensen and Michael Raynor draw a similar conclusion regarding the incubation of disruptive innovations in large incumbent firms in their book *The Innovator's Solution* (Boston: Harvard Business School Press, 2003).

10. E.F. Schumacher. *Small Is Beautiful: Economics as if People Mattered.* (New York: Harper Torchbooks, 1973) page 150.

11. My thanks to Dick Cahoon, Director of Cornell's Center for Technology, Entrepreneurship, and Commercialization, for this opportunity.

12. Among the few efforts to explore the leadership and organizational challenges associated with sustainability are Bob Doppelt, *Leading Change Toward Sustainability* (Sheffield, UK: Greenleaf Publishing, 2003); and Dexter Dunphy, Andrew Griffiths, and Suzanne Benn, *Organizational Change for Corporate Sustainability* (London: Routledge, 2003).

13. Jim Collins and Gary Porras, *Built to Last* (New York: HarperCollins, 1994).

14. Clayton Christensen and Michael Raynor, *The Innovator's Solution.*

15. My thanks to Kate Fish and others at Monsanto for giving me the opportunity to work with the fledging Sustainable Development Sector.

16. Personal communication, Jan Oosterveld, Group Management Committee, Royal Philips Electronics, July 2004.

17. Robert Frank, *What Price the Moral High Ground?* (Princeton, NJ: Princeton University Press, 2004).

18. John McMillan, *Reinventing the Bazaar: A Natural History of Markets* (New York: W.W. Norton. 2002).

19. I am indebted to Bryan Smith for this approach to personal action planning, which draws from his work with Peter Senge and the Society of Organizational Learning.

INDEX

"Great schools have…endeavored to do more than keep up to the respectable standard of a recent past; they have labored to supply the needs of an advancing and exacting world…"

— **Joseph Wharton,** *Entrepreneur and Founder of the Wharton School*

The Wharton School is recognized around the world for its innovative leadership and broad academic strengths across every major discipline and at every level of business education. It is one of four undergraduate and 12 graduate and professional schools of the University of Pennsylvania. Founded in 1881 as the nation's first collegiate business school, Wharton is dedicated to creating the highest value and impact on the practice of business and management worldwide through intellectual leadership and innovation in teaching, research, publishing and service.

Wharton's tradition of innovation includes many firsts—the first business textbooks, the first research center, the MBA in health care management—and continues to innovate with new programs, new learning approaches, and new initiatives. Today Wharton is an interconnected community of students, faculty, and alumni who are shaping global business education, practice, and policy.

Wharton is located in the center of the University of Pennsylvania (Penn) in Philadelphia, the fifth-largest city in the United States. Students and faculty enjoy some of the world's most technologically advanced academic facilities. In the midst of Penn's tree-lined, 269-acre urban campus, Wharton students have access to the full resources of an Ivy League university, including libraries, museums, galleries, athletic facilities, and performance halls. In recent years, Wharton has expanded access to its management education with the addition of Wharton West, a San Francisco academic center, and The Alliance with INSEAD in France, creating a global network.

Wharton
UNIVERSITY *of* PENNSYLVANIA

University of Pennsylvania

www.wharton.upenn.edu

Academic Programs:

Wharton continues to pioneer innovations in education across its leading undergraduate, MBA, executive MBA, doctoral, and executive education programs.

More information about Wharton's academic programs can be found at:
http://www.wharton.upenn.edu/academics

Executive Education:

Wharton Executive Education is committed to offering programs that equip executives with the tools and skills to compete, and meet the challenges inherent in today's corporate environment. With a mix of more than 200 programs, including both open enrollment and custom offerings, a world-class faculty, and educational facilities second to none, Wharton offers leading-edge solutions to close to 10,000 executives annually, worldwide.

For more information and a complete program listing:
execed@wharton.upenn.edu (sub 4033)
215.898.1776 or 800.255.3932 ext. 4033
http://execed.wharton.upenn.edu

Research and Analysis:

Knowledge@Wharton is a unique, free resource that offers the best of business—the latest trends; the latest research on a vast range of business issues; original insights of Wharton faculty; studies, paper and analyses of hundreds of topics and industries. *Knowledge@Wharton* has over 400,000 users from more than 189 countries.

For free subscription:
http://knowledge.wharton.upenn.edu

For licensing and content information, please contact:
Jamie Hammond,
Associate Marketing Director,
hammondj@wharton.upenn.edu • 215.898.2388

Wharton School Publishing:

Wharton School Publishing is an innovative new player in global publishing, dedicated to providing thoughtful business readers access to practical knowledge and actionable ideas that add impact and value to their professional lives. All titles are approved by a Wharton senior faculty review board to ensure they are relevant, timely, important, empirically based and/or conceptually sound, and implementable.

For author inquiries or information about corporate education and affinity programs or, please contact:
Barbara Gydé, Managing Director,
gydeb@wharton.upenn.edu • 215.898.4764

The Wharton School: http://www.wharton.upenn.edu
Executive Education: http://execed.wharton.upenn.edu
Wharton School Publishing: http://whartonsp.com
Knowledge@Wharton: http://knowledge.wharton.upenn.edu

The Fortune at the Bottom of the Pyramid
Eradicating Poverty Through Profits
BY C. K. PRAHALAD

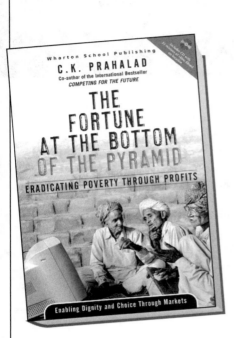

The world's most exciting, fastest-growing new market? It's where you least expect it: at the bottom of the pyramid. Collectively, the world's billions of poor people have immense entrepreneurial capabilities and buying power. You can learn how to serve them and help millions of the world's poorest people escape poverty. It is being done—profitably. Whether you're a business leader or an anti-poverty activist, business guru Prahalad shows why you can't afford to ignore "Bottom of the Pyramid" (BOP) markets.

ISBN 0131467506, © 2005, 432 pp., $28.95

The Enthusiastic Employee
How Companies Profit by Giving Workers What They Want
BY DAVID SIROTA, LOUIS A. MISCHKIND, AND MICHAEL IRWIN MELTZER

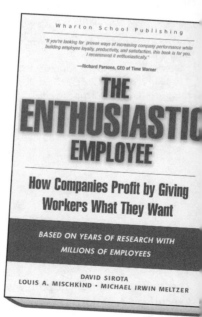

This book is about employee enthusiasm: that special, invigorating, purposeful and emotional state that's always present in the most successful organizations. Most people are enthusiastic when they're hired: hopeful, ready to work hard, eager to contribute. What happens? Management, that's what. This book tells you what managers do wrong, and what they need to do instead. Drawing on more than 30 years of employee attitude research, the authors detail exactly how to create an environment where enthusiasm flourishes and businesses excel.

ISBN 0131423304, © 2005, 400 pp., $26.95

11305